spatial questions

To Sophie and Bohdana

spatial questions

cultural topologies and social spatialisations

rob shields

Los Angeles | London | New Delhi
Singapore | Washington DC

Los Angeles | London | New Delhi
Singapore | Washington DC

SAGE Publications Ltd
1 Oliver's Yard
55 City Road
London EC1Y 1SP

SAGE Publications Inc.
2455 Teller Road
Thousand Oaks, California 91320

SAGE Publications India Pvt Ltd
B 1/I 1 Mohan Cooperative Industrial Area
Mathura Road
New Delhi 110 044

SAGE Publications Asia-Pacific Pte Ltd
3 Church Street
#10-04 Samsung Hub
Singapore 049483

Editor: Chris Rojek
Editorial assistant: Martine Jonsrud
Production editor: Katherine Haw
Copyeditor: Rosemary Campbell
Marketing manager: Michael Ainsley
Cover design: Wendy Scott
Typeset by: C&M Digitals (P) Ltd, Chennai, India
Printed in India by Replika Press Pvt. Ltd.

Library of Congress Control Number: 2012934972

British Library Cataloguing in Publication data

A catalogue record for this book is available from
the British Library

ISBN 978-1-84860-664-7
ISBN 978-1-84860-665-4 (pbk)

table of contents

list of illustrations

about the author

Dr Rob Shields is Henry Marshall Tory Chair and Director of the Faculty of Extension's City-Region Studies Centre and teaches in the Departments of Sociology and of Art and Design at the University of Alberta. Before being awarded the Tory Chair, he was Professor of Sociology and past Director of the Institute of Interdisciplinary Studies at Carleton University.

His focus has been urban cultural studies, particularly the social use and meanings of *Places on the Margin*, urban spaces and regions, including tourist destinations and place identities. In co-edited collections such as *Rereading Jean-François Lyotard*, and *Demystifying Deleuze* and in texts such as *Lefebvre, Love and Struggle*, Shields considers changing spatialisations. This intellectual project has been extended through a peer-reviewed journal, *Space and Culture*, *Curb* planning magazine and many talks on the city, the *Strip-Appeal* of malls and other *Ecologies of Affect*, and the importance of intangibles and *The Virtual* to everyday life.

preface and acknowledgements

This book is a work of thresholds, edges and folds: a topology in many senses – it explores spatial distinctions and boundaries established by markers such as a doorway, as well as less tangible distinctions such as near and far or cultural divisions between social fields. It marks a threshold of new research that shifts from space as a constitutive dimension and spatialisation of social life and personal identities to understanding competing and contested time-space milieux which are elaborated by social interactions, texts and institutional relationships. This shift from questions of social spatialisation to time-space topologies structures the sequence of chapters in this book.

We begin by shifting from the discourse of 'space' to social spatialisation from the beginning. For a detailed discussion of social spatialisation, the reader is refered to *Places on the Margin* (1991), with its case histories of how social action and place-images plays out as a nuanced geography of interlinked places and regions. Here, 'social spatialisation' or just 'spatialisation' is used to capture the sense in which places are 'cast' as 'places-for-this' or 'places-for-that'. 'Spatialisation' in French and English popular usage has meant 'making spatial'. In Chapter 2, 'social spatialisation' redefines 'space' as a problematic term by locating its partiality and identifying the cultural role that it plays by constructing a crucible and arena for the play of capital, art and technology. It seeks to not only translate but move beyond Lefebvre's Marxist-Hegelian analysis by stressing its Leibnizean, Nietzschean and even structural qualities and drawing on Foucault and Deleuze's equally Nietzschean engagements with cultural and psychological structures of power. Their debt to twentieth-century French thought – Durkheim, Cassirer, Bachelard and Canguilhem – is well established despite their critiques and denials. However, spatialisation takes on a distinct meaning in my usage given that Foucault and Deleuze tend to use the term 'spatialisation' in its French sense as localisation, 'placing'.

A 'Glossary' is appended after the last chapter to provide a ready reference to the terminology used in this book. Terms such as the 'virtual', 'material', 'actual', 'real', 'ideal', 'possible', 'abstract' and 'probably' are ontological aspects of events and objects drawn from *The Virtual* (Shields, 2003, 2006b). They stand in the relation to each other described by Proust's definition of memory, developed in part by Deleuze, as virtual: 'real but not actual, ideal but not abstract'.[1] Any aspect of spatialisation could profitably be developed on its own or its relationships explored, for example the process of the realising of fictional place-images as the character of a place or the actualisation of that quality in a built environment such as a tourist attraction. Although none occur purely, for example a virtuality in isolation from material object or vice versa, the terms can be diagrammed as a four-part ontology:

	Real	Possible
Ideal	**Virtual** (memory, intangibles, spatialisations)	**Abstract** (representations, maps, place-images, borders)
Actual	**Concrete or material** (tangible objects, constructions, material boundaries, fences)	**Probable** (statistical %, e.g. risks, political economics of values)

Rather than 'either-or', this table is a synopsis of a set of modalities of existence that co-occur and provide the stations of a continuously changing reality, where objects appear of use at hand in their capacity to occupy all of these positions, that is, to be simultaneously 'actually' one thing but 'as if' something else, 'possibly' effective for other uses and 'metaphoric' of others. Table 1.1 is thus marked by continuous movement between its categories: realisation of the possible, actualisation of the ideal, virtualisation of the actual, and so on, and also illegitimate transformations such as from the abstract to the concrete, described as the 'miraculous' in everyday speech (see Shields, 2003). 'Syncretic' phenomena that are undecidable, hovering on the boundary between categories are also of great interest.

Since its presentation in *Places on the Margin*, spatialisation seems to have provided a tool-kit for geographical analyses of a much broader set of phenomena (Shields, 2006a; see for example, the usage in Hall, 2003: 151). The term has been disseminated as a keyword across human geography in particular. Contributors to a recent reference book use the term over a hundred times in 350 pages to profile *Key Thinkers on Space and Place* (Hubbard et al., 2004). Historically, one might ask whether or not it constitutes a paradigm shift in geographical thought? The argument pursued in this book goes further. Do questions of spatialisation in turn lead to questions of time, history and memory that demand a less genealogical, more topological approach to space-time? The affective quality of hoped-for futures and nostalgic pasts has been the topic of previous collective research by the Space and Culture Research Group at the University of Alberta, culminating in the edited book-work *Ecologies of Affect* (Davidson et al., 2011). This research group of students, colleagues and so many students who have become colleagues, continues in the writing groups, theory retreats, visiting speakers and conferences on a wide range of topics. These recollected and anticipated spatialisations set the stage for the introduction of topology.

The survey of the development of non-Euclidean understandings of topology will inevitably strike mathematicians as crude and social theorists as incomplete, but to my knowledge it represents the only non-algebraic introduction to topology in plain English to outline both the history and the implications of this approach. Other efforts at this time include work on social networks and special issues of *Space and Culture* and of *Theory Culture & Society*. My efforts to go beyond the metaphorical usage of topological terms by connecting-up cultural studies with the rigour of topological concepts also benefitted from comments at symposia organised at Cultural Studies centres at the University of Western Sydney and at Monash University in Melbourne Australia in 2010, and at Shanghai International Studies University in 2011 and the University of Toronto's Semiotic Circle in 2012. I deeply appreciate the efforts of organisers and funders, including the Henry Marshall Tory Chair fund that I have benefitted from abroad, at the University of Alberta, and the support of the Social Sciences and Humanities Research Council of Canada.

Many of the chapters in this book are the result of almost three decades of work. Some have appeared in earlier versions that anticipated the presentation here. However, all have been revised and updated and include orienting commentary that shows how they form the building blocks of a larger edifice that itself has matured over time. In particular they have benefited from discussion at the Space and Culture Research Group at the University of Alberta over the last four years and in sessions organised at the American Association of Geographers Conference in 2011, and the Bristol Symposium on Event Space sponsored by the World University Network in late 2011. Many individual conversations over coffee have provided food for thought. In Chapter 1, while I alone am liable for problems resulting from the too brief treatment of the ancient Chinese text *Shan Hai Jing*, this has benefited from the critique and commentary of scholars including at the Chinese Academy of Social Sciences in Beijing in September 2011. Professor Jin Huimin and Professor Xu Dejin provided valuable context. I am most grateful for this and many others' academic and personal hospitality.

In as much as this book draws on a long period of research, students and colleagues in Sociology, Cultural Studies and other Departments at Lancaster, Carleton, and University of Alberta; a sabbatical at the Faculty of Communications, Universidad Federal da Bahia, Salvador Brazil; professional networks of the City Region Studies Centre in the Faculty of Extension and its research staff including Dr Kevin Jones, and visiting academics such as Professor Hamid Abdollayan, Professor Sergio Benicio di Melo, and Professor André Lemos; networks through the American Association of Geographers, the Association for Cultural Studies, the editorial group of *Theory Culture & Society* and the all-important virtual network of the journal, *Space and Culture* have all added to the shape of this work. I am especially grateful to all those who hosted these symposia or took the time to talk with me. It is impossible to thank everyone personally or properly. My family have given me the most benefit of patience and tolerated travels to the events mentioned above, or family holidays that turned into proof-reading days or detours to archives. I am especially grateful for Bohdana and Sophie's willingness to take on the challenges of travel and dislocation. Thank you.

Edmonton, Alberta Canada, 19 May 2012

Note

1   In Shanghai, Beijing Professor Huang Zhuo Yue reminded me of the critique of Storch's defence of the bourgeoisie and nobility as engaged in immaterial production (such as service, or knowledge work) as discussed in Marx's *Capital* Vol. 4 (online Ch. 4 Section 16). However, the virtual is not intended as an activity in and of itself but an aspect of all historically located activities and objects, including material products. Immaterial labour has received much critical attention recently, notably in the work of Maurizio Lazzaratto and in relation to the accumulation and potlatch of excess in the work of Georges Bataille.

1

overtures

The ill-defined concept of 'space' itself presents an immediate problem. 'What space is' is of universal social interest and the topic of some of the most historic knowledge projects and texts produced by human cultures. How is space known? How might we take stock of our spatial knowledges, placemaking and spatial practices across cultures? What are the elements of a topology of space? If history and geography have a descriptive bias, a genealogy of space would go in a different direction, attempting to avoid describing within an unquestioned framework, while critically exposing the conditions for discourses on space and the framing effect of spaces. A 'critical topology' might take this even further, to ask how different formations or orders of spacing might coexist and not succeed but modify or warp each other. Borrowing from the insights of mathematics and theoretical physics, it would deploy a spatial method: a dynamic, set-based and topological rather than stratified approach. This book develops a 'cultural topology' as a critical theory and method for social science and geography by considering the recurrent quality of orders of spacing and placing – what I will call 'spatialisations'. These will be presented as 'virtualities': intangible but real entities. Cultural cases, including the history of philosophies of space, will be used to illustrate the diversity of social spatialisations and their impacts. This chapter introduces social spatialisations by considering two historical cases, as presented in the ancient Chinese text, the *Shan Hai Jing*, and in the *Kitab Nuzhat*, an encyclopaedic atlas produced for Roger II of Sicily in the first half of the 1100s.

From the *Shan Hai Jing* to Herodotus' *Historiae* and to Idrisi's *Kitab Nuzhat*

The first geographers are mythographers then travellers; their books are histories then atlases. One of the first books, *Shan Hai Jing*, or *The Guide to the Ways through Mountains and Seas*, is a perfect illustration (P'o Kuo (Guo Pu), 1985). As a text it pre-dates not only books but printing. Though misinterpreted and embellished as a mythology by later generations, it was originally a book of geography describing the character of regions at the edges of the Zhou Dynasty empire (approx 1046–771 BCE) although elements are said to date from the first Hsia dynasty (twenty-second century BCE). Historians divide the text into a core 'Classic of Mountains' (*Shan Jing*) and later sections, 'The Classic of Seas' (*Hai Jing*) and 'Classic of Great Wastes' (*Da Huang Jing*). Divided into short passages, each entry describes locations grouped in geographical areas to present a comprehensive account of the world as the Warring States and the Han knew it. However, the places discussed are never sites of everyday life but mountains and distant regions where strange races and monsters dwell. They are metaphors of unknown hinterlands, the sorts of liminal zones discussed in *Places on the Margin* (Shields, 1991), and frontiers where social and cosmological order breaks down. Divinities, strange plants and hybrid beings populate an atlas of 'interfaces between the animal, the human and the divine' (Lewis, 2006: 285).

> As a result, such writers as Sima Qian and Ban Gu[1] dismissed the work as nonsense. In the earliest catalogue of Chinese texts it was classified under the section 'Calculations and [Mantic] Arts,' under the subcategory of 'Methods of Forms' (*xing fa* ...) This category contains books on the physiognomy of men and animals as well as early examples of what would evolve into the science of environmental influence known as *feng shui*. The classification thus indicates that the *Shan hai jing* was viewed as a manual for divination based on the physical shape of the world ... It may also reflect the fact that the text contains numerous accounts of natural prodigies and what they foretold.
>
> In the twentieth century, the work was treated as a geography, a compendium of myths, an early ethnohistory, and a set of labels for lost illustrations [or maps]. A large literature has also attempted to gloss the places mentioned with modern or historical names. (Lewis, 2006: 285)

Spanning recorded history and the history of printed books, commentaries on *Shan Hai Jing* mirror change in successive dynasties (see Figure 1.1). Its classification changed in Chinese historiography between travelogue, strategic guide, bestiary and mythology, depending on the extent to which it was found to be useful to the Imperial court as an empirical reference in dealing with neighbours, its peripheries and foreign contacts. These included trade routes such as the Silk Road connecting China with the Middle East and Europe. Contemporary Chinese scholarship understands the text critically as a document dictating Imperial rituals binding the regions of Ancient China together. At the same time in contemporary China mountain parks and temples such as Wu Tai Shan (a key site in Buddhism) are being rediscovered as tourist and pilgrimage destinations for Chinese citizens.

Following Dorofeeva-Lichtman, Lewis argues that none of these classifications exactly capture the basic nature of the text as a cosmology which assigns every being and even ancient legend to a place in a sacred geography (Dorofeeva-Lichtmann, 1995).

> The *Shan hai jing*, despite the impression given by the exact distances between sites, does not depict the world's physical form. Instead it is a 'conceptual organisation of space' conveying fundamental ideals about the world through its overarching schema ... the world [and cosmos] is square, oriented in the cardinal directions, balanced if not symmetrical ... and clearly distinguished between centre and periphery ... in which there is a progressive decline as one moves away from the centre through a series of concentric squares. (Lewis, 2006: 285)

Mountains in the *Shan Jing* are interfaces to the divine, distant seas of the *Hai Jing* are uncanny regions of strange beings 'separated from the centre in both space and time' (Lewis 2006: 285). History and geography are integrated into an atlas. The *Shan Hai Jing* is also a text integrated into the cults and politics of its time. Mountains are interfacial, in-between sites of spiritual potency where celestial and hybrid beings are expected. Distance equates with barbarism signalled by the monstrosity of the peoples. As Lewis notes, 'remoteness ... became part of an ideology of power' (Lewis, 2006: 301). Peripheries are conflated with primitiveness and also with lesser-developed societies in a manner similar to the exoticism of nineteenth- and twentieth-century European ethnology and anthropology. Lewis argues:

> the shift toward the horizontal dimension ... focused on the distinction between inner and outer by structuring the earth according to the diverse peoples on its surface rather than the mountain chains that linked it to the sky. This shift away from the vertical is also marked by the abandonment as a structuring principle of the hierarchy from beasts through men to spirits marked by the relations of consumption and feeding. Instead it emphasized ... beings sharing a common nature varied across space through the influence of custom. (Lewis, 2006: 295)

The *Hai Jing* and *Da Huang Jing* look not upward but outward to exotic peripheries. In part, the horizontal structure of the later sections coincides with the shift of attention to their borders and beyond by an expansive Han dynasty. However, these accounts are not detailed,[2] but serve the self-definition of the Chinese (a strategy used throughout history (Lewis, 2006: 297)):

> There is the state of the Zhi people. The god Shun sired Wuyin, who descended to the land of the Zhi. They are called the Shaman Zhi people. The Shaman Zhi people are surnamed Fen. They eat grain. They wear clothes that are not woven or sewn, and eat food that they do not plant or harvest. Here there are birds which sing and dance; simurghs that spontaneously sing and phoenixes that spontaneously dance. All varieties of four-legged creatures assemble here, and all types of grain can be gathered. (Lewis, 2006: 299)

This is also a processual itinerary similar to even more ancient Chinese legends such as the *Yu Gong*. As noted above, these texts are a prescription and model for the performance of actions that organise space (Lewis, 2006: 286), situating the reader and providing the basis for efficacious, strategic action. This is similar to annual royal processions of ancient Chinese rulers, ritual visits to mark sovereignty by making sacrifices on specific mountain tops, and seasonal duties in temple complexes which were followed as a means to authority (Lewis, 2006: 286).

Within the overall text known as the *Shan Hai Jing*, the *Shan Jing* is more empirical than the *Hai Jing* or *Wan Jing*. These appear to be written at different times rather than being one manuscript, although it was

Figure 1.1   Illustration from the *Shan Hai Jing*

in its final form by the time of the Han Dynasty (206 BCE–220 CE). For contemporary Chinese scholars, the text is neither a unitary mythology nor a 'cosmology', even if it has been treated as such within China historically and by modern scholars outside of China. Chinese scholars have argued that the entire nature of mythology is different in China compared to Western Europe: it is not as closely articulated with everyday life but treated as an abstraction. It does not represent 'mainstream' historical Chinese cultural geography texts (such as the Confucian classics *ShangShu* (*Book of Changes*), *Lifi* (*Record of Rites*) or *ShiJing* (*Book of Poetry*). With its changing reception over time, it cannot be used as an atlas or index of historical events. For example, the *Shan Hai Jing* has no mention of Confucius or other historical figures. Nonetheless, the *Shan Hai Jing* provides an example of a text of rituals where the changing reception of the text over time suggests shifting 'cultures of space' or spatialisations.

Mediterranean Geographies

Although over 2000 years older, the *Shan Hai Jing* uses the same method as Renaissance and Islamic cosmographies that listed 'marvels and curiosities under the place they were found and structured the presentation by moving from place to place while locating each site only in terms of the direction and distance from the preceding one' (Lewis, 2006: 286). While previous theorists of space such as Lefebvre (1991b) have preferred a linear teleology in which one 'mode of production of space' (or reified spatialisations) surmounted the previous modes, these texts illustrate the absence of a linear historical development of spatial understanding, where history is full of reversions to older perceptions and never fully refuted conceptions of space. Hand in hand with this heterodoxy goes alternating social practices.

The widely travelled Athenian historian, Herodotus (Bodrum and Athens c.484–c.425 BCE), remarked on Hecataeus of Miletus' (c.550–c.476 BCE) work *Periegesis* or *Periodos Ges*, '*A Voyage Around the World*'. Hecataeus' world map was structured, like Miletus itself, on pure geometric forms (circles, squares), which influenced how the Earth was understood as a flat plane (Herodotus, 1962 IV: 36). These remarkable maps can be understood as *diagrams* – more like a subway map than the contemporary cartography we are used to. Our Mercator projection may one day be seen as just as distorting a representation as that of Hecataeus. Hipparchus and Ptolemy's later concepts of latitude and longitude were related in part to an interest in defining *Klimata* – ecologico-ethnological regions (Ptolemy 1969) but became a coordinate structure. Bands of latitude were not only climatic, but were characterised by different flora, fauna and societies including different races of humans. This is one of the origins of the idea that a region's inhabitants embody its qualities.

> The maps included in the original edition of Ptolemy's *Geography* have been lost. However, that barely matters. The text is absolutely lucid and can be read with profit even today ... Ptolemy's *Geography* was largely forgotten for many years except by a number of Muslim scientists. In Palermo, in the multicultural court of the Norman King Roger II, al-Idrisi (c. 1100–1165 CE) used an Arabic translation of the great work and improved on Ptolemy's calculations. The Greek text was ... not rediscovered until a Byzantine monk, Maximus Planudes (c. 1260–1330 CE), found a manuscript copy without the maps ... This became the basis of the first printed Ptolemy atlas, which was published in Bologna in 1477 in an edition with five hundred copies. Columbus owned a copy and studied it carefully. (O'Shea, 2007: 15)

Figure 1.2   Mappa Mundi from Al Idrisi, *Kitab Nuzhat*, c.1154. This map is from a manuscript copied by Alî ibn Hasan al-Hûfî al-Qâsimî in Cairo in 1456, preserved in the Bodleian Library, Oxford (Mss. Pococke 375 fol. 3v-4). [Public domain, available on Wikimedia.org]

By the twelfth century, *the* most voluminous undertaking of its time with respect to knowledge was another geographical work, Al Idrisi's encyclopaedic *Kitab Nuzhat*[3] (Al Idrisi and Sezgin, 1988) commissioned by Roger II of Sicily from a team of famed twelfth-century scholars led by Al Idrisi (Ibn Rushd also known as Averroes). Idrisi is included in Raphael's '*School of Athens*' as the turbaned figure on the left (see Figure 3.3). In effect, Roger II's kingdom based in Palermo represented the intersection of feudal Christian and Moorish societies. The *Kitab Nuzhat* built on previous Arab geographical texts and experience but also involved teams that did fieldwork and gathered data. Although this masterwork was unknown in Europe until the sixteenth century, its organisation of research and its presentation as a narrative and cartographic representation of knowledge – including a large circular silver map (destroyed 1160) – were world views which influenced far more than cartographic practice. It inspired European global ambition and probably stories of it inspired Columbus. The *Kitab Nuzhat* anticipated the organisation of strategic state knowledge-enterprises in later centuries, from the Inquisition to the collecting and profiling practices of Napoleonic armies to Royal Commissions and state inquiries of our time.

Spatialisation and Space-Time

Geographies scaffold presuppositions about not only the world but the cosmos. Despite the official hesitation of dictionarians and philosophers, we find an unexpected cornucopia of spatial references embedding space and time in everyday life: elaborate expressions and elegant spatial metaphors. Not surprisingly, what appears to communicate most in slogans, theoretical description and ideological diatribes are precisely spatio-temporal allusions; they place us 'in situ' in innumerable, politicised, socio-spatial/socio-temporal contexts and in partisan relationships to other groups, individuals, objects, social processes and ideas, without necessitating the explicit enunciation of this partisan relationship. They place us in a space in which we are 'to the Left' or 'to the Right' of a political issue, for example, and in a time in which futures are presented before us as consequences of the present, or where we are asked to learn from the past, referring back and forth between tenses. In this, 'space' (and time) evidently plays an important role in knowledge and in knowing the world. It is political. When we turn to our daily speech, read the headlines of our newspapers, scan learned journals, we draw on our experience and understandings of spatiality and temporality.

Conceptions of space are intimately linked to those of time, and are intrinsic in the intellectual ordering of our lives and to our everyday notions of causality and experience. Time-space is very much the stuff of common-sense as well as physics. It spills over into practice. Presuppositions about the broad context we live in – that the world is flat or round, or that time is directed to a specific, teleological endpoint or simply unfolds as a trail of the present – form actions and responses to situations.

Is space not a cultural artefact in its own right, a socially produced framework which may become a self-fulfilling prophecy by structuring actions? Nearly every philosopher and social thinker has dealt in some way with space or spatiality. However, analysis is further complicated by the intangibility of physical space. It is not a concrete object, but a 'virtuality' or set of relations that are real but not actual (see Shields, 2003). 'Space' is also translated in different ways (see Chapter 2): engineers conceive of space as a void; physicists, conceive of it mathematically as a set of dimensions (e.g. from two dimensions of a surface up to 11 dimensions in particle physics). And, in the late twentieth century, social scientists began to understand space as a qualitative context situating different behaviours and contending actions as a thoroughly social factor.

However empirical and concrete writers have attempted to be, there has been no consistent historical consensus on the nature of space that would establish an unequivocal philosophical position or a cartographic method once and for all. Statements of the 'problem of space' by Aristotle, Euclid, Descartes, Leibniz and Newton, Kant, Hegel, Nietzsche, Husserl, Merleau-Ponty, and Heidegger along with Lefebvre, have marked out entire epochs in the treatment of space. Enlightenment philosophies of space depended on Euclid's geometry and presumed a three-dimensional *extensio* known through geometry. However, the Aristotelian tradition casts space as a mental category by which objects are named and classified. And by contrast, Kant cogently argues that space is neither cognitive nor subjective (Kant, 1953: 41–51).[4] Privileging only relations over a geometrical reality involves attributing to space relations that are proper to objects. But if all continuous motions in a three-dimensional space are as real as objects are, not much is saved by denying the reality of space itself. It may not have the tangible actuality of material objects, but it has the ideal reality of a medium, intangible object or social fact (an ideal but real analytical object, similar to mathematical sets, social groups, brands, etc.; see Chapter 3 and 4 and Shields, 2003). At a minimum, space can be successfully argued to be an intangible but substantial bearer of topological properties whose consequences we can notice in ordinary experience (see Chapters 5 and 6).

If this discussion challenges nominalist, commonsensical notions of our spatiality, it remains a problem that classical approaches emphasising three-dimensional space break down in everyday usage as well as in physics and the mathematical modelling of space. Theorists of globalisation speak of 'space-time compression' in a routine manner to convey the experience of a shrinking globe, even if it is not actually changing. This is not a mental experiment. It illustrates that we live in a nuanced, changing spatialisation that is certainly distinct from the cosmology of the *Shan Hai Jing*. More significantly, it is clear that social science orthodoxies of globalisation are not based in a Euclidean space but in a 'rubber sheet geometry' of the sort which is only possible in an elastic topological space. This spatialisation is continuously changing – even since Lefebvre, Harvey (1987) and Jameson (1984) described capitalism as an 'Abstract Space'. The art of Escher demonstrates the paradoxes of mathematical '*phase spaces*' which may have any number of dimensions or may be conventional spaces warped by added factors. These are *topologies* (see Chapter 5) that depict variables as dimensions (thus a simple graph is a two-dimensional space of x and y axes). Physicists and mathematicians envision an infinite number of spaces, all in motion with respect to each other. By early in the twentieth century, the work of Lobachevski (2005) and of Riemann (1854) opened up a relativist plurality of spaces and helped legitimate the possibility that the history of the earth and its discoveries might be construed differently in different sociocultural spaces.

Before these mathematical innovations, non-Euclidean geometry was only encountered in optical illusions and visual parlour tricks. These remain and most people will have experienced the effect of a fish-eye lens on a simple object such as a triangle whose sides balloon and whose angles are similarly distorted. If these were measured with a regular protractor, the angles of the corners would be found to add up to more than 180°. However, in historical examples, one could always remove the lens, revealing the 'real' shape to be an unchanged triangle where the sum of its angles always add up to 180°. The fish-eye experience was an adventure into fictional representations of the possible, not the real. The legitimate commitment to exposing the real, rather than representations and ideologies explains nineteenth-century social science rectitude and resistance to the virtual (see Chapters 3 and 4). The twenty-first-century world depends on technologies and mathematical analyses that turn on non-Euclidean spatial modelling (i.e. representations) and on the effects of extra-dimensional phenomena at the subatomic scale where Euclidean norms do not pertain. It is not that we suddenly live in an Escher-like world, but consider that when we speak of globalisation as 'space-time compression' we are tarrying with spatialisations and topologies that are neither Euclidean nor illusory. If they have tangible effects, how might we acknowledge this while maintaining our footing in the real world of experience? How might we reflect critically on the nineteenth-century commitments to privilege one 3D spatialisation over all others in the name of truth – the one that social and spatial sciences still maintain? How might we conduct an immanent critique of the language and Euclidean rhetoric of our geography, planning and architecture?

Ever since the development of non-Euclidean geometry, Cartesian absolute space has become just one topological space that describes the human experience of embodiment. Other mathematical topologies may better describe the social configurations of those bodies in everyday life, the various perceptive and bodily capacities of other species (von Uexküll, 1909), or of wider socioeconomic processes of human populations. We are led to examine alternatives that might more appropriately describe the complexity of global culture than the common sense, Euclidean 'spatialisation'. Here, *social spatialisation* is a unity of practice, theory and presuppositions that casts the world as the play of volumes and planes in three, and only three, universal dimensions (see Chapter 2). But in a plurality of spaces, it makes sense to talk of *multiple* simultaneous social spatialisations which could be different and which gain meaning as changing topologies that map affinities between bodies, meanings and sites in time (Mach, 1901: 94; Poincaré, 1952: 50–8). The historicity of social spatialisations shown in the cases of the *Shan Hai Jing* and the *Kitab Nuzhat* continues with the admission of time as a dimension in representations of 'space-time' made by theoretical physicists since the end of the nineteenth century.

At the beginning of the twentieth century, Durkheim audaciously proposed a correspondence between social structure and society's notion of space laying the ground for structural anthropological studies. He provided the example of the Zuñi Indians, concluding that their space was nothing else than, 'the site of the tribe, only indefinitely extended beyond its real limits' (Durkheim and Mauss, 1973: 12). One could venture from reports of Aboriginal conceptions of space as the 'Dreamtime', that landscape can become more than sedimented traces. It can be a historiography, read through embodied presence, perigrination and pilgrimage. This view of social space and place is topological. As social spatialisation, it has an over-dimensioned quality – affect, memory, interaction exceed any 'physical' datum. For example, against my impoverishment as a monadic subject orphaned from my involvement with a material world that is practico-inert, such cultures and practices emphasise qualitative heterogeneity, varying not only from place to place (some being perhaps sacred, others profane); but they are also not locked within one topology: spatialisations are contested within societies or are held and contested by clans. Heterogenous social space must be produced and reproduced as a real and lived, tangible and intangible cultural artefact.

The multiplication of spaces was deeply disturbing to the common-sense mind of the nineteenth century European Left and Right. The implied subjectivity and relativism threatened the stability of objective reality, of what could be taken for granted. Space, it was argued, must 'exist before social groups can be perceived to exhibit in their disposition any spatial relations which may then be applied to the universe; the categories of quantity have to exist in order that an individual mind shall ever recognize one, the many, and the totality of the division of his society' (R. Needham, 'Preface', in Durkheim, 1976: xxvii). The reduction of 'social space' to 'physical space' re-aligned late twentieth-century social science with early nineteenth-century natural sciences. This was crucial to the nineteenth-century achievement of a homogenous spatialisation allowing and legitimating the power practices of an expansive European imperialism (Lefebvre, 1991a).

Piaget's experimental research challenged the Kantian assertion that space and time are *a priori* modes of conception:

> space is not the vague and indeterminate medium which Kant imagined; if purely and absolutely homogeneous, it would be of no use, and could not be grasped by the mind. Spatial representation consists essentially in a primary coordination of the data of sensuous experience. But this co-ordination would be impossible if the parts of space were qualitatively equivalent ... To dispose things spatially there must be a possibility of placing them differently, of putting some at the right, others at the left, these above, those below, at the north of or at the south of ... space could not be what it is if it were not, like time, divided and differentiated ... All these distinctions evidently come from the fact that different sympathetic values have been attributed to various regions ... and that almost necessarily implies that they be of social origin. (Durkheim, 1976: 11)

Knowledges of 'space' are part of social and cultural processes. Yet social space is not just a cognitive mapping (cf. Lynch, 1956). It cannot be derived entirely from forms of social solidarity. This would render space entirely cultural, whereas some aspects of spatial experience and embodied interaction are neuropsychological (such as the optical reversal of left and right in mirror images), dependent on mathematical laws of topology and on physical forces (see Chapter 5). How might one understand conflicts over social space or the production of '*counter-spaces*' of resistance and reversal of the dominant spatial logic? The concept was introduced by Lefebvre (1991a: 381–2; see Harvey, 1987) to help understand juxtapositions within social space and nested spaces within spaces in which very different rules apply (cf. Jameson, 1984).

In the late 1960s, Lefebvre turned Durkheim's hypothesis of countless social spaces back on the West to consider class struggles over the organisation and meaning of space. What are the relations masked and who is disadvantaged by the spatial common sense of a Cartesian absolute, *a priori* and ineffable 'social space'? Is this contradictory and paradoxical structure not a type of cultural 'signature' of a dominant technocratic and capitalist social spatialisation? This made social space appear to be a homogeneous, smooth order. 'Distance' became its most important feature. Rigorous discussions of the spatialisation of this system were marginalized, though influential writers of the first half of the twentieth century had prioritised the geographical expansion of capitalism as an imperialistic 'fix' for systemic contradictions and inefficiencies. The importance of non-Euclidean mathematical spaces in science set the stage for late twentieth-century re-appreciations of social space. We need to know about 'spacing' and the spatialisations that are accomplished through everyday activities, representations and rituals. How is space not just about distance between elements but an order of difference that is heterogeneous and unfolds temporally. This book asks, how is this spatialisation changing, not simply in the truisms of a shrinking world but in the sense of new digital dimensions of the internet, social software, GPS and spatial data that change the qualities and functionalities of specific places and spaces?

The Argument of this Book

The argument presented over the course of a review of the nature of space as spatialisation and the history of theories and cultural representations of space, is that we require a set of theoretical tools to analyse multiple spatialisations at the same time. We need to be able to also analyse these as time-spaces: flows of matter, time and energy, not to mention interests, ideas and bodies. This toolset is provisionally referred to as *cultural topology*. We need to be able to work with our everyday three-dimensional interactive environment, at the same time as understanding what new media theorists have called an 'augmented reality' of digital representations and wider so-called 'spaces of flows'. Non-propinquitous communities of practice and networks of influence and inscription have material effects. These are not merely socially constructed but will be argued to be real if not actual or tangible to the body. Other space-times, other dimensions enter the sensorium of the local. Explanations that cast situations predominantly in one sole spatialisation are doomed to incompleteness. We need to seek the topological coordination and entraining of multiple spatialisations around situations or events, futures and pasts.

Notes

1   Sima Qian (c.145 or 135 BCE–86 BCE) was one of the founders of Chinese history. His history covered more than 2000 years of early China, based on fieldwork and travels to verify myths. Ban Gu's (32–92 CE) geographical history influenced later gazetteers and geographies of China.
2   Unlike some other Han writings such as Chao Cuo's (c.200–154 BCE) memoir that compares and contrasts northern and southern people in a human geography which might rival that of Herodotus: 'The land of the northern barbarians is a place of accumulated darkness. The tree bark grows three inches thick, and the ice pack is six feet deep ... The people are compact and solid, while the birds and beasts have down and dense hair, so by nature they can endure the cold. ... To provide clothing and food the northern barbarians are not

attached to the ground, so their circumstances are conducive to causing disorder at the frontier. How can I prove this? The northern barbarians eat meat and drink milk fermented. They wear leather and skins. They have no settled abode inside city walls or in dwellings in the fields, so they are like flying birds or running beasts in the vast wilds. When there is excellent grass and fresh water they stop ... ' (Lewis, 2006: 298).

3 *Kitab nuzhat al-mushtaq fi ikhtiraq al-afaq* (The Recreation for Him Who Wishes to Travel Through the Countries) by Idrisi Muhammad ibn Abd al-Aziz c.1150CE.

4 See histories of philosophical definitions of space such as Koyré's cosmology *From the Closed World to the Infinite Universe* (1957), Câpek's history of 'space' as used in mathematics and physics, *The Impact of Physics on Philosophy* (1976), and surveys of 'space' as used in the social sciences in Kolaja's *Social System and Time and Space* (1969) and Sack's *Conceptions of Space in the Social Sciences* (1980).

2

spatialisations

Space as Problem: Etymology/Translation

The *Oxford Dictionary* presents more than 17 definitions for 'space', which is (like the French *espace* and the Italian *spazio*) etymologically descended from the Latin *spatium* but whose English-language meaning is often more closely related to the Latin *extensio*. Hindu philosophy defines *Akasa* (*akasha* – space/ether; Sanskrit, from *kas*, 'to shine') as an infinite, indivisible but imperceptible substance that has as its sole nature to be a static principle of extension (in contrast to movement, *prana*), or an eternal matrix or context of accommodation (*kham-akasa* see *Khândogya-Upanishad* I. 9, 1). Italian and French writers such as Lefebvre (1981a), Castells, Bachelard (1961) and Zevi have felt at ease with using the full range of meanings of '*spazio*' and '*l'espace*'. In the *Dictionnaire Larousse*, '*l'espace*' denotes 'place' (*lieu*), 'site' or an area, 'surface', or 'region'. '*L'espace*' does not mean just 'space'. By contrast, English-language theorists have often limited their appreciation of space to a quantitative definition with reference to distance and to time (and vice versa e.g. graphically on a calendar).

Twentieth-century philosophers of space first focused their attention on the category of time. It was claimed that there was a 'consequent devaluation' of space in favour of time (Foucault, 1980: 69). For most of the social sciences, it has remained the exception rather than the rule when philosophers or social scientists have examined space from angles other than as purely a neo-Kantian *a priori*.[1] Space is just there (and thus colonised): a context that will be ignored by most analysts in favour of the objects it contains and their interaction and development. Even in architecture, a profession that deals intimately with the formation of spaces, discussions of space numbly concern the boundaries of spaces (walls, property lines and so on). When space does catch our attention as an object of analysis, we discover that social science vocabulary in particular works against us; we are blinkered at an apparently profound level.

Definitions of 'space' have often collapsed into a mathematical and geometrical discussion designating a morphologically-specific arrangement of a set of elements, where *distance* and *form* are pre-eminent. This, however, is a jarring case of Eurocentrism. For example, to make *distance* the basis of the sociological appreciation of space, of spatialisation, reifies distance as an invariant concept. Anthropologically speaking, the understanding of distance varies culturally depending on factors such as different cultural conceptions of time and different rhythms of life (Martins, 1982: 181). Only in Cartesian rationalism is distance fixed as just a quantitative measurement. In such a scheme, the possible 'politics of arrangements' – that x is beside y instead of z; that a noise-producing freeway could be planned beside an area of state-welfare-supported accommodation rather than a high-priced residential development – is evacuated from the discussion. This is in stark contrast to the apparent comfort writers in other cultures and historical moments have felt at the use of the full range of meanings of space and spatialisation even in the most rigorously self-critical of texts. '*L'espace*', as used in urban studies texts written in and translated into French, denotes 'place' (*lieu*), 'site' (in the sense in which one might speak of the green spaces of a city, where 'space' could just as well be replaced by 'place': the green places), 'surface', and 'area' or 'region' (a 'stretch of land': *une étendue*). Economic region can easily be expressed as *espace économique*.

The truth easily lost in translation is, of course, that 'l'espace' does *not* mean just 'space'. The failure to address this translation problem leaves most recent authors who wish to build upon Lefebvre's work or to introduce it to English-speaking audiences vulnerable to the criticisms that, firstly, they do not provide a clear conceptual framework to support their claims of providing a 'dramatic' or 'radical' reconceptualisation of social science approaches to 'social space'. Secondly, they do not clearly indicate to their readers that they have a defined object of inquiry: they fail to answer the question 'what is space?'. For this reason, the work of Martins and many others (Martins, 1982), the popularisation of Lefebvre by Jameson (1984), the work of geographers and others appear somewhat overstated, even after the most sympathetic readings.

The traditional discourses are plagued by their reference to the ill-defined terms 'space', or 'social space'. These deflect analysis away from 'space' itself, away from any confrontation with the significance of the term, towards its acceptance as a neutral void. It is significant that there is no precise definition of the word – its meaning changing with the context of its use and the accompanying (modifying) words which surround it. In many cases, space is defined with reference to time (Jammer, 1960), as in 'a "space" of time', denoting a lapse or extent of time between two definite points. J.B. Priestley stresses this spatialisation of time (Priestley, 1964: 105). Durkheim provides the brilliant example of the typical Western calendar where, by convention, the passing of time in days is denoted not only by the numeric system of dates but also by movement from top to bottom and left to right along rows on visual calendars (Durkheim, 1976: 11–12).

Similarly, Durkheim suggests that the circular calendars of the Mayans correspond in their form to a cyclical temporality. 'Space' also signifies duration, linear distance, a proper place (as in a 'parking space') or relationship, area (in two and three dimensions), any stretch, section, extension around a point, portion, or extent within limits. There is literary space, the space between words, problem spaces, the spacing of musical notes, leisure time ('having "space"' to do something), and a host of metaphorical usages: 'spaced-out', 'in time and space', 'inner space', 'social space' and 'problem space' (*Oxford English Dictionary*, 1976).

Translation difficulties, and the vagaries of translation from older texts into the modern vocabulary (which, it could be argued, has its own historically specific preconceptions about 'spatiality') pose formidable problems.[2] Based on the lack of any systematic approach in this area, and the divergent citations of historical precedents with respect to the definition and treatment of space, it is fair to note that social scientists (for example, Sack, Lefebvre and Kolaja) dealing with 'space' make a series of apparently arbitrary decisions regarding whom they view as the seminal thinkers with respect to space (for example, compare the above histories with Kern (1983), with Harbison (1977); and with Lefebvre's equally selective compilation (Lefebvre, 1981b). In 1980, Soja went as far as to write:

> while such adjectives as 'social', 'political', 'economic', and even, 'historical' generally suggest, unless otherwise specified, a link to human action and motivation, the term 'spatial' typically evokes the image of something physical and external to the social context and to social action, a part of the 'environment', a context for society – its container – rather than a structure created by society. (Soja, 1980: 210)

Nonetheless, our semantic confusion does not stop us from using the word in almost any context as one term in a helpful metaphor, or as an analogy for an abstract concept (to indicate the 'passing' of time). 'Space' proliferates in our discourse. If we do not use the word 'space', *per se*, then we use *spatial* descriptions, such as Heidegger's 'clearing' in the forest as a metaphor for becoming and emergence, or Kojève's illustration of his ontology using the image of the gold ring whose hole is as essential to its existence as is its gold (Kojève and Queneau, 1947: 214). Despite the official hesitation of dictionarians and philosophers, we find an unexpected cornucopia of spatial references, elaborate expressions and elegant spatial metaphors when we turn to our daily speech, read the headlines of our newspapers, scan the philosophical journals, eavesdrop on the small-talk of the early morning commuter and the scripts of the afternoon TV soaps. These are most often the key 'catch-phrases', the essential philosophical card trick of the wily writer who wishes to provoke a sudden deep breath of insight – the 'ah hah!' moment.

In what became a global *lingua franca*, rigorous discussions of capitalism and modernity as spatial regimes were marginalised, though influential writers of the first half of the twentieth century prioritised geographical expansion of capitalism as a 'fix' for system contradictions and inefficiencies. Partly as a result of its nebulous status, 'space' has been appropriated as a metaphor for countless abstract concepts. The major theorists who will be considered in this book also encounter this difficulty but often fail to resolve it. A direct encounter with the multitudinous meanings of 'space' and an acceptance of the legitimacy of the various appropriations of the term to explain, describe, and understand it is necessary. The fact that spatial metaphors are used in theories of organisational structure, or as key legal and social science concepts such as 'alienation' (in which the dual roots of (1) estrangement/belonging and (2) the being 'of' some other *place*, are fundamentally entwined) is considered a significant shading of an overall conceptual system which calls on 'space' (and 'time') to structure and orient the entire system of thought and culture toward subjects and toward the 'world'.

Tracts of literature exist for us to refer to if we are interested in understanding a study of geographic space (perhaps the impact of distance and dispersion on cultural formations, or perhaps the quantitative description and measurement of urban commuting regions, or perhaps, again, a study of patterns of corporate concentration 'in space'). However, for those interested in mounting a rigorous inquiry into the position of space in cultures – as a metaphor, as a cultural medium of ritual, or as a socially created bearer of meanings encoded as distance, geometry, separation and relation, in other words, as a whole social spatialisation – space seems a suddenly inaccessible territory. Words fail; the most articulate of texts fall dumb. The linguistic-epistemological problem in English is that it has difficulty in treating 'space' itself as an object of inquiry. Abuse and not a small degree of fuzzy thinking has led to the term 'space' being almost useless for rigorous discourse:

> [w]e really do not have a widely used and accepted expression to convey the inherently social quality of organized space, especially since the term 'social space' has become so murky with multiple and often incompatible meanings. (Soja, 1980: 210)

This situation has slowly changed in the English language literature with recognition of the importance of globalisation in social science and geography, the translation of works from French and an engagement with literary sources that describe social spaces and spatialisation qualitatively. Over the last 30 years, the translation of the work of Lefebvre has been a barometer of this changing awareness.

'L'Espace Lefebvre'

In contrast, Henri Lefebvre begins his inquiry into 'space' with the explicit aim of contributing to the revolutionary and emancipatory project of Marxism. In the late 1960s, Lefebvre began inquiries into urban space with the explicit aim of discovering the role of space in maintaining a political-economic order. He refuses to privilege biology or nature (as environmental determination), or to consider social forms of territory as universal. He turns Durkheim's hypothesis of countless social spaces around to consider struggles over the organisation and meaning of space as a problem for social and political research. Is not the near hegemony of the 'absolutist' view of social space only one possible stance among many? What are its structural linkages with the theoretical spaces of physics and the 'real' spaces of everyday life? What are the real relations masked by the spatial phantasmagoria of a Cartesian absolute, *a priori* and ineffable 'social space'? Is this contradictory and paradoxical structure not a type of cultural 'signature', of a dominant 'modern' technocratic and capitalist social spatialisation?

Much has been written on Henri Lefebvre's (1901–1991) important critique of Enlightenment spatialisation, which renders space merely a container or void to be filled (Lefebvre, 1991b, see Shields, 1999). In *La Production de l'espace*, first published in 1974, Lefebvre responds with a synthesis of the positions outlined above, drawing on his training as a philosopher, his experience founding France's first Sociology Department (Strasbourg), his work with planners and his engagement with counter-cultural critics (from his early days, Dada and Surrealism, through the Situationists such as Debord and the architect Constant in the 1950s, and Parisian students of May 1968). If not directly building on earlier figures, Lefebvre's career path and his acquaintance with German ensured that he engaged with the positions of not only Marx and Nietzsche, but also others such as the sociologist Max Weber (cited directly and paraphrased indirectly) and the literary theorist Bakhtin (translated into French in 1970 with a preface by Kristeva (Bakhtin, 1970)), or the historian of human sciences, Foucault. His work also directly and indirectly critiqued other theorists, including Kristeva, Derrida, Sartre, Barthes, Althusser.

His discovery, after Nietzsche, of the fundamental importance of space in maintaining (reified) epistemological categories leads, in turn, to a re-examination of the epistemological legacies of the Enlightenment, including Marxism. An important Nietzsche scholar and translator in his own right (Lefebvre, 1939, 1959, 1962, 1967) Lefebvre identifies Nietzsche as one key historical figure for a re-examination of space. Unlike Hegelian space which is a residue of a past-ward moving Time, Nietzsche's Space is the substrate of force and being. From this, Lefebvre attempts to develop specific strategic ideas for emancipation within the spatial context of the twentieth-century urbanised nation-state (Lefebvre, 1970b, 1973, 1974, 1978: Ch. 5, 2009), which are based on his earlier contributions to the theorisation of the spatial activities of 'daily life' (Lefebvre, 1947, 1961, 1962, 1968a).

Written in the aftermath of the student occupation of key institutions in Paris during the six weeks of the countercultural 'moment' of May 1968, 'La Production de l'espace' (1974) is a product of the early 1970s reflection on the failure of the May '68 occupations to achieve lasting change. Lefebvre sought to synthesise his work over a decade on the relationship between the urban and revolutionary resistance. The book presents a historical study of the overarching creation of a spatial order and dynamics to cities and surrounding territories. Although read and parsed by a few scholars, it was not translated into English until some 18 years later (1991a; cf. Shields, 1986). Prior texts such as *Revolution urbaine* (Lefebvre, 1970a translated as Lefebvre, 2003) and *Le Droit à la ville* (Lefebvre, 1968b) as well as subsequent texts such as the four volume *De l'Etat* (Lefebvre, 1978 excerpted in translation in Lefebvre, 2009) are essential reading for understanding the specificity of urban and national scales, respectively. As it stands, *La Production de l'espace* is insufficient.

Lefebvre refers to his project variously as a 'spatiology' and 'architectonics' (cf. Lefebvre, 1991b: Ch. 3). Essentially, his thesis is that 'space' is a collectively produced or elaborated 'social space', which is better translated as a social spatialisation. While Lefebvre does use the French '*spatialisation*' (only twice in *La Production de l'espace* (1981b: 117, 234). He uses it in opposition to '*localisation*', or fixing in place. The term stresses relationships and settings: 'The vertical and height will always spatially manifest the presence of a power capable of violence. In relation to the spectator, this very particular spatialisation ...' (1974: 117).

For Lefebvre, 'space represents the realm of flows of capital, money, commodities and information ... place comprises the locus and a sort of stopping of those flows, a specific moment in the dynamics of space-relations under capitalism' (Merrifield, 1993: 525). In section 3.8 of his Chapter on 'Spatial Architectonics' in *La Production de l'espace*, Lefebvre emphasises the psychological significance of the body itself as a space of consciousness from which the ego subtracts itself to establish identity: 'This operation, inextricably magical and rational, sets up a strange interplay between (verbal) disembodiment and (empirical) re-embodiment, between uprooting and re-implantation, between spatialisation in an abstract expanse and localisation in a determinate expanse' (Lefebvre, 1991b: 203; cf. Lefebvre, 1981b: 234 (s III.8)).[3]

Lefebvre's '*place*' has been read as, 'the delimited order of inter-related elements that are prescribed in a distinct location ... A space, on the other hand, exists only when mobile elements (implying direction, velocity and time) intersect, and it is this relationship of movements that produce space'

(Zieleniec, 2007: 71). Merrifield refers to place as the 'thingification' of 'material flows', grasping for a sense of how things change as their dynamics slow from global circuits to local relations in which capitalism is enacted in everyday labour and local events. A stronger argument, however, would be that the nature of places is forged out of real but intangible relationships between participants in capitalism over time and over distance, intersecting and coming into specific relationships vis-à-vis tangible goods and material processes, all grounded in a particular location. That is, place is a combination of actualising virtualities, such as social and commercial relationships, and realising abstractions, such as ideologies of planning or representations of particular regions (as diagrammed in the Preface). It surpasses location and takes on the qualities of the social spatialisation that it materialises.

La Production de l'espace does not separate spatialisation completely from place as localisation in the way that Castells attempts to do with his vision of a dynamic space of flows in which place is dominated as a mere static, parochial node of localisation. Spatialisation includes the translation of elements of identity into grandiose surrogates in a spatial counterpart to alienation:

> Verticality and great height have ever been the spatial expression of potentially violent power. This very particular type of spatialisation, though it may seem 'normal' or even 'natural' to many people, embodies ... a twofold strategy ... a metonymic logic consisting in a continual to-and-fro movement ... By constantly expanding the scale of things, this movement serves to compensate for the pathetically small site of each set [or part] ...

> The second 'logic' embodied in this spatialisation is a logic ... of metaphorisation. Living bodies, the bodies of 'users' – are caught up not only in the toils of parcellized space but also in the web of ... images, signs and symbols. These bodies are transported out of themselves, transferred and emptied out, as it were, via the eyes ... with doubles of themselves in prettified, smiling and happy poses; and this campaign to void them succeeds exactly to the degree that the images proposed correspond to 'needs' that those same images have helped fashion. (Lefebvre, 1991b: 98; compare Lefebvre, 1981b: 117–18)

Alienation is at the centre of Lefebvre's work in general, and his interest in space in particular, because Abstract Space establishes the ground and frame for other alienations (Shields, 1999: 42; Gardiner, 1999).[4] Against those who argue that Lefebvre simply restates Marx's position my argument is that he goes beyond both Marx and Engels in offering additional elements that transcend a political economy of alienation and reification. In particular, his analysis includes the little analysed discussion of 'intelligence of the body' itself, reminiscent of Deleuze and Guattari's critique of

the dissection of the body into functions but as applicable to the body of a
spider as to a human (Lefebvre, 1981b: 204; 1991a: 174): the body as 'first
nature' that has been forgotten. He is important for reconnecting the question of consciousness to political economy and to the body in a manner that
unifies frame and content, form and matter.

> The object produced often bears traces of the materiel and time used: the
> operations that that have modified raw material. One can thus recon-
> struct them. However, productive operations tend to erase their traces;
> some even see this as their goal: polishing, varnishing, facing, plaster-
> ing etc. Once construction is finished, scaffolding is taken down ... This
> way, products and even works have a further characteristic: to detach
> themselves from productive labor. To such a point that one forgets this,
> and it is this forgetting – or, as a philosopher might say, this mystifica-
> tion [or reification] – that makes possible the fetishism of goods: the fact
> that commodities imply social relationships and lead to their misappre-
> hension. ('qu'elle implique des rapports sociaux et qu'elle entraîne leur
> méconnaissance' – Lefebvre 1981b: 134 my translation, cf. 1991a: 113)

Lefebvre defines 'l'espace' as 'l'espace social', as 'social space'. But a 'social
space is not a socialized space (pace Matoré, 1962) ... the "socialisation" of
whatever precedes society' (Lefebvre, 1991b: 190). 'L'espace' is produced but
not as a 'thing among other things': '(Social) space [L'espace (social)] is ...
an outcome of a sequence and set of operations ... itself the outcome of past
actions, social space [L'espace social] is what permits fresh actions to occur,
whilst suggesting others and prohibiting yet others' including production,
consumption and knowledge or meaning (Lefebvre, 1991b: 73; cf. Lefebvre,
1981b: 88–9). Space mirrors and then perpetuates socioeconomic divisions
and hierarchies. Social space,

> ceases to be indistinguishable from mental space (as defined by the phi-
> losophers and mathematicians) on the one hand, and physical space (as
> defined by practico-sensory activity and the perception of 'nature') on the
> other ... constituted neither by a collection of things ... nor by a void –
> packed like a parcel with various contents ... (Lefebvre 1991b: 27; cf.
> Lefebvre, 1981b: 30)

'L'espace' is all embracing, seeking what could be influenced by spatialisations in different historical epochs rather than simply defining and delim-
iting the spatialisation of one particular time or place. I suggest this is at
root a social spatialisation, which includes (1) a set of spatial relations (i.e.
space proper) between and on which core elements of the mode of production (and consumption) depend; (2) the arrangements of architecture
and the landscape; (3) understandings and representations of that logic; and

(4) cultural forms of social space that include the body and its gestures and comportment. The translation of '*l'espace*' as spatialisation has stuck (see e.g. Zieleniec, 2007: 76), but it is worth noting Lefebvre's own use of '*spatialisation*' (above).

Lefebvre's '*l'espace*', moreover, is analytical and methodological in nature. Lefebvre identifies three dialectical moments or theses of '*l'espace*', embedding his analysis within an enlarged and unorthodox but still recognisably Hegelian and Marxist assessment of domination and resistance:

1 'Practices of Space' involve producing and enacting spatial order in every action, challenging the constructions we engage in. Elsewhere he refers to these as '*l'espace perçu*' of commonsensical action and 'perceived space'.

2 'Representations of Space' (or 'Discourses on Space') are found in narratives, such as the idea that space is an a-political neutral void, or theories of the planning professions or cartographic conventions that assume that the landscape can be rationally planned and subdivided – especially into planning zones for different uses. These discourses require argument and refutation. He also refers to this as '*l'espace conçu*' or 'conceived space'.

3 And, finally 'Spaces of Representation' (or 'Discourses of Space') frame our understandings of what is possible and how our senses and bodies are embedded in space. These more insidious habits of understanding are the special purview of radical artists who must challenge the ways we see the world and ourselves. Elsewhere he refers to the potential of this most intangible of aspects of spatiality to become '*l'espace vecu*' or 'lived space': a kind of Nietzschean, fully engaged and unalienated identification of the actor, their actions and activities, with the environment itself.

All three influence and tug at each other, producing '*l'espace*' as a dialectical synthesis at any given historical mode of production. Marx's modes of production become modes of production of space. If anything is a mark of Lefebvre's analysis, it is the combination of totalisation and periodisation.

Respecting Lefebvre: Critical Tensions

We pay creative thinkers such as Lefebvre no respect by enshrining his work as a new *doxa*, something that risks happening in geography amongst a particularly American industry of translators and whips concerned about gaining Lefebvre epistemological and professional legitimacy. There are a number of key themes in Lefebvre's theorisation of space. These, however, are often rendered, both in his *Production de l'espace* and in the secondary literature, in an uncritical shorthand which leaves them not up to par with either his ambition or the way he presents them in other works.

1. *Periodicisation:* In Lefebvre's analysis, spatialisations are presented as a set of historical periods, whose boundaries cannot be clearly defined. This divides history into a set of hypostatised epochs glossed and characterised in a manner akin to stereotyping. It sweeps diversity into univocity under the umbrella of a single narrative. These reify historical experience. Dependent on the quality of historical research at the time of writing, Lefebvre inadvertently produces his own Representation of Space. However dialectical, each of his spatialisations is set up as a signature of a given epoch. The reliance on periodicisation neuters the dialectic in a snapshot of each period. Ironically, on the dynamism of history, Lefebvre is *not dialectical enough*. Or, as will be argued, his analysis flattens heterogeneities into a narrower repertoire of difference than required for a progressive critique, into dialectics at a rather grand scale rather than the nuances of lived experience.

According to Lefebvre's thought, it becomes impossible to theorise the change from one epoch to another except as revolution. In this model of historicity, a particular type of praxis is produced that emphasises revolutionary projects that alter the mode of the production (and mode of production of space) as the most significant basis of historical change. Politics is first and foremost, and most urgently, one of class struggle against the social basis of the system that produces space: 'its role in the production of space is a cardinal one in that this production is performed solely by classes ... inscribed in space. Indeed it is that struggle alone which prevents Abstract Space from taking over the whole planet' (Lefebvre, 1991b: 55). New alliances against risk and around the environment and commonly held goods become less likely to be understood as the first line of political intervention. However, important to Lefebvre's contribution is that he locates classes as spatial as well as historical agents with a rare clarity.

2. *Totalisation:* Lefebvre conceives of '*l'espace*' as all-encompassing, operating at multiple scales, from the body to international airspace. Even if fractured by resistance and carrying the inheritance of previous modes of production (of space), every epoch has its mode of production (of space) that dominates the necessities and practicalities of the vast majority of the population and of the territory. As colonialism and globalisation expanded the reach of capitalism and its associated forms of modernity, one globalised 'hypercapitalist' mode of production began to dominate the entire globe, entangling everything and everyone in matrices of association and exchange that are informational and physical. Lefebvre concludes *La Production de l'espace* on the challenges of this '*espace planetaire*'.

Nonetheless, his analysis centres on 'the interplay of everyday experience and interactions within historical modes of production' (Zieleniec, 2007: 85). 'Everyday life' (*la vie quotidienne*) is his parallel project to '*l'espace*' that spans four separate volumes between 1947 and 1981 as well as numerous articles over a broader period (Lefebvre, 1947, 1961, 1968a, 1981a; see Shields, 1999).

In a critique of Heidegger, Lefebvre argues that everyday life is not simply 'everydayness' (alienation, *Alltäglichkeit*), not simply repetition or routine as the manner Being is dominated (Heidegger 1962: 422 ss.II.4 ¶71) but *recurrences* of otherwise unique events, *cycles* of reproduction and seasonal celebration, and wholly particular and unique '*moments*' in which all aspects of '*l'espace*', of consciousness and embodiment are unified in a oneness with an unfolding experience (see Lefebvre, 1959 and Harvey, 1991). Lefebvre adds to Heidegger the insight that the 'everyday' is sociologically and politically important as a ground of possibility, not just an existential actualisation of a philosophical ideal that should be displaced nor simply a fallen manner of being in which 'everything is all one and the same... In everydayness Dasein can undergo dull "suffering", sink away in the dullness of it, and evade it...' (Heidegger, 1962: 422).

This eventually culminates in Lefebvre's final text, written with Catherine Régulier-Lefebvre, on '*Rhythmanalysis*' that stresses the flow and changeable quality of affects such as alienation, hope and enthusiasm. Out of alienation, boredom and meaningless repetition, can arise transformative 'moments' of dis-alienation that hold a potential as the seeds of collective change (Shields, 1999 69ff.; Davidson et al., 2011). If modernity is a cultural system of signs, then everyday life is a 'compound of insignificances' (Lefebvre, 1971: 24) – in-sign-ificant gestures given importance when brought together under the concept of space. 'Everyday life, the social territory and place of controlled consumption, of terror-enforced passivity, is established and programmed; as a social territory it is easily identified' (Lefebvre, 1971: 197). Everyday life is a specifically modern geography of sites where we endure bored distraction, but also engage in fantastic daydreams. It lies within the realm of consumption and the social reproduction of labour that we inhabit in our daily journeys through time and space.

The body grounds everyday life in its routines and relations to the environment. Indeed, Lefebvre is one of the first theorists of cultural understandings of the body. He offers a Freudian psychoanalysis of spatiality. The body provides the pivot between spatial and social orders. Although he has been critiqued for his heterosexism and his alignment of the feminine with the passive, he is not as 'phallo-happy' as the English reception has suggested (see Shields, 1999: 174). He is writing ahead of critiques of heterosexuality and insights on cultural embodiments offered by gay, lesbian and queer theorists and now deepened by trans theorists. However, by neglecting gender, he offers a frustratingly incomplete critique of the body's spatiality. Not only are women missing except as domestic labourers, this undermines the specificity of men as the other pole in Lefebvre's heterosexual assumptions.

In effect, we get a gender-flattened topology smuggled into his history of modes-of-production of space in which an essential aspect of the politics and the affect of places is removed, leaving only Lefebvre's romanticised discussions of infatuated love as a spontaneous experience in which space may contract and time stands still experientially. What Lefebvre could have produced would unknot the heterodox quality he values in any place. This reflects the diversity of intentionalities and plans, intersecting flows and relations to other places, and remnants of past moments taken up again in current social action and spatial projects. This allows the space itself to be understood as non-unified and heterological, multidimensional and evolving in different ways at the same time. That means that different logics of sexuality, for example, different 'pitches' to interaction, can coexist in the same space and time to radically different (and conflict-provoking) ends. Analysis of such a space would not look for unity or historical periodicisation, but the dissonantly sonorous co-presence of difference. However, Lefebvre would require a different analytic toolkit to get to this degree of resolution than even a three-part dialectic – for which the final chapter will propose a cultural topology.

3. Production: Lefebvre makes a very significant theoretical intervention into Marxism by revising the definition of the production of cities, landscapes and territories to refer more to the production of works of art or to 'the work of nature' than of commodities and other products. Smith summarises Lefebvre's understanding of the trialectical production of space:

> Space is *perceived* through involvement in 'social practices', *conceived* in 'representations' of that space, e.g. architecture, and *lived* through the association of images and symbols with specific 'representational spaces' that acquire and communicate meanings and are the loci of passions, e.g. the home, the wilderness and so on. Each aspect of this triad of spatial relations is in a dialectical relation with the others. For example, Lefebvre argues that the manner in which any space, real or imagined, is *represented* constitutes an intervention in the social fabric through its attempt to set out and construct a model of that society and what it might become. (Smith, 2001: 36)

The city, like a sculpture or painting, is an *oeuvre* according to Lefebvre. The quality of such 'works' is preciousness and an artist gives themselves totally to the process by which their works are created. This theoretical move makes everyone a creator and contributor to the production of the city, of space, and a stakeholder, an inheritor of a patrimony, a 'right to the city'. It underlines the totality and coherence of '*l'espace*' against the reigning practice of dealing with spatial issues by planning particular buildings, sites, and assuming the interchangeability of these lots as property.

4. Oeuvre has been barely examined in the subsequent literature on social space and spatialisation. For example, Maria-Carolina Cambre draws attention to Godard's warning 'I do not believe in the concept of "a work." There are works, there are some that are new, but the work as a whole, the great work, is something that does not interest me, I prefer to talk of a journey' (my translation, Godard in Lañamme and Kaganski, 2010: online; see Cambre, 2011). One stands back from the artistic work, the *oeuvre*, often to either contemplate or criticise, but rarely to inhabit, demolish or recreate. Does Lefebvre's concept help us do this? Does it help us man*ouevre* tactically in the city or is it really an abstract intervention into a theoretical debate within Marxism? We need to know much more about the apparent tactility of *l'ouvre* and how it sits within and shapes time and space, for example as memories and relations.

Missing also is a sense of artifice or play in cities as artefacts, in architecture and in tactical appropriations of space. Roman Jakobson identified artifice as a distinct mode of signs that applies when one thing avowedly poses as something else – for example, participants in costume at a masked ball. They are dressed as an animal, for instance, but one knows they are human and engages in the play of signification. Rather than a factual relation, here meaning is imputed (Preziosi, 2003: 143; Jakobson 1980). Artifice is 'the only self-conscious sign type and the only ... whose intention is to represent something other or ... more than what it seems to. Like disguise or camouflage (McCarthy, 2002), once it is seen-through ... it ceases to act in that way' (Cambre, 2011: 29ff.). Rather than a factual relation, meaning is imputed (Preziosi, 2003: 143); what appears to be one thing is actually another, but virtually it passes as if something else. That is, it operates as virtually and actually real in contradictory ways.

When meaning in the environment points in different directions at the same time, the result is a double entendre. One not only engages in the intrigue: people are forced to consider the alternatives or switch back and forth between levels and modes of meaning. This movement of understanding that is part of unstable meanings introduces a dynamism to how we interact with environments and social spaces: it destabilizes the sense of equilibrium in social spatialisations as cultural formations. The to-and-fro between the literal sense of a place and its unofficial or habitual meanings and uses pits actual usages against intangible conventions and meanings.

This epistemological fluidity of *ontological mobilities* is referred to as *syncresis* (Davidson et al., 2011: 119–21). Where there is a movement between the virtual and concrete, a liminality is introduced at the interface between the two that opens up the bond between tangible and intangible aspects of commodities, bodies and places (see the diagram in the Preface). Jokes, puns, tactical acts of resistance, *détournements* and parodies work this boundary. Ontological mobility refers to the impossibility of fixing a phenomenon as either-or concretely, actually-real, or virtually, ideally-real (see Table 1.1 in Preface).

To code this diagram in Lefebvre's terminology, there is a dialectic between different actually real Practices of Space, contending ideal and possible

Representations of Space and various ideal yet real Spaces of Representation that form intangible, or 'virtual' images of a place as a site with certain qualities or appropriate to certain activities. It is possible to find Practices of Space such as buying and selling on a street, contrasting with official Representations of Space that insist trading shall not happen on thoroughfares, and unofficial Representations of Space that depict that same street as a local destination for specific purchases. All these might again confront contradictory Spaces of Representation that cast that street as a market or that commerce as a regulated activity carried out in the interior of licensed shops. A survey might find that the probability of any actually-possible activity or a particular understanding is distributed amongst passers-by depending on class or time-of-day. Hence the proposal for a rhythmanalysis of moments, routines and cycles in these spaces (Lefebvre and Regulier-Lefebvre, 1992), but semiotic insights already applied in urban and architectural research could invigorate geographical understandings of Lefebvre's work with a sense of dynamism.

There is an *art* to living spatialisations that involves negotiating the play of this artifice and adapting oneself to the different roles they provide for bodies to engage with each other and the environment. Cambre notes the resort to adequation in our judgements – good enough logic – rather than conclusive identification and decision. That is, we engage on a pragmatic and provisional basis, accepting that change may be necessary (Preziosi, 2003). Depending on one's experience and local knowledge one might expect fundamentally different social spaces. Lefebvre claims a democratic 'right to the city'. Which of these is part of the city to which one has a right? Which of these several, superimposed and flickering street scenes is part of 'your' city?

The appropriation of space depends on arts of spatialisation: for example, loitering in a shopping mall but posing as a bona fide consumer. Hanging out on street-corners and in other public spaces may also fall under this category. Squatting might be a further example. Criminal activity often relies on dissimulation that must be decoded by potential clients. Such dialectical levels are essential to understand the hijackings and appropriations that add complexity to the meaning and the function of everyday spaces in the city and in rural landscapes. This doubling or layering of spaces is intrinsically political and aggressively intervenes against legal and administrative regimes. It is as important in urban contexts as the official and legitimated shapings of place and space. These insights set up a 'problematique' but it is up to the reader to work out the answers. The theory doesn't quite get to the street. Fisher, drawing on the work of María Lugones (2003), argues that if theory is abstract and produced from an objective distance, but resistance is concrete, embodied and produced in the moment, in the midst of oppressive spaces, then how can a resistant theory exist. It is of little help to theorise strategy:

> If people resist and abstract theory does not include embodied people
> as active subjects, then abstract theory cannot comprehend or express

resistance. Abstract space produces '"users" who cannot recognize them-selves within it, and a thought which cannot conceive of adopting a criti-cal stance towards it' (Lefebvre 1991b: 93). The erasure of active subjects from the abstracted position of ... strategists results in what Lefebvre calls 'the *entire* problem: the 'silence of the "users"' (1991: 365). My claim is that the users are speaking, moving, and producing space(s). The problem is that their voices and movements and productions are not registered from the abstracted position.

> According to Lugones, the solution to this problem is the creation of tactical strategies – a blend of theory and practice. Tactical strategies are positioned concretely, on the street. Lugones argues for streetwalker theorizing that sees the world close-up, street level, yet deeply. (Fisher, 2008: 163)

5. *Differential Space*: differential space-time, which became the preferred term in Lefebvre's more widely read *Production de l'espace* (Lefebvre, 1981b) transcends the spatial distinction of the near and far, allowing the urban – and by extension the city – to function as a site of exchange between different parties, forces and elements. Different networks are juxtaposed and superim-posed (Lefebvre, 2003: 121). It is above all the urban that is 'informed' by difference (Lefebvre, 2003: 133). Heterotopias are both precluded and inter-woven in the urban: ordered times and spaces are separated by crossroads, neutral spaces, freeways, revolutions and liminal moments. The status of the urban is not merely an abstraction, a theory, but a logic that is temporal and spatial. The rules of private property and surplus value are integral to it, but the urban is not reducible solely to them; its sociality exceeds these economic and political processes. Settlements not only involve coordination around the tolling of bells and clock time but have distinctive temporal rhythms that correspond to the coordination of urban populations: rush hours, open-ing and closing times of businesses and schools, market days, festivals and parade days, curfews, to name only a few. Lefebvre thereby initiates a debate later joined by Castells and later writers on the powers and utility of the urban as a problematique (Castells, 1977; Saunders, 1981). In the city, sev-eral spatial logics meet head on: consumption, the state, production and the residuum of everyday life. Lefebvre refers to this as an 'isotopia'. It produces the historical-cultural form of the city. The urban designates this 'differential' space: each place or locale exists only within the whole through contrasts and oppositions which connect and distinguish it.

> Superficially it may appear that I have been describing and analyzing the genesis of the city as an object ... But my initial concern has been with a virtual object which I have used to describe a space-time axis. The further illuminates the past, the virtual allows us to examine and situate the realized.

The complexity of the urban phenomenon is not that of an 'object' ... presented as *real* prior to any examination ...

> Rather than being an object that can be examined through contempla-
> tion [i.e. abstractly] the reality of the urban phenomenon would be a *vir-*
> *tual object*. If there is a sociological concept, it is that of 'urban society'.
> (Lefebvre, 2003: 23, 57, 58)

Although his work is dated in some of its assumptions, there are outstanding insights to be gained from Lefebvre's texts. At the same time, the overwhelming stress on aligning spatialisation with Marxist historiography – via the notion that modes of production are in effect modes of spatialisation – introduces periodisations that rely on ideal types such as 'Feudalism' or 'Primitive Com-munism' rather than the diversity of empirical evidence. While some have noted that space is cut off from time, the problem is that Lefebvre's spaces are tied to a particular temporality of historical periods that is itself a deeply entrenched narrative of modernism and the triumph of the West. It is no surprise that colo-nies and global peripheries go so often unmentioned in Lefebvre's work. By using a nineteenth-century historiography, Lefebvre's system of thought denies his radically enlarged three-part dialectic. In addition, it ties '*l'espace*' and spa-tialisation to a model of extrinsic periods derived from economic rather than spatial analysis. While we can agree that spatialisation is an ongoing process of production that is also a concretised product or *oeuvre*, this dynamism is not reflected in the series of periods that seem to be all about equilibrium. This is reached in the logic and regime of spaces and spacings, whether that be during Feudal times or during Industrial Capitalism.

Contra Lefebvre, spatialisation has a dynamism which escapes the theo-retical abstraction from everyday life that he joins Marx in imposing. This is a Space of Representation nestled like a creature in a seashell, at the inner-most turn of Lefebvre's Representation of Space. It is that we turn to a post-Lefebvrean but still Lefebvrean representation of space as not only spa-tialisation but as *topological*, which provides an integrated context for the analysis of temporalisation and spatialisation. This allows us a more critical understanding of the need for a dynamic rather than periodised understand-ing of spatialisation. Perhaps because of such limitations, we need to seize the spirit of Lefebvre's project: his works are 'open spaces' that must be occasions for new approaches.

The Spatialisation of Places and Regions

Senses of place and region transcend the purely 'natural' and material, and we must look beyond the environment of the site – and beyond the site itself to properly understand a 'sense of place'. Spatially, any site is obviously interconnected with other places. Temporally, historical patterns may extend into the future as projected trends. However, we can go further to say that these are part of overall, relational networks of similarly mythified sites and regions in which each place or region is distinguished not only by its proper place-myth but by its distinctiveness and contrasts with other sites. This *geography of difference* is socially constructed over the long term and constitutes a spatialisation of places and regions as 'places-for-this' and/or 'places-for-that'. That is, each site or area is construed as appropriate for certain social activities and behaviours – and this is central to its identity. Places and regions are cast – or spatialised – as certain types of place: romantic, harsh, warm, boring, polluted, foreign, and so on. The 'first nature' of topology is reconstructed as a 'second nature' (Lefebvre, 1991b). Place is not just a matter of real estate or landed property; it is intellectual property, cultural property. What might merely be notable or strategically advantageous land is only the geological foundation of a mythic landscape of historic national events, or a memory of a nationalist history, not to mention advertising images. Visual representations, literature and folk tales, small and tall, are aspects of the spatialisation of a site or region. This is hardly a fixed system of coordinates, rather it is a relational network of differences which provides the principle and rationale for movement between places and regions.

This second nature is only barely a fixed system of coordinates; it is a relational network of differences which provides the principle and rationale for movement between places and regions. Rather than a fixed structure, the process of *spatialisation* is a process and a horizon of meanings. To contrast with most tourist literature which refers to the elements and crowds assembled at a site to create its ambiance, spatialisation theory equally stresses what is excluded and what remains elsewhere as contrasts and as distant places – a tourist's home – in relation to which the tourist's experience is constructed. Each of these place-myths is the locus of intense struggle over its meaning. Places are taken up from the raw topological diversity of the land and integrated into a meaningful human geography which is nonetheless contested. This *social spatialisation* lies at the core of tourist destination choices (Shields, 1991), attempts at place-marketing, and is the basis of our geographical sense of the world as a space of difference and distance.

Even if a site is already remarkable, the topology is also over-written with often-contradictory 'place-images' (Shields, 1991) to create a general 'place-myth'. 'Image' is meant in the sense of not only a representation but a virtual image, a cultural *imago* (Castoriadis, 1987). 'Myth' is meant here not as a possibly-fictional origin-story; rather it denotes the *mythic* in the original sense of *mythos* as a qualitative understanding of the 'nature' or capacity of a place. Before we encounter a specific place or region, we generally have some information and preconception about it. We can elaborate on this cultural or informational spatial sensibility by distinguishing between the identity of a place or region itself consisting of distinguishing 'natural' features, histories of habitation, meaning-making and development. But a consciousness of the particularity of a region is different: it is not solely a result of individual perception of its distinguishing features but also a result of the ongoing and public pedagogy including all of the mechanisms of the production of collective identity and interpellation of individuals to social worlds through imagined communities (Anderson, 1991) and learned, prosthetic memories (Cohen, 1982).

What and who are missing can be counter-intuitive questions but they reveal regional, geopolitical struggles over what is present. Spatialisation can be a vehicle of repression in subtle ways. Constituting regions is closely related to constructing hierarchical relations of centre and periphery. The framework of regions is not only put in place as an act of geopolitical power but is part and parcel of the consolidation and reproduction of power relations. Spatialisations are the subjects of struggle because of their power to influence social reproduction in a manner in which it is difficult to trace the authorship of its normative arrangement of places, regions and entire states. Hence the battle for spatialisation is not just a question of perpetuating memories but of framing the future.

Each place-myth is the locus of intense struggle over the meaning and significance of place. There is a geopolitics to place and region which appears to be reflected in the various findings of the significance of green space, local access to resources, environmental toxicity and resiliency of local communities as ecosystems noted in the geography literature. Significant places are taken up from the raw topological diversity of the land and integrated into a meaningful human geography that is contested by individuals and different cultural groups (Shields, 1991). This differential social spatialisation is the basis of our geographical sense of the world as a space of distinctions, difference and distance. While policy makers may want to treat this as a structure for operational, administrative reasons, for more expert purposes it is not a unified system, merely a 'regime' of spacings which are often contested. This play of major and minor spatialisations against each other or in complex, nested inter-relation is a source of specific (sub)cultural and community needs.

Spatialisation ties together the cultural conception of the environment with individual bodies to sediment, in a practical and physical manner, social reproduction in line with place-myths (however contested or only pretending to the status of the hegemonic). It embraces not only spatial patterns but temporal rhythms. *Place is a memory-bank for societies* inscribed and read in ways which are sometimes ritualised but always much more embodied than merely visual. Place takes on this memory-function by virtue of retaining and displaying the inscribed traces of rhythmic repetition of routines in time and space in a manner which is relatively difficult for a single individual to erase or for a small group to change in a short time without the investment of a great deal of effort (the wholesale and total destruction of a city).

In the process of social spatialisation, places are not only over-coded, but inter-related via classification schemes and reifying divisions into locals' and tourists' parts of a city, safe and dangerous areas, ours and theirs, work and leisure places. They are categorised colloquially in ways that overwrite mere topography and even location with cultural values 'the "right" and "wrong" side of the tracks'. More than mere function is at issue. Categorisation can amount to the creation of a local network of spaces and places that reflect and also tend to reproduce values and activities anchored in a mosaic of sites. This patchwork may conform to typical topological patterns, such as divisions of centre and margin ('capital and province'), simple binaries ('us and them') as well as more complex networks, all of which tend to be reflected in an uneven and unequal distribution of resources.

Spatialisation, the 'production of space' concerns social and cultural reproduction and interaction. People learn the comportment associated with a place as well as with their social status and gender. Spatialisation is not only a matter of sites and networks of space but exists at all levels to tie the micro scale of the body to the macro scale of the region. Bodies are 'spaced': the performative carriage of the body, the gestures, actions and rhythms of everyday routines deemed socially appropriate to a particular site are etched onto place and into the somatic memory of individual inhabitants. Such a practical, somatic *hexis* is usually not recalled except with an awkward self-consciousness when one finds oneself 'out of place', as the idiomatic expression puts it. Spatialisation is written and read practically by bodies as much as metaphorically through the conceptual operations of discourse. Goffman has referred to these as 'meaning frames' (1974) and others have referred to habitual routines (Bourdieu, 1977) and to 'scripts' for everyday interaction – however contested or renegotiated 'on the fly' (Smith, 1987). At the core of spatialisation is a process of simplifying for cognitive purposes, and of stereotyping as a pragmatic strategy for everyday life.

Spatialisations of places within complex webs of social meaning are abstractions and '*virtualisations*' of the concrete materiality of given places. Whereas urban or 'place images' might be abstractions or other representations of a place, in the previous chapter, I argued that 'spatialisation' connects places and regions so that they are systematically understood with respect to each other. The place image of one city is directly related to the contrasting place image of another city. In this cultural formation, places are legitimated only for certain types of socioeconomic and cultural action – places cast as 'places for this and places for that' (Lefebvre, 1981b; see Grönlund, 1993). This involves representations which legitimate or de-legitimate social action.

This is a contrast to naïve materialist approaches that divide the world into things and ideas or abstractions that are generally treated as secondary and non-causal, epiphenomenal. It is also a contrast with approaches which emphasise the causal power of the imaginary or of a cultural '*imago*' that may be more complex and nuanced but is also ideal in the sense of 'ideational', conceptual or imagined. By contrast, if spatialisation is a theoretical abstraction, space itself will be argued to be very much real, only intangible in that it cannot be literally touched or picked up like a physical object. Other examples of virtualities would include groups, communities and all social facts.

Virtualisation is a creative process of questioning which opens up problem frames to critically question cultural formations, 'the way things happen'. Virtualisation moves from situations ('*l'actuel*') to create problems (in the sense of a problematique) – a knot of 'constraint and finality that inspires our acts' (Lévy, 1998: 174). The virtual is neither absence nor an unrepresentable excess or lack.[5] But it troubles any simple negation because it introduces multiplicity into the otherwise fixed category of the real. The tangible, actually real phenomena cease to be the sole, hegemonic examples of 'reality'. The logical identity of the real with these phenomena is broken apart, allowing us to begin to conceptualise processes such as becoming in terms of emergence and dialogism (cf. Bakhtin, 1981) rather than only as a dialectic, as a negation of existing identities (Laclau, 1996: 20–46). Phenomena take on an irreducible pluralism, continually differentiating themselves (Deleuze, 1988a/b: 101, 104).

Using topological language, Deleuze poses the relation between the virtual and the actual as one of folding over a surface to double it up, to complicate the surface (Rajchman, 1998; see final chapter of this volume). Thinking, knowing, experiencing is the unfolding and refolding of actual materiality to reveal a multiplicity of virtualities. These are unformed, unfinalised functions and relations of force that constantly destabilise or problematise the material.

Memorial and Anticipatory Spatialisation: Time-Spaces

If place is a memory bank, one might usefully think of sites as the points in a folded temporality where an older temporal region is folded to touch the present. This space-time structure of place-based memory and '*memorial spatialisation*' is a topological structure that will be examined in the concluding chapters. Similarly, larger-scaled regional space-myths may be imposed generalisations that amount to self-fulfilling prophecies. In effect, a future quality of life in a region is imputed to a given location in the present. This is an '*anticipatory spatialisation*'. Both the past and the future are drawn into spatialisation through topological operations that involve place and region space-images and myths and practices of space through the governance of bodily comportment as ways of framing the present.

Lefebvre called this a space of representation. Spatially, these connect the near to the far, and temporally, they connect pasts, presents and futures. For example, a foreign agenda can be imposed by being placed 'as if' it was a local future that frames initiatives in the present within a space of representation that is very much concerned about the temporal, rather than simply the spatial. This then suggests relations of power and a mode of politics that works through weaving these virtual pasts and futures with material actions and concrete places.

An anticipatory mode of power is distinctly different from the present-tense and localised spatio-temporal matrix of the society of discipline which Foucault found encapsulated in Bentham's Panopticon (Foucault, 1979; see also O'Connor, 2003). Rather than focusing on direct discipline in the context of encounters in the present, or attempting to direct how we define the present ideologically via sets of abstract ideas, anticipation attempts to pre-structure the present by intervening in the 'near future' of actualisation and becoming. Anticipatory power is proscriptive rather than responsive; it is surveillance extended into the future. It relies on simulation and moves the terrain of politics forward into the near future, the tense of the 'next' (DeLanda, 2002). The desire to structure choice, to simulate situations (virtually), to spot the actualisation of risk (probabilistically) as it becomes a clear and present danger (a concrete materiality), suggests that acknowledging the virtual ushers in a new model of governance, the so-called 'societies of control', which seek an anticipatory edge on the future (Deleuze, 1992; Hardt and Negri, 2000). Massumi refers to these virtualities as 'future affective facts' (Massumi, 2005) – 'what will have been' – an example of which was George Bush Jr's administration's projection of future terrorist events as threats that were used to justify present actions such as surveillance and reductions in civil freedoms. In this, Massumi's analysis is indebted to his translation of Lyotard's discussion of postmodernity as the paradox of the future (*post*) anterior (*modo*), a desire for nostalgic dreams. This pitches the future as a recapitulation of a past that is believed to be better than the present (Lyotard, 1980).

The mutability of place-images in spatialisations and their susceptibility to poetic licence and witty manipulation demonstrates their 'deep' role in cognition. To choose only one of hundreds of possible literary examples, Solzhenitsyn opens his *Gulag Archipelago* (1977) by playing on the super-structural and ideologically-charged 'second nature' of otherwise explicitly empirical, geographical 'space'. This shift from the geographical to the social betrays the tensions of power relations and hierarchies of privilege and 'social place':

And the Kolyma was the greatest and most famous island, the pole of ferocity of that amazing country of Gulag which, though scattered in an Archipelago geographically, was, in the psychological sense, fused into a continent – an almost invisible, almost imperceptible country inhabited by the 'zek' people. And this Archipelago crisscrossed and patterned that other country within which it was located, like a gigantic patchwork, cutting into its cities, hovering over its streets. Yet there were many who did not know of it ... (Solzhenitsyn, 1977: 1)

One can also see that this is a nested structure where larger spaces can be contained in smaller spaces as well as vice versa. In this 'sack' or 'case' logic (*valise*, cf. Serres, 1982), the global can be stuffed into the local. The system of imprisonment and exile exhibits an almost *territorial* unity and presence which is obscured, however, by the omnipresence of (socially defined) 'reality' – that of empirical landmasses, and natural science-defined notions of space. This 'reality' insists that the carceral system of the Gulag was spatially separate from the civilised heartland of Soviet society. The power of Solzenitsyn's for-mulation was to break through the polar opposition of the concrete practices of space in quotidian life (everyday life, the Euclidean space-time of positiv-ism), on the one hand, and the supposed non-existence (no-place-ness) of the internal prison system, on the other. By throwing them against each other, the prison system is made visible (hence analysable, visible to the 'eye' of reason, as a virtuality). It becomes 'placed' through the giant conceptual metaphor of 'as if' an 'Archipelago', where before it could not be perceived and was displaced to the Siberian periphery.

Attributes that may appear to be natural are not necessarily rooted in the nature, the topography or geology of a place. Spatialisations are as much about the absence of activity (spatialised elsewhere in spatial-temporal net-works of distance and difference) as they are about presence. Images of places and regions travel easily via electronic media, extending the hold of spatiali-sations on material cultures. As a cognitive and practical *habitus*, social spa-tialisation is a source not only of social algorithms (cf. Bourdieu, 1972) but of allegorical solutions. This involves attempting to solve new problems or cultural conundrums by metaphorically assimilating them to established rou-tines or to the implied nexus of behavioural codings implicit in a place-myth. Spatialisations are also the sources of differentiating categories (for example, 'right' versus 'left' and 'near' versus 'far') and conceptual shortcuts including stereotypes and 'metaphors we live by' (Lakoff and Johnson, 1979).

Vieux Québec: The Example of Tourist Practices

Tourism maps are part of tourist texts and media representations of time-space – that is, of history and places – which may be classed along with guidebook narratives and a panoply of inscriptions ranging from arrows, plaques posted by heritage authorities, and indicators of what may be observed from scenic lookouts or in a panoramic view. Through quoting, summarising, and imitating, these texts are closely related to full histories, paintings of famous events, 'tourist art' and souvenirs. The purpose of many of these texts is to allow a past to be actualised in part by giving direction or illustration, and in part by fitting together with other tourist texts. This crucial quality of both intertextuality and of seamlessness informs itineraries, re-enactments, observed re-stagings of historical events and dramas on site. Place images depend on textual integration. A tourist map must work together with a guidebook narrative, which in turn must not clash with an actor or animator in period costume describing their lives – the distances they might walk each day.

Québec City, the touristy walled-capital of Québec, has long been described in poetic terms that cast it as 'a piece of Europe', a medieval fragment in the present, an unlikely site of difference to North America. European opinion-makers, guides and travelogue-writers sought to conjure up and place the city in a single aphorism so that it might be, on the one hand, known, and on the other, expected or anticipated. Presenting Québec City as an anachronism and a minor cultural enclave, they have strikingly reduced the grandeur of the site and the geopolitical delights of the sovereign view with diminutives. The liberal American orator Henry Ward Beecher called Québec 'a populated cliff' and 'a small bit of medieval Europe perched upon a rock and dried for keeping – a curiosity that has not its equal in its kind on this side of the

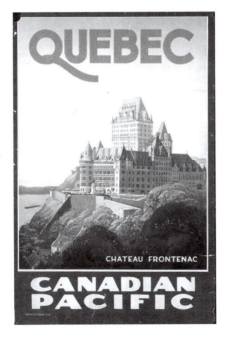

Figure 2.1 Panoramic view. Historical poster of the Chateau Frontenac c.1926 (Canadian Pacific Archives)

ocean' (cited in Canadian Pacific Railway, 1926: 6; see Figure 2.1). Tourist guidebooks produced by the Canadian Pacific Railway or CPR cast Québec as European, even if in a patchwork of places: 'Strolling in Lower Town one might fancy himself [sic] in Amiens ... and along the Grand Allée, running right across the Plains of Abraham, you might be in Brussels or Paris, only that Clifton Terrace seems to recall Kensington' (Canadian Pacific Railway, 1926: 7). Charles Dickens, on a trip that helped popularise the practice of honeymoons there, wrote for his readers:

> The impression made upon the visitor by this Gibraltar of America, its giddy heights, its citadel suspended, as it were in air, its picturesque steep streets and frowning gateways and the splendid views which burst upon the eye at every turn is at once unique and lasting and make it a place not to be forgotten. (Canadian Pacific Railway, 1926: 6)

Codings of places and regions have political effects. Appearing in the popular media of the nineteenth century – in talks attended by thousands and in widely read newspapers – representations are treated by social actors and institutional decision-makers as nature, as *a priori* material objects. In Québec, it is as if the historical place-myth was as solid as the high bluff on which the city walls sit. But its double-sided möbius qualities set up a contradictory topology that is folded rather than planar and Euclidean. The ironic miniaturisation in discourse of the powerful view and site sets up an ideal milieu of play, of tourism and leisurely delight.

Not only does Québec City still stand out today as the object of intensive efforts to create a place myth and to articulate and actualise a memorial spatialisation, as a particularly significant node within an overall spatialisation of Canada and of Québec as the site of historic events between English, French and even American imperial ambitions. It is an exemplary site of French Canadian settlement where cultural history and nationalistic political projects are sedimented, like geologically layered events and sites of memory (Shields, 1991, 1997). Québec City – and, for that matter, the touristic 'Old Quebec' within the walled city – takes on its importance in relation to other spaces and places. The ritualised tourism practices of Old Québec as a site of memory known through walking through small winding streets and gazing out over the views is governed by an indexical structure in which archaeological traces, historic sites and monuments refer to another, vanished Québec. It is in relation to the people and territorial province of Québec, and of Canada, that the Québecois political history at Québec City is significant. This significance is furthermore not merely an issue of history, but of present governments and of the future. Travelling to 'Old Quebec' as a tourist, one cannot but be aware of the political project, oriented towards a future Québec State, of which the city would likely remain the capital. As one looks out on the commanding view from the battlements across the St Lawrence River, one has a sense of a deliberate staging of power effects:

> 'Beyond' signifies spatial distance, marks progress, promises the future; but our intimations of exceeding the barrier or boundary – the very act of going *beyond* – are unknowable, unrepresentable, without a return to the 'present' which, in the process of repetition, becomes disjunct and displaced. The imaginary of spatial distance – to live somehow beyond the border of our time – throws into relief the temporal, social differences that interrupt our collusive sense of cultural contemporaneity. (Bhabha, 1994: 4)

The tense möbius spatialisation of the touristic place-myth of 'Old Quebec' – a time-space that twists back on itself like a 'Klein Bottle' whose neck snakes over back through the body – and the political place-myth of 'Vieux Québec' sometimes loses both its dialectical balance and its purchase and control over the site as the stress shifts from intrinsic, fixed references focused on the site to extrinsic, 'centrifugal' comparisons and contrasts to other sites. In temporal terms, this shift may be a reversal from the emphasis on the past into a future-directed projection of new spatialisations – a new space of distance and difference. The historical linkages to hemispheric struggles between rival nations remain as a latent circuit that can be quickly brought back to life in times of crisis. The result is a dialectical tension within the tourism maps and an unstable identity through its links to other sites. These elements make Québec into a particularly acute switching point, a liminal threshold between the local and the global, in which particular attractions, and even the entire historical city centre can find itself caught betwixt and between everyday life and the historic drama.

In the process of spatialisation, the local is related to the distant by virtue of the interconnected quality of place-myths which depend on a structural principle of other, contrasting place-myths in order to take on a (comparative) significance. But spatialisation is also memorial and anticipatory. It represents a form of *spatially-projected discipline* that yokes time to space to political belonging. This can be understood as a specific form of power and network of governance practices that supplements and expands Foucauldian visions of Panoptic, disciplinary power into the future. O'Connor argues that this is a form of 'montage', exemplified in an operation by which relations are constructed between the seen and what 'could be seen' or what 'will have been seen' next. These structure and form actions that follow on from a present situation. They exclude other actions or responses (O'Connor, 2003). The effect is more than spatial. It is an interleaving of space-time where the past and future are involved in the present formation to imply certain immediate and longer-term futures but not others.

Notes

1   Such investigations are often greeted with surprise – as recorded in Etiènne Gilson's prefatory comments to Bachelard's *La Poétique de l'espace* (Bachelard, 1959: vii–ix).

2   It is worthwhile turning to the efforts of others working in languages which are more conducive to examining 'social' spaces as objects of inquiry. This chapter thus focuses on work that was once largely unavailable to the reader of the English literature. I will concentrate on French and German sources, but there are also important Italian (Portoghesi, 1982; Tafuri, 1976, 1980; Zevi, 1969) and Japanese writers (Azuma, 1981; Chang, 1984). It is important to note, however, that all of these writers pose notorious translation difficulties (attempt to read Tafuri (1976) in English!) to such an extent that there remains much disagreement as to what English terms should be used and what the original author's intent was (see the ongoing debate among geographers as presented in Soja, 1980: 20).

3   'Indistinctement magique et rationnelle, l'opération introduit un étrange mouvement de *disincarnation* (verbale) et de *réincarnation* (empirique), de déracinement et d'enracinement, de spatialisaiion dans une étendue abstraite et de localisation dans une étendue spéecifiée' (Lefebvre, 1974: 234 (ss. III.8)).

4   It is important to focus on the distinctiveness of Lefebvre's exploration of alienation. He treats it as a central feature of Marxism, even in contrast to later theorists of class struggle who narrow their sights. For example, 'The *division of labour* is the economic expression of the *social nature of labour* within estrangement' (Marx, 1973a: 3rd manuscript, online). Across his many works on the topic, Lefebvre is widely understood to have enlarged Marx's theory of alienation (Monferran, 2003: 2). Some English-language textbooks (e.g. Hadden, 1997: 77) focus on 'alienation' (*entäussern*) counting three forms in Marx's *Economic and Philosophical Manuscripts* and leaving aside 'estrangement' (*Entfremdung*), Marx's fourth form (alienation from 'species-being'). Lefebvre (in line with current scholarship) counts all four and stresses them. I have been misquoted on this point and although I leave it for a later engagement, enumerating facets of Lefebvre's work or arguing that his work cannot be understood outside of its relation to other philosophers risks dragging him back into academic philosophy despite his lifelong struggle to overcome the isolation of radical ideas within the prison of 'scholarship': 'when taken ... speculatively, outside of *praxis*, the theories of alienation and totality become transformed into systems which are very remote from Marxism – into neo-Hegelianism' (Lefebvre, 1991a).

5   The virtual is not a form of the Real in Lacan's sense. For Lacan, the Real is an unrepresentable actuality which figures in language as excess and lack, but which can never be adequately represented. It therefore constantly troubles and undermines the authority of representations of self-identity (see Widder, 2000: 118; Žižek, 1989).

3

histories of spaces

Both everyday and professional understandings of space have a history of gradual change which cannot be understood without studying changes in philosophy and in mathematical representations of space. Changes in experience and philosophy have altered spatial perception and thought, changing social behaviour, architecture, planning and settlement patterns, several times since Pythagoras (Croton, c.570–c.495 BCE), Euclid (Alexandria, c.325–265 BCE) or Descartes (Netherlands, 1596–1650). This chapter is a capsule survey of this history from the point of view of the early twenty-first century when the sense of the spatial has begun to reflect not only European but East Asian cultural viewpoints and traditions.

In general, there is a lack of systematic, non-specialist histories of the theories and mathematics of space that also form parts of the historical repertoire of spatialisations that persist and seem to be drawn upon depending on the situation. Surveying across history, advances in understandings of space and spatialisation advance and retreat, are proclaimed and lost for centuries. Figure 3.1 (on pp. 54–5) attempts to present this knotted path up to relativistic understandings of space and time as a chronological list. However, it will be clear to any schoolchild that Euclidean geometry remains relevant as what we teach as core scientific and mathematical knowledge. There is no progress at this scale of historical time. Many of the key figures were polymaths who are better known for other contributions that in fact depended on their grasp of geometry, trigonometry and topology to allow them to solve practical questions in their time. History demonstrates that every understanding of space and spatialisation also has had practical, military and political implications.

One expects a history of theories of space to present a series of triumphs of scientific insight and of human advancement. Although there are eureka moments where pure intellectual genius grasps the nature of reality in a way which leads us to reorganise our understanding of the entire cosmos, in truth the history of space as much as that of time is a convoluted story of local advances which were later forgotten, practices that continued the errors of forebears, and of the persistence of primitive understandings and habits which may place the modern user of an iPod on the same level as a Phoenician sailor, despite the technical advancement of our gadgets.

Mediterranean Geometric Space

Although Greeks, Phoenicians, Egyptians and Romans depended on Sumerian and Babylonian astronomy and mathematics, and despite Chinese and South Asian contributions, the systematic investigation of the properties of spatiality and the development of a geometry that described the property of objects and relationships in space is intriguingly centred around the Eastern Mediterranean, hence the subtitle of this section as 'Mediterranean Geometric Space'. As lines linking philosophers to places in Figure 3.2 map out, the geography of innovation in spatial thinking shifts over time from place to place. This is dominated by European centres of thinking, illustrating the power of institutions to attract scholars and encourage the systematisation, recording, collection and communication of ideas. Even short-lived centres, such as at Tus in the north of modern-day Iran, represent institutions such as observatories. And, where works have been lost, they are known through the citations of other scholars at these institutions and the collections of institutions further afield.

Space as Geometric Area

Greek theories of time, space and place remain touchstones in many discussions. It has been a tendency to choose an arbitrary starting date with the Greeks and cast everything prior to this as primitively irrational and bound to oral traditions of myth (Jammer, 1960: 8). However, the archaeological and textual evidence demonstrates otherwise. For example, the Sumerian *še* (grain) was a measurement of space, used as a monetary instrument based on the quantity of seed used to sow a given area. The spatial foundation of economics reflected the stability that could be attributed to material territory as a basic form of capital (see Chapter 4 below).

> In general, the Greek and early civilisations were much better equipped to handle invariant spatial relations than temporal variables. [This is due to the fact of] the Greeks' ... idea of a finite and stable universe whose spatial and tactile relations were almost equilibrated aesthetically and proportionally ... Euclidean geometry certainly expresses the dominant spatial character of Greek civilisation. Moreover, time was structured not only by the Greeks but also by others as a recurrent cyclic phenomenon and in that sense time was as bound and finite as was the universe of Aristotle. (Koyré, 1957: 86–87 cited in Kolaja, 1969: 4)

Pythagoras, Aristotle (Macedonia and Athens c.384–c.322 BCE) and Euclid may be the best known, but Stoic philosophers such as Zeno of Elea (possibly Athens, c.490–c.430 BCE) and Democritus (Abdera, N. Greece c.460–c.370 BCE) are recurrent figures in historical texts, including Epicurus (Athens, c.341–c.270 BCE) (as summarised by the Roman, Lucretius (Rome, c.99–c.55

BCE)) and Ptolemy (Claudius Ptolemeus, Alexandria, c.90–c.168 BCE). Paradoxically, Euro-American cultural notions of space and time depend on these figures, yet their philosophical and mathematical conceptions of space and time are quite foreign to ours. As the dates and locations of these figures tabulated in Figure 3.1 and mapped in Figure 3.2 demonstrate, the array of thinkers, and their movements all over the Eastern Mediterranean, blurs the conceit that 'our' philosophical origins are simply 'Greek' and not more complexly also Egyptian and Sumerian.

Thebes and Alexandria were key centres for mathematics, geometry and astronomy. Due to his early formative experiences in Egypt, Pythagoras was able to draw on this Egyptian heritage. He had a lasting influence on later followers such as Philolaus (Thebes, c. 470–c.385 BCE). The Pythagorean school in Croton (modern day Crotone, Italy) was to found an influential lineage of thinkers, mapmakers and explorers. The Pythagoreans believed that the Earth was spherical and these later followers proposed that the Earth, sun and stars orbited an unseen centre to the universe. Eratosthenes (Alexandria, c. 275–c.195 BCE), the third Head of the Great Library at Alexandria, produced a map of a spherical world and proposed a method for verifying it. This was done by using the differences in the angles at which one sees the sun at the same time of the day in different locations. He measured the difference between the elevation of the noon-day sun at Alexandria and Aswan, about 600 km south on the Nile to accurately estimate the circumference of the Earth. Later, Hipparchus (Rhodes, c.190–c.120 BCE), founder of trigonometry and considered the greatest of the ancient astronomical observers, brought Babylonian astronomical observations (Kidinnu (also referred to as Cidenas), Chaldes, circa fourth century BCE) into Greek thought. He proposed that the Earth circled the sun, established latitude and longitude measurements by dividing the Earth into 360 degrees and providing accurate, quantitative models for the motion of the Sun and orbit of the Moon. The role of trigonometric triangulation was to become central to debates on the curvature of the Earth and to determining the topological properties of time-spaces from inside of them (see Chapter 6). Ptolemy collated this knowledge into an encyclopaedic *Geography*, including the topological problem of projecting a spherical Earth onto a flat map.

The importance of geometry may have been in part linked to its central position in ancient mathematics from Pythagoras to Archimedes and beyond. For Pythagoras, numbers had a spatial property such that physics was treated as geometry. There is some evidence that Greek and Egyptian mathematicians had a method of calculation that involved converting numbers and problems into geometrical equivalents, drawing the geometric figures in sand and measuring the results. This would be similar to doing calculations using a slide-rule or clock-like mechanisms (such as would have been familiar to Archimedes in the third century BCE, for example the Antikythera Mechanism, an orrery or astronomical clock made in Syracuse

(Sicily) that also indicated cyclical festivals such as the Olympics) where one reads the result as precisely as possible from measurements on the ruler itself. Euclid's *Elements of Geometry* could be read not just as a set of proofs but as a text of methods (Euclid, 1998).

The Elements proceeds from *axioms*, for example: a 'point' is 'that which has no part'; or, 'a line is a breadth-less length' and from common notions, such as 'things which coincide with one another are equal to one another', to *proofs*. Four of Euclid's five *postulates* are axioms – assertions assumed to be true without proof. The fifth, 'Parallel Postulate', is necessary to maintain a familiar planar geometry, but not necessarily required for all geometries. The fifth postulate cannot be deduced from the first four. However, whether or not this 'chink' in the chainmail of *The Elements'* clever and relentless logic was necessary was the focus of much later debate and the beginning point for non-Euclidean geometries and topologies (see 'Dimensionality' and 'Flatness' below in this Chapter, and see Chapter 6). Euclid's axioms are:

1 There is a straight line from any point to any point.

2 A finite straight line can be constructed in any straight line.

3 Circles have any centre and any radius.

4 All right angles are equal to each other.

5 If a straight line crosses two straight lines in the same plane at 90 degrees, they are parallel (they never meet). 'If a line segment intersects two straight lines forming two interior angles on the same side that sum to less than two right angles, then the two lines, if extended indefinitely, meet on that side on which the angles sum to less than two right angles' (Euclid, 1998: ss. 20–3).

Space as Void

For the early Greek poets, Hesiod's (Boeotia, c. late eighth century BCE) 'Chaos' (Greek *Cha-* yawning, gaping void) was a seminal conception of space as a dark void (Hesiod, 1914: 116). In this uncrossable, formless, bottomless abyss any object would fall endlessly, without the possibility of orientation. Hesiod's genealogy of the Gods formalised earlier oral traditions, adding other *Protogenoi* such as the male *Eros*, firstborn Light, the creative urge or desire for bringing into being and ordering all things in the cosmos, and *Tartarus* the deity of the underworld. Earth, *Gaia*, emerged from this 'womb of darkness', which is widely found in creation myths. The Greek mythical universe is founded on this apprehension that Earth or ground, the *terroir* or terrain of everyday life, is separated from the formless space and governed by an emergent force of time.

The Pythagoreans refined the conception of spatial vacancy (*pneuma apeiron*) or void (*kenon*) between individual numbers and elements (cf. *Metaphysics*,

Aristotle, 350 BCE: 1080 b 33), allowing each numeral a unique identity. From simply 'air' or the 'space between', this becomes more and more abstracted into a distinction between space understood as place (*topos*, location, site) and matter: 'Every body occupies some place, and cannot exist unless its place exists ... A characteristic property of space is that all things are in it but it is never in something else ... setting frontiers or limits to bodies in it' (cf. Simplicius, 1992, Alexandria, c. 490–c. 55 BCE).

This left the question of infinity and finitude, which gave rise to enduring debates summed up in the repeated question of whether one could go to the 'end' or edge of space and reach out beyond it. Even Locke (Oxford, 1632–1704), in the 1600s argues that 'if God placed a man at the extremity of corporeal beings, he could not stretch his hand beyond his body' (Locke, 1690: II, ss. 13, 21 in Jammer, 1960: 13). This problem occurs as a category mistake when space is objectified, understood as tangible and as in some way bounded.

Gorgias (Lentini [Leontini] c.487–c.376 BCE) proposed the first clear argument that space and matter belong to different categories. Because he conceived of space as finite (i.e., it must be located to exist), Gorgias' conception maintains a place-like quality (*topos*).[1] For the widely travelled atomist, Democritus (c.460 BCE–c.370 BCE), who was in touch with Egyptian and Persian mathematicians and philosophers, space was *kenon*, conceived as an infinite empty extension which contained an infinitude of atoms but which did not influence their motion in any way and did not penetrate these atoms. Subsequent Atomists, such as Leucipus (Abdera, c. early fifth century BCE) and later Epicurus, make clear that space is the void between. However, by the time of Lucretius' (Rome, c.99–c.55 BCE) summary of Epicurean philosophy around 50 BCE this idea has shifted to bodies placed in space itself: 'All nature then, as it exists, by itself, is founded on two things: there are bodies and there is void in which these bodies are placed and through which they move about' (Lucretius, 1997 in Jammer, 1960: 12, fn 10). Despite the abstract quality of their non-material concept of space as void, or *kenon*, the Atomists understood gravity as an integrated feature of infinite space, giving it a concrete directionality, an up and a down. 'It is a strange coincidence that the very founders of the great materialistic school in antiquity had to be "the first to say distinctly that a thing might be real without being a body"' (Burnet, 1920: 389, cited in Jammer, 1960: 13).

Space as Medium

Plato (Athens, c.429–c.347 BCE) asks for more than this ontology by attempting to tell us what space is (*Physics* Aristotle, 1970: 209b; *Timeus* Plato, 1925). He proposes that space is an undifferentiated material substrate, which becomes stratified and differentiated through the motion of becoming. Physics becomes geometry; geometric structure is the final cause of an ordering process whereby 'like attracts like'. Drawing on Pythagorean thinkers (eg. Philolaus), in *Timeus*, Plato assigns elements specific spatial forms which give them different degrees of stability, immovability and so on – air is an octahedron, fire a pyramid, earth a cube (Plato, 1925). This view of space dominated up until the twelfth century. It was formulated in commonsensical terms that seemed to require little further investigation. However, Castoriadis argues that the Kantian and Hegelian tradition that develops space as a form of *a priori* has led us to underestimate the power of Plato's argument that space is not a void but a receptacle, *chora*:

> For what is a space? People were led to believe that Plato had said all he had to say when, suddenly [in *Timeus*] he stops, retraces his steps and says that everything has to be begun all over again ... in addition to always being and always becoming, a third term must be posited: *chora*, 'space'... *receives* 'what' is-becomes, that 'in which' exists everything that is ... and which is neither intelligible, like always-being, nor sensible, like becoming, 'a third incorruptible kind that we grasp as in a dream'. (Castoriadis, 1987: 189)

The indiscernibility of what is contained from the container (*dechomenon*) in Plato's 'invisible formless *eidos*' (1925: 50 b) is eschewed by Kant (Königsberg, 1724–1804), following Aristotle, who 'posits that we represent time by means of pure non-time, that is, by means of a line [a one-dimensional spatial construction]; Hegel (Berlin, 1770–1831) will continue along this same path' (Castoriadis, 1987: 189; Aristotle, 1970: IV, 10–14 esp. 219 b, 16–25, 220 a, 9–21, 222 a, 13). Kant (1953), 'will believe that these forms can be separated ... from any content *whatsoever* ... that is a space and a time as the pure possibility of the self-difference of identity ... which ... leads to the impossibility of a genuine distinction between space and time' (Castoriadis, 1987: 189–90; see Kant, 1965 s. 6 b; Shields, 1992) The two must be defined in terms of each other. Space is fundamentally choratic:

> a form/aspect, hence a formless form, an invisible aspect; 'tangible, outside of any sensation, to a bastard reflection' – sensible insensible, unthinkable thought. *Aporotaton*, superlatively intractable: we do not feel space, Plato says, and yet we touch it (*hapton*); we touch it, not with our hands but with a bastard reflection ... addressed to something that partakes of the intelligible, that is incorruptible ... based on a vision 'as in a dream' ... as it *must* be separated from what is found 'there' and from what takes place 'there' and at the same time this separation *cannot* really be made. (Plato, 1925: 48 a–52 e, cited in Castoriadis, 1987: 189)

Space as the Sacred

Given its cosmological implications, there is also a spiritual aspect to casting Creation in one spatial form versus another. First century BCE Judaic thought adopted the Hebrew 'place', *makom kadosh*, as a name of God (Arabic *makam* 'holy place'). This notion was later imported into Renaissance thought via the immigration of many Byzantine Greek scholars who moved west to find refuge in Italy and Spain after the fall of Constantinople in 1453. Just as Pythagoreans had seen mathematics as a key to understanding the powers of the Gods, mathematical patterns, series, and space were the subject of mystical speculation. For example, Jewish Cabalistic thought associated the numbers of positions of each letter in the Hebrew alphabet with mathematical demonstrations of the Divine. Because space was understood via the Aristotelian model of higher, divine spheres, this theological influence in spatial thought persisted through to the time of Newton (London, 1643–1727).

The European legacy of such ideas turns on the work of early Italian Renaissance scholars such as Telesio (Cosenza, 1509–88) and Campanella (Naples, 1568–1639). They melded the Platonic and Cabalistic to argue that space is a real, absolute, almost spiritual entity; it is homogeneous, undifferentiated, immovable and incorporeal without reference to cardinal directions or intellectual differentiation between up and down, right and left (Campanella, 1620). Campanella's space is penetrated by matter, allowing the co-location of mobile entities. As such, this ideal-but-real spatiality establishes a firm basis in the virtual for legitimising mathematical speculations about the nature of the divine, laying the basis for the empirical studies and calculations of Newton, Locke and others. With light as an incorporeal attribute further relating space to the divine in philosophical writing, space came to play the role of a mediator between the natural world of the early Renaissance and the spiritual inheritance of medieval thought. Ironically, the interest in establishing the divine nature of space propelled not only mathematical investigations but inspired a range of interests in experiments, from thirteenth-century optics (cf. Grosseteste c.1175–1253), which contributed to the development of the telescope, through to sixteenth-century debates between Descartes and More (London, 1478–1535) on the possibility of an absolute vacuum, leading to Boyle's Law of gases.

However, just as they were unaware of Arabic cartography and geography (see the first chapter, Idrisi Muhammad ibn Abd al-Aziz (Al Idrisi), 1990), Europeans working in Latin were largely unaware of the work of Biruni (Ghazna, 973–1048), Avicenna (Hamadān, c. 980–1037) and Al-Razi (Ragha, 865–925) on the existence of voids and vacuums (Jammer, 1960: 91). These are evidence of the importance of experimental evidence stretching back to Aristotle which were ignored in Europe. For Al-Razi, the void is not only a cosmological principle but an actual 'substance of emptiness' endowed with a force of attraction which explained the tendency of light bodies to rise (Jammer, 1960: fn 93).

Although Bacon (London, 1561–1626) criticises the concept of empty space endowed with forces, it is significant that the theological influence in Scholastic spatial thought persisted further. For Newton, space was the sensorium of the omnipresent divine – god being 'the place of all things'. The weight of theological preoccupations on Newton's work is much discussed (Jammer, 1960: 112). In effect, the primary problem of space from Judaic and early Christian era through to the Enlightenment was to reconcile Aristotelian conceptions of space as full, finite and characterised by motion with the absolute conceptions of the divine as outside of time and space. How could Aristotle's set of nested spatial spheres contain space and yet be in motion? What space was this cosmos moving through? 'Where is the universe?' asked Giordano Bruno (London, 1548–1600). The concept was demonstrated to be fallacious on the scale of a mill wheel, but the reality was continually avoided by Scholastic philosophers. Ironically, this dilemma and the impasse of theological control over thought spurred materialist investigations and ultimately a new synthesis – the birth of modern science.

Even Ockam (Oxford, c.1288–c.1348), the famous fourteenth-century nominalist and rationalist deferred to Aristotle's definition of space as an immobile containing place or a concave surface, although insisting that while place could move or be transformed vis-à-vis the greater sphere that in turn contained it, each place remained nonetheless formally in place in the overall order of the universe. In an important step, however, this formal place is defined as a '*metric*' of 'distance from the centre and the poles of the universe' (where a metric is any rule for specifying distance cf. Ockam, 1494). The solution of a non-material, immobile and infinite spatiality was a radical conception which philosophers were loath to accept because of its heretical theological implications and the unquestioned authority of Aristotle. The exceptions, as proposed by thinkers such as Crescas (Saragossa, c.1340–1410) and Cusanus (Kues, 1401–64), were ahead of their time and neglected due to political instability. Even at a later date, Copernicus (Frombork, 1473–1543) and Giordano Bruno caused considerable controversy.

Metric Space and Place

The distinction of high and low was fundamental to medieval spatialisations. For example, the medieval order of saints established a ladder-like progression from the lowest creature to the most divine of saints and ultimately the divine. These ranked orders and spheres are typically depicted in the tiers of statues which form the facade of medieval cathedrals. The conception is the basis of the organisation of Dante's *Divine Comedy* (c. 1308–21) which presents a graded hierarchy from sin to grace.

Southern European philosophers such as Crescas and the itinerant Giordano Bruno emancipated the concept of space from the scholastic substance-accident scheme of natural places (Jammer, 1960: 83). These natural philosophers moved towards modern theories of space by making the motion of the Earth relative rather than absolute, and rejecting a hierarchy of values or spatial spheres. Where the Archbishop of Canterbury lampooned, Bruno adhered, and was burned at the stake for, 'the opinion of Copernicus that the earth did go round, and the heavens did stand still; whereas in truth it was his own head which rather did run round, and his brains did not stand still' (George Abbot c.1585 in Weiner, 1980).

Crescas proposes that infinite, homogeneous space is a vacuum which provides Aristotle's outermost sphere, the firmament, with the possibility of motion. This means that the movement of the stars can be accounted for. But Cusanus, also known as Nicholas of Cusa, proposes that universal motion has no centre, nor is the earth at the centre of the cosmos. All bodies are in motion relative to each other, rather than in absolute motion around a fixed central point. This relativism allows him to reject the hierarchy of values based on different concentric spheres of the universe. Cusanus arrives at a rudimentary cosmological principle, 'wherever in the heavens anyone may be placed, it would seem to them as if they were the centre of the universe' (Nicholas of Cusa [Cusanus], 2001[1514]: 92 in Jammer, 1960: 83–4). The universe presents the same aspect from every point – laying the basis of the postulate that space and time are the same everywhere, allowing experimental results to be repeated from one place to another (a law that holds at neither the quantum nor the cosmological scale, where space and possibly time may be warped). This was the basis for Cusanus' ethics and a theory that marks him as a founder of modern cosmology, despite his insufficient astronomical measurements which would have to wait for the optics and empiricism of Copernicus.

> The break-up of [Greek] ... anthropo/geo-centric cosmologies with the discoveries of Galileo and Copernicus resulted in a radical change whereby 'infinity' and a notion of space as unbounded gained ground eventually to become the Cartesian res extensa. More recently, the empty-receptacle of Newtonian space has given way to 'organic theories of the multiplicity and relativity of space and time'. (see Sorokin, 1937–41: I, 39–46, cited in Kolaja, 1969: 17; see also Bergson, 1948)

Only at the end of the sixteenth century is the Aristotelian relationship between mathematics and physics reversed: Patritius (Ferrara, 1529–1597) proposed that space is ontologically as well as epistemologically the primary basis of all existence. It is neither corporeal nor incorporeal as these are only ways of characterising things in space, which is rather a necessary condition (Jammer, 1960: 86–7). This emancipates space from the Aristotelian doctrine of categories. Building on this, Campanella (Naples, 1568–1639) argued that space is:

> homogeneous and undifferentiated, penetrated corporeally and penetrating incorporeally. Its homogeneity excludes such differentiations as 'down' or 'up,' which attach to the diversities of bodies, rather than to space ... the existence of 'natural places' is emphatically rejected. God created space as a 'capacity', a receptacle for bodies ... divested of all inherent differentiations or forces. ...

> Place does not affect the nature of things, it has no bearing on their being at rest or being in motion. (Jammer, 1960: 90–1)

Copernicus concluded that either 'the definition of "place" had to be revised, or the dogma of the motion of the outermost celestial sphere [the universe] had to be repudiated' (Jammer, 1960: 72–3). Early versions of his manuscript cite the fourth century BCE Greek Pythagoreans, Aristarchus (Samos, 310–c.230 BCE) and Philolaus, who proposed a heliocentric view of the universe. In addition, he used the mathematics of Muslim astronomers, especially the works of Nasir al-Din Tusi (Tusi-couple, Tus, 1201–74), Mo'ayyeduddin Urdi (Urdi lemma, Maragheh, d. 1266) and Ibn al-Shatir (Damascus, 1304–75) and cited the theories of Albategni (Al-Battani, ar-Raqqah, 835–929), Ibn Battuta (Tangier, 1304–69), Arzachel (Al-Zarkali, Toledo, 1029–87) and Averroes (Ibn Rushd, Cordoba, 1126–98). Copernicus supported the contention that motion should be attributed to the contained body rather than to the container (Copernicus, 1949) and then demonstrated by observation that the Earth revolved around the Sun and therefore changed its position and could not be the centre of the universe. The Copernican revolution was a grand synthesis which reached beyond European knowledge to other, Islamic traditions. It reorganised the spatialisation of the universe and allowed new navigational practices, thereby destabilising the sense of the centrality of the human world and the certitudes and European institutions built on this understanding.

In summary, by the mid-1200s Aristotle's *Physics* came to replace Plato's *Timeus* as a standard text in European theories of space. As Aristotle puts it in his *Categories*, 'space is conceived as the sum total of all places occupied by bodies, and "place" (*topos*) conversely, is conceived as that part of space whose limits coincide with the limits of the occupying body' (Aristotle, 2007: 5 a, 8–14). The *Physics* concentrates on topology or place, rejecting the general conception of space as an empty void. Place is an *accident*, a 'context' which is real but not independent in the sense of a substantial or material being, and therefore has no physical implications. We can note that this is an important qualification; in effect, space is not concrete like an

actually-real object but '*virtually*' real (see below). This can be summarised
by four axioms drawn from the *Physics*:

- The place of a thing is no part or factor of the thing itself, but is that
  which embraces it;

- The immediate or 'proper' place of a thing is neither smaller nor greater
  than the thing itself;

- The place where a thing is can be quitted by it, and it is therefore separable
  from it; and,

- Any and every place implies and involves the relational correlatives of
  'above' and 'below', and all the elemental substances have a natural
  tendency to move towards their own special places, or to rest in them
  when there – such movement being, for example, 'upward' or 'downward'
  (Aristotle, 1970).

This last point gives *topos* an important metaphysical role as the foundation
of 'natural' motion, which makes it very different from realist Euro-American
understandings of 'place' today (Sayer, 1985). It is more like a normative 'sense
of place', of 'just place', placement and belonging to a place, making *topos* the
opposite not of time (*chronos*) but of *kairos* – *the* 'right time' or 'good timing'.
But from these, Aristotle deduces a definition of 'place' as the adjacent boundary of a containing body. In his *Physics*, like a series of spheres, these containing bodies are contiguously nested and centred on the Earth's centre. Aristotle
likens space as a geometrical structure of places to a field of forces: 'the trends
of the physical elements (fire, earth, and the rest) show not only that locality
or place is a reality but also that it exerts an active influence; for fire and earth
are borne, the one upwards and the other downwards ... each towards it own
"place"' (Aristotle, 1970: 208 b).

The strength of the definition in the *Physics* is that it avoids previous
criticisms by not confusing content and container as in Zeno of Elea's paradoxical 'Everything is in place; this means that it is in some thing; but its
place is something, then place itself is in something ... ', ad infinitum. In
fact, this remained the basis for all debates and theories of space until the
fourteenth century. Stoics such as Chrysippus (Athens, c.280 BCE–c.207
BCE) modified Aristotle's notion of the geometric continuity of matter. As a
School they developed the debate into two topics: an active tension (*tonos*)
amplifying the sense of space of the material universe as a field of forces
between bodies (such as gravity); and a discussion of a uniformly empty
void. As evidence, Posidonius (Rhodes, c.135–c.51 BCE) demonstrated the
relation between the moon and lunar tides as an ostensible proof. Aristotle's followers, the later Peripatetic School (founded in 335 BCE), proposed
that an upper sphere forced matter to cohere (*hexis*) and remain together.
However, there is a tendency to reduce spatial thinking to Euclid's planar

geometry: bodies are understood in terms of their surfaces and faces rather than their three-dimensional measure:

> The idea of coordinates ... seems to go back to ... the ancient Egyptian hieroglyphic symbol for 'district' (hesp) being a grid. It would therefore be only natural to expect some reference to spatial coordinates in Greek mathematics. But in the whole history of Greek mathematics, no such reference is found. Longitude (*mekos*) and latitude (*platos*) as spherical coordinates ... being the ideal two-dimensional system for concentric spheres in Aristotle's world of spherical symmetry. Simplicius mentions ... that Ptolemy ... demonstrated that bodies can have three dimensions ... The use of a three-dimensional coordinate system, and in particular of a rectangular spatial coordinate system, was not thought reasonable until the seventeenth century (Descartes, Frans van Schooten, Lahire and Jean Bernoulli) when the concept of space had undergone a radical change ... how could Euclidean space, with its homogeneous and infinite lines and places, possibly fit into the finite and anisotropic Aristotelian universe? (Jammer, 1960: 26)

Substantivalist, Reductionist and Virtualist Theories of Space

European Enlightenment philosophies of space depended on Euclid's geometry and presumed a three-dimensional extension known through mathematics. This contrasted with the Aristotelian tradition of space as one of the mental categories by which the objects of the world were named and classified. And in another contrast, Kant cogently argued that space is not mental or subjective (Kant, 1953: 41–51): the first problem of space as Kant outlines it in an early essay is the question of whether space is (1) a substance, (2) an attribute or relations, (3) an entity, or (4) a void/non-entity (Kant, 1968). Does space 'exist'? Or, is it only a chimera? That is, is it only a fictitious entity that expresses positively real relationships of positively existing and actually-real matter? Voids describe absences or gaps in spatial relations, but if voids are accepted as things that are present, then space takes on the qualities of some sort of object like an ether.

As an attribute, space would only be the dimensional qualities of objects or their separation at specific distances and in geometric relationships (a position adopted by late twentieth-century 'realist' thinkers). In the classical discussion, space was not allowed any status as a non-tangible but real entity, similar to a set in mathematics, or a medium in communications studies – all referred to as virtualities by later philosophers). Privileging relations over a topological reality involves attempting to attribute to space the relations of objects. If all continuous motions in a three-dimensional space are real, not much is saved by denying the reality of space itself. At a minimum, space could be successfully argued to be an intangible substance and the substantial bearer of topological properties whose consequences we can notice in ordinary experience.

Capek maintains that the later, 'Substantivalist' theories of time and space found few adherents prior to the Renaissance, with most philosophers backing a form of reductionism – a position which continues to be revived in realist geography's focus on space as the relation or distance between objects alone. Our brief survey of the historical texts supports this judgement. The classical Greek view foundered on conundrums such as the possible existence of space in the absence of any bodies entails that space is ontologically distinct from and independent of the bodies it contains. This is further extended by the rising focus on energy rather than matter in contemporary physics – there is no longer a search for the smallest grain of matter, which dissolves into particles that are virtually energy states, not 'things' which fit with a commonsense view of everyday objects (Futch, 2008: 10).

In Substantivalist theories, space and time are structures that exist and have properties independent of the existence of objects located in space and time. Spatial and temporal features such as 'a moment' or 'a place' are ontologically independent of, and prior to the things that occur during or in them. That is, space and time are said to have an intrinsic structure on which events and processes of things are dependent. Against this position, Reductionists deny that space and time have an existence in and of themselves: they are merely relations of 'really existing' objects. Space is 'an order of co-existences, as time is an order of successions' (Leibniz and Clarke, 2000: LC 3.4, in Futch, 2008: 7). 'Time' and 'Space' are not 'things' but better understood as spatio-temporal relations (Futch, 2008: 7, n. 3). Without material things, temporal and spatial relations would not exist. The substantivalist and reductionist concepts of space may be contrasted as follows: (a) space as a positional quality of the world of material objects; and (b) space as a container of all material objects. In case (a), space without a material object is inconceivable. In case (b), a material object can only be conceived as existing in space; space then appears as a reality that in a certain sense is superior to the material world (Einstein in Jammer, 1960: xv). Aristotle understood that physical change is more fundamental than abstraction such as time or something merely changing status from being future to being present to past (Newton-Smith in Futch, 2008: 7).

This is an enduring paradox: on one hand, one wishes to refer to space and time as existing in and of themselves – as real if not palpably tangible. On the other hand, the existence of space and time as entities is counter-intuitive because of their intangibility, their ideal quality. A solution is to consider space and time as real but not actual virtualities. Like a mathematical set or series, their status exists above and beyond individual elements that are their members. They are not concrete. Such virtualities are intangibles but are not merely abstract ideas or conceptual representations: they have real causal powers and effects. A *Virtualist* position could thus resolve the stalemate between Substantivalist and Reductionist positions (Shields, 2003).

Who	When	Schools/Key Work	Where*
Hesiod	c.late C8 BCE	With Homer, the earliest surviving Greek poetry	Boeotia
Kidinnu	c.C4 BCE	Babylonian Astronomy	Chaldes
Pythagoras	c.570–c.495 BCE	Pythagoreans, Mathematician	Croton
Zeno of Elea	c.490–c.430 BCE	Sophism	Athens
Gorgias	c.485–c.380 BCE		Athens
Leucippus	c.early C5 BCE		Abdera
Philolaus	c.470–c.385 BCE	Non geocentric cosmology	Thebes (?)
Democritus	c.460–c.370 BCE	Atomism, Socratics	Abdera
Plato	c.429–c.347 BCE	Platonism	Athens
Aristotle	c.384–c.322 BCE	Aristotelian Geocentric cosmology	Athens
Epicurus	341–270 BCE	Epicureanism	Athens
Euclid	c.325–c.265 BCE	*Elements of Geometry*	Alexandria
Aristarchus of Samos	310–c.230 BCE	Heliocentric cosmology	Samos
Archimedes	c.287–c.212 BCE	Mathematician, Engineer, Hydrology	Syracuse
Chrysippus	c.280–c.207 BCE	Stoicism	Athens
Eratosthenes	c.275–c.195 BCE	Cartographer, Founder of geography, Librarian of	Alexandria
Hipparchus	c.190–c.120 BCE	Founder of Trigonometry, Astronomer	Rhodes
Posidonius	c.135–c.51 BCE	Stoic, geographer	Rhod
Lucretius	c.99–c.55 BCE	Epicureanism	Rome
Ptolemy	c.90–c.168 CE	Geocentric cosmology	Alexandria
Al-Battani	835–929	Mathematician, Astronomer	Ar-Raqqah, Syria
Al-Razi	865–925	Rationalism	Ragha
Al-Biruni	973–1048	Trigonometry, Geography	Gazni Afghanistan
Avicenna (Ibn Sina)	c.980–1037	Medicine *Laws of Medicine*	Hamadan, Iran
Al-Zarkali	1029–1087	Astronomer	Toledo
Al-Ghazali	1058–1111	Mystic	Tus, Iran
Averroes (Ibn Rushd)	1126–1198	Aristotelian	Cordoba
Nasir al-Din al-Tusi	1201–1274	Geographer, Astronomer, Spherical trigonometry	Tus, Baghdad
Mo'ayyeduddin Urdl	d.1266	Empiricism Engineer	Maragheh, Azerbaijan
Ibn al-Shatir	1304–1375		Damascus
Ibn Battuta	1304–1369	Traveller *Rihla (The Journey)*	Tangier

Figure 3.1   Table of philosophers of space (*Indicating places that thinkers' works are associated with)

Who	When	Schools/Key Work	Where*
Occam	c.1288–c.1348	Scholasticism	Oxford
Crescas	c.1340–c.1410	Rationalism	Zaragossa
Cusanus (Nicholas of Cusa)	1401–1464	Mysticism	Brixen (Tyrol) Italy
Copernicus	1473–1543	Heliocentric cosmology	Frombork
More	1478–1535	Humanism	London
Telesio	1509–1588	Empiricism	Cosenza
Patritius	1529–1597	Neo-Platonism, Historian	Ferrara
Bruno	1548–1600	Non-heliocentric cosmology	London
Sir H. Savile	1549–1622	Translator *Acts of the Apostles, Kings James Bible*	Oxford
Bacon	1561–1626	Empiricism	London
Galileo	1564–1642	Astronomer, heliocentric cosmology	Padua
Campanella	1568–1639		Naples
Gassendi	1592–1655		Aix en Provence
Locke	1632–1704		Oxford
Descartes	1596–1650	Rationalism	Netherlands
Newton	1643–1727		London
Leibniz	1646–1716		Leipzig
Clarke	1675–1729		London
Kant	1724–1804	*Critique of Pure Reason*	Königsberg
Hegel	1770–1831	Idealism *Phenomenology of Spirit*	Berlin
Gauss	1777–1855	Mathematician, Surveying, Differential geometry	Göttingen
Lobachevsky	1792–1856	Hyperbolic geometry, Topology	Kazan
Riemann	1826–1866	Non-Euclidean geometry	Göttingen
Mach	1838–1916	Positivism	Prague
Poincaré	1854–1912	Time-Keeping, Cartography, Topology	Paris
De Cyon	c.1842–1912	Physiologist	St. Petersburg
Von Uexküll	1864–1944	Biologist, Ecology, *Umwelt*	Mihkli
Lenin	1870–1924	Marxist Materialism	Geneva
Bogdanov	1873–1928	Medicine, Utopian Science Fiction	Moscow

Northern Europe: Mathematical Space

Newton, in his correspondences with Clarke (London, 1675–1729; see Câpek, 1976), appears to have been one of the first Renaissance scholars to have empirically examined space qua space to attempt to determine its exact status. In his investigations, Newton assigns to space the status of a real entity. However, the question of whether space is known directly or indirectly, through things and events is left unanswered. What sort of 'scale' exists to assess the measure and structure of space? How could it be recognised (Goldmann, 1971: 65)?

Newton published his *Principia Mathematica* in 1687, an epochal year for natural science. He differentiated any observer's setting of apparent objects and events from a set of laws of nature independent of location – whether on earth or in heaven – and of observers. The laws remain the same throughout the different spheres of the universe, the effects only appearing different because of different initial conditions. Newton's absolute space is a pure, infinite volume set above and apart from the objects of the universe that it contains. Together the relative positions of objects make up their relative space and their velocities with respect to each other. This founded a very science of mechanical interaction and of physical forces which was successful from a practical point of view. It explained Galileo's laws of free fall and everything from the action of complex machinery to the orbits and perturbations of the planets.

The *Principia* sets out to demonstrate the existence of true motion and absolute space (Newton, 2009: 12). Beyond its importance as a synthesis and the usefulness of his mechanics to physics and astronomy, absolute space and time find a place in the *Principia* because as attributes of God they brought a level of cosmological completeness and perfection to his more prosaic mechanics. Their inclusion as first principles at the beginning of the text lent an important theological legitimacy to physics and mechanics (Jammer, 1960: 115, fn 37). It conformed with the view that science shed light on Nature as God's work. Subsequently, the factual and experimental aspects of Newton's system gained ground while the divinity of space was accommodated as a matter for theologians. Echoing the spiritual interest in space to this day, the *Principia* continues to provide a template for the expectation that science in some way will be able to shed light on metaphysical questions such as the existence of God, while it also provides an enduring cultural template which separates out the 'sciences' from the arts or 'humanities' in institutions of knowledge.

Although, or perhaps because Newton appears to understand the distinction between deductive theory and practical application, an abstract geometry is impossible: 'the description of right lines and circles, upon which geometry is founded, belongs to mechanics' (Newton, 2009: Book 1,

Scholium, Prop. 69: 121). Spatiality is strictly empirical and not an object of theory, but rather a precondition of theories such as mathematics. This gives the *Principia* a fundamentally realist ontology in that the primary concepts and laws Newton uses are not presented as hypothetical nor are they abstractions to be correlated to subsequent observation and experimental verification. Rather they are considered facts of immediate experience (despite occasionally being referred to as axioms, by which Newton appears to mean points of departure for his investigations not arbitrary assumptions: '*lex tertia ....per theoriam comprobata est*' (Newton, 2009: Scholium, *Axiomata*: 23).

Given that space is real for Newton but experientially intangible, his realism is a compromise. For Newton, despite his use of relative spaces or coordinate systems, space is absolute and immutable in epistemological and ontological terms. He developed Campanella and Gassendi's (Aix en Provence, 1592–1655) concept of an infinite, homogeneous and isotropic space, independent of the bodies it contains. It is a basis for conceptions such as a state of rest and the postulate of the universal validity of repeatable experimental results. This standardisation of space and its qualities, such as three-dimensionality, are essential for experimental method, where an experiment in one place holds for the same procedure in another location. In contrast to Descartes, Newton follows Galileo's (Padua, 1564–1642) conception of matter as fundamentally characterised by mass as a 'mass-point' rather than by extension. This allows him to separate objects and forces from space. Despite methodological shortcomings, he believed he had proved that objects occupy just part of space and not another part of space without reference to any other bodies in the universe.

However, as Leibniz (Leipzig, 1646–1716) and many others including Einstein objected, the Substantivalist assumption that absolute empty space existed as a physical reality remained counter-intuitive. Newton's absolute space acted in a mysterious, non-contact manner and could not be defined in the terms that governed the science of mechanics. Absolute space and time was the seat of acceleration conceived as a property of bodies themselves (Sklar, 1974) which hinted at their absolute motion, quite different from the observable motion of a ship relative to a headland. The status of bodies with respect to absolute space could only be detected in cases of rotation. For example,

When we see the seats attached to a carnival ride [such as a calliope or merry go round] slowly rise as the apparatus turns, Newton's mechanics tells us that this is due [not] to its motion with respect to the fairgrounds ... but, rather, to its motion with respect to absolute space. (Genz, 1999: 148)

Figure 3.2 Map and reverse chronology of key thinkers on space

Henri Lefebvre (1901–1991) – Paris
Maurits Cornelis Escher (1898–1972) – Baarn
Albert Einstein (1879–1955) – Zurich
Alexander Bogdanov (1873–1928) – Moscow
Vladimir Ilyich Lenin (1870–1924) – Geneva
Henri Poincaré (1854–1912) – Paris
Élie De Cyon (1842–1912) – St. Petersburg
Ernst Mach (1838–1916) – Prague
Bernhard Riemann (1826–1866) – Göttingen
Nikolai Ivanovich Lobachevsky (1792–1856) – Kazan
Georg Wilhelm Friedrich Hegel (1770–1831) – Berlin
Immanuel Kant (1724–1804) – Königsberg
Johann Bernoulli (1667–1748) – Basel
Gottfried Leibniz (1646–1716) – Leipzig
Isaac Newton (1643–1727) – London
Lahire (1640–1718) – Paris
Thomas Locke (1632–1704) – Oxford
Frans van Schooten (1615–1660) – Leiden
René Descartes (1596–1650) – Netherlands
Pierre Gassendi (1592–1655) – Aix en Provence
Tommaso Campanella (1568–1639) – Naples
Galileo (1564–1642) – Padua
George Abbot (1562–1633) – London
Sir Henry Savile (1549–1622) – Oxford
Giordano Bruno (1548–1600) – London
Franciscus Patricius (1529–1597) – Ferrara
Francis Bacon (1521–1626) – London
Bernardino Telesio (1509–1588) – Cosenza
Thomas More (1478–1535) – London
Nicolaus Copernicus (1473–1543) – Frombork
Nicolaus Cusanus (1401–1464) – Kues
Hasdai Crescas (ca. 1340–ca. 1410) – Saragossa
Ibn Battuta (1304–1369) – Tangier
Ibn al-Shatir (1304–1375) – Damascus
William of Occam (ca. 1288–ca. 1348) – Oxford
Mo'ayyeduddin Urdi (??–1266) – Maragheh
Naṣīr al-Dīn al-Ṭūsī (1201–1274) – Tus
Robert Grosseteste (ca. 1175–1253) – Oxford
Averroes (Ibn Rushd) (1126–1198) – Cordoba
Al-Ghazali (1058–1111) – Tus
Arzachel (al-Zarqālī) (1029–1087) – Toledo
Avicenna (981–1037) – Hamadān
Biruni (973–1048) – Ghazna
Al-Razi (865–925) – Ragha
Albategni (Al-Battani) (835–929) – ar-Raqqah
Simplicius (ca. 490–ca. 560) – Alexandria
Ptolemy (ca. 90–ca. 168) – Alexandria
Titus Lucretius Carus (ca. 99–ca. 55 BCE) – Rome
Posidonius (ca. 135–ca. 51 BCE) – Rhodes
Chrysippus of Soli (ca 280–ca 207 BCE) – Athens
Archimedes (ca 287–ca 212 BCE) – Syracuse
Aristarchus (310–ca. 230 BCE) – Samos
Euclid (ca. 325 –ca. 265 BCE) – Alexandria
Peripatetic School (ca. late 3rd century BCE) – Athens
Epicurus (341–270 BCE) – Athens
Aristotle (ca 384–ca 322 BCE) – Athens
Archytas (428–347 BCE) – Tarentum
Plato (ca. 429–ca. 347 BCE) – Athens
Democritus (ca 460–ca 370 BCE) – Abdera
Philolaus (ca. 470–ca. 385 BCE) – Thebes(?)
Leucippus (ca. early 5th century BCE) – Abdera, Thrace
Herodotus (ca. 484–ca. 425 BCE) – Thurii
Gorgias (ca. 485–ca. 380 BCE) – Athens
Zeno [of Elea] (ca. 490–ca. 430 BCE) – Athens
Pythagoras (ca. 570–ca. 495 BCE) – Croton
Hesiod (ca. late 8th century BCE) – Boeotia
Sumerian Kingdom (6th–2nd millennium BCE) – Sumer

For Newton, no energy had to be spent to maintain the rotation of a frictionless object.

> Whenever we attempt to set masses in motion ... those masses will offer resistance ... In order to speak of absolute space, Newton also had to find differences between various motions that are free of forces, in his system of mechanics ... distinguished from all 'relative motion'. (Genz, 1999: 149)

Leibniz rejected Newton's theory of an absolute space as the 'organ of God' (cf. Jammer, 1960: 114, fn 35; Leibniz collection of papers, Leibniz and Clarke, 2000: 3) in favour of a network of relations among coexisting things, similar to the lines relating persons on a genealogical chart. However, this conception of space (and of time) as a network of relations between created bodies is found even earlier in the work of Muslim philosophers such as Al-Ghazali (Tus, 1058–1111) who was active in the eleventh century (Al Ghazali (Algazel), 1927). Leibniz, in his correspondence with Clarke exploited Newton's metaphysical space, the divine 'place of all things'. This ruled out any divisibility of space because this would suggest the divisibility of the substance of a Christian God. In contrast, Leibniz argues that space is a simple expression of relations. Although he accepts absolute true motion, the essence of Leibniz's spatial critique is that Newton hypostatises a set of relative positions in a system of relations (such as a family tree) as an absolute system for

Figure 3.3   Raphael, *School of Athens*, 1505. Including from left to right figures said to be Epicurus or Democritus; Pythagoras (foreground writing in a book); Plato or Archimedes; Aristotle; Euclid (or Archimedes) bent over with a compass on the right) and Ptolemy (turned away on the right). (public domain courtesy Wikimedia Commons)

which there is no ultimate proof. Because Newton's system worked well – it served the purposes of astronomy, physics and everyday mechanics into the twentieth century – Leibniz's critique was largely ignored.

Newton's and later Locke's theories of space originated in part, at least, in the Byzantine diaspora that had happened almost two centuries before them. They depended on Gassendi's natural philosophy which was an empiricism rooted in readings of the classic texts and correspondence with key challenges to medieval understandings of the relationship between subjects and objects via perception (cf. Campanella, 1620). We also find the Empiricists' emancipation of space from the Aristotelian tradition of space as container in the work of Gassendi's better known colleague, René Descartes. Space ceases to be a mental or conceptual category by which the objects of the world were named and classified. That is, space ceases to be merely an abstraction or representation of spheres and voids (Kolaja, 1957: 16). Rather than being a category of experience imposed on our perceptions of the world, in Cartesian reason Space enters the realm of the absolute. Descartes' *res extensa* dominates the senses and body, the *res cognans*, which it contains (see Descartes, 1901, as cited in Koyré, 1957).

This oppressive divide between the objective cosmos and the thinking subject spurred Kant to attempt to move beyond the polarity of the subject alienated from an outside world. In 1769 Kant was to categorise space and time as *a priori* synthetic judgements. Here the 'a priori' flags the crisis-point of deduction. It stands 'before' reason, like a philosopher's 'big bang', before and beyond which it is impossible to extrapolate back further. *A prioris* form the substratum of experience, always pre-existing and external to the knowing subject. 'Pure intuition, space and time, constitute precisely that formal totality which is the first condition of knowledge by the understanding and reason' (Goldmann, 1971: 159). In effect, Kant attempts to reconcile Leibniz and Newton: 'to investigate whether there is not to be found in the judgements of extension, such as are contained in geometry, an evident proof that space has a reality of its own, independent of the existence of all matter, and indeed as the first ground of the possibility of the compositeness of matter' (Jammer, 1960: 132; see Immanuel Kant, 1910: II, 37).

Dimensionality: Three, Four or More?

Classical approaches emphasising three-dimensional space break down in everyday usage and metaphor as well as with the mathematical exploration of anomalies in Euclidean geometry: mirror images or 'Incongruous Counterparts' and the 'Parallel Postulate'. In the first case, mirror reflections or left and right hands are similar in the spatiality of our everyday experience but Euclidean geometry cannot superimpose one side on its counterpart.

Mirror image incongruity fractures the simplicity of the everyday world each time we look in a mirror. Looking in a mirror and brushing our hair, we must resort to a practised habit of imagination by counterposing left and right sides of our images with the right and left sides of our bodies. Prisms were required to correct this inversion. Mathematically, this problem can only be resolved by constructing a geometry with more than three dimensions. This is an excellent example of how our everyday embodiment in a '3D' world, which we take to be natural, relies on unnatural imaginative gymnastics that leads to flaws in our representations of the world linguistically and scientifically. This suggests to Kant that space cannot be 'real' but is rather a form of 'outer intuition' – a synthetic judgement (Kant, 1953: 41–51). Nonetheless, Kant does make an argument for absolute space as an entity with a definite structure and properties, integrated to time. It cannot, however, be known empirically.

The problem of left-right geometric incongruity may be taken as an indicator of the *dimensionality* of space. Such a superimposition could be easily accomplished if space were four-dimensional, or non-dimensional (for example, if space was really like a möbius strip, see Jammer, 1960: 131–2). Despite the fact that we cannot tell in strictly logical terms which hand is which, we do know that they are *different*. If space were simply the relations between objects then this would not be possible (Lucas, 1984: 144).

For Kant, this refutes Leibniz's argument that a simplified definition can be given such that, 'Space denotes, in terms of possibility, an order of things which exist at the same time, considered as existing together (Alexander 1956: 26; See Leibniz, III s. 4, and cf. V s. 104). Such a 'relationism' would point to the conclusion that, 'Space is nothing but the collection of actual and possible spatial relations between actual and possible material objects' (Sklar, 1974: 285). These material objects would implicitly exist in a Cartesian three-dimensional framework, thereby locking analysis into a single kind of Foucauldian *dispositif* or cultural formation – an 'order of things'. While Kant may be taken as only proposing a middle ground against Leibniz's monadology, Kant's formulations provide a powerful weapon against relationist approaches.

[In] the principal stages of Kant's pre-critical thought, it seems to me that the earliest element is the assertion that to physics and to bodies on the one hand, and to mathematics and to space and time on the other, correspond two entirely different kinds of knowledge ... [I]n geometry ... the individual and the limited can only be understood as a part of a greater whole. Space is infinitely divisible precisely because it forms a whole which is not made up of individual monads. (Goldmann, 1971: 61)

Goldmann (1971) draws a link between Kant's spatial analysis and the more sociological problem of *totality*. For example, space in Hegel's scheme also occupies a transcendent position. 'Historical Time engenders Space, in which the State exists. Man (the Concept) is Time: the "Concept which is there in the [spatial] empirical existence of Nature (*der Begriff der da ist*)"' (Kojève and Queneau, 1947: 133). For Kojève, Hegel's Space is the (four-dimensional) natural, 'real Space', 'extended Matter' (Kojève and Queneau, 1947: 135–7), that which exists positively or actually (as opposed to the temporal past and future). One cannot conclude that 'space merely consists of external relations of the parts of matter which exist alongside one another' (Kant, 1968: 48). Although Kant does not develop his arguments for absolute space, years later he continued to interrogate the concept of space: 'Either space contains the ground of the possibility of the co-presence of many substances and their relations, or the latter contain the ground of the possibility of space' (Kant, 1910: XVII, 3790).

'*Spatium* and *tempus* are *tota analytica*, bodies *synthetica*.' (Kant, 1910: XVII, 3789). In *Space and Incongruence*, Buroker (1981) locates the origins of Kant's idealism in this problem of incongruence. As Lucas (1984: 148) points out, the need for the relationists to invoke *possible* objects and relations is open to objection on the same grounds as Sklar criticises *space*. Possible objects are as ethereal as they criticise space as being. If all continuous motions in a three-dimensional space are real, not much is saved by denying the reality of space itself (Lucas, 1984: 148). Privileging relations over a topological reality involves attempting to attribute to space the relations of objects:

> Since the topological properties of space affect the spatial features of objects, we can expect to characterize the former in terms of the latter but, in so doing, we have to invoke principles and complexities that deprive the relationist account of its claims to economy and simplicity. (Lucas, 1984: 148)

Space can be said to be, at minimum, a substance: the substantial bearer of (topological) properties whose consequences we can notice in ordinary experience (Lucas, 1984: 146). However, what type of substance remains debatable. A conception of virtuality rather than materiality is required to do justice to space as a relational medium in which a particular ordering and regularity can be found.

Flatness

Recall that Euclid's fifth 'Parallel Postulate' defines planes by stating that through one point in a plane it is possible to draw only one straight line parallel to a given straight line in the same plane. Planes thus have a singular flatness. Many aspects of geometry are related to this. If one accepts the first four postulates (see Chapter 5) and one result such as the Pythagorean theorem or that the sum of the angles of a triangle is two right angles (180°), then the fifth postulate follows. Conversely, accepting all five postulates constructs a geometrical space of representations in which the mathematics and the representations of space by Pythagoras and other ancient mathematicians, surveyors and geographers surveyed above function.

As early as 1621 Sir Henry Savile (Oxford, 1549–1622) noted that the Parallel Postulate was a blemish in Euclid's system. It can be violated if the three-planar dimensions of Euclidean space are warped – such as the geometries of Gauss (Göttingen, 1777–1855), Lobachevsky (Kazan, 1792–1856) and Riemann (Göttingen, 1826–66) produced in the first half of the nineteenth century. Lobachevsky announced a two-dimensional hyperbolic space in 1830. Bernhard Riemann produced his elliptical space in 1854, distinguishing space from geometry, but also added distance to Euclid's basic terms such as points and lines. For Riemann, regardless of how many dimensions a space, or manifold, has, straight lines are geodesics, or lines that minimise distance between points – like 'great circle' routes between cities on the globe, or 'as the crow flies' one might say (see Chapter 4). Straight lines allow one to form triangles and triangulate not only location but relative speed and to sum the angles at the points of triangles to check for curvature in the space. Surfaces or manifolds where the angles of triangles do not equal 180° are not flat, but curved.

Conversely, this means that curvature (change in the shape of a manifold) expresses deviation from the 180° sum of the angles of a triangle – a key point for Einstein who was to show that matter deformed space around it. Light from a star passing the sun bent from the expected straight line to observers on the Earth. However, it is space that is warped; light is merely following the actual shortest path, a geodesic in space-time. But this creative insight depended in more ways than this on Riemann. He is the one who established a distinction between actual, material or physical reality and ideal, virtual, mathematical reality, opening up a topological laboratory for experiment that was to thrive in the late nineteenth and early twentieth century abstraction of European academic mathematics departments. The art of Escher demonstrates the paradoxes of these mathematical and logical 'phase spaces' – more projected topographies of mathematical solution sets than any Euclidean 'lived space'. Ever since, not just Euclidean but Cartesian absolute space has become just one of many topological spaces.

Historically, it is in this fin-de-siècle plurality of *spaces* that the term 'social space' finds a place, becomes admissible and gains meaning as a qualitative cultural topology of affinities between bodies, meanings and sites (Poincaré, 1952: 50–8; Mach, 1901: 94). However, as Lefebvre commented, 'Les mathématiciens *s'emparent* de l'espace ... ' (Lefebvre, 1981b: 8, my emphasis), likening it to a hijacking or kidnap scene. The radical difference of topological spaces from the social space of everyday life aggravated all the problems of 'knowing' the truth of social space. Space becomes an abstract equation. There is no final method which will make a theoretically consistent leap from these mathematical *spaces* of logic to the spaces of society. Social space is thus born in abstraction and presents social sciences with a struggle that takes much of the twentieth century to integrate with embodied practice in culturally meaningful places.

Relativistic Space

Ernst Mach (Prague, 1838–1916) followed shortly after Reimann with arguments for visual, auditory and tactile spaces; each varying according to the sensitivity and reaction time of the organ involved. This, it was argued, was a physiological foundation for the cognitive development of understandings of geometric space. 'Notions of space are rooted in our physiological organism' (Mach, 1901: 94). This naturalises – or biologises – the understanding of space, removing the intellect and replacing it with psycho-biology. Mach argued that symmetry could be traced to bodily sources and the coordinate system of Cartesian geometry to the right-left orientation of the body. For Mach, measurement had anatomical origins, where surfaces were understood like skin, 'the analog of a two-dimensional, finite, unbounded and closed Riemannian space' (Mach, 1901: 9).

De Cyon (St Petersburg, 1842–1912) extended the case for physiological origins of the experience of space. Clinical research was advanced to show that the sense of space is rooted in the semicircular canals of the ear: dimensions are in direct relation to the number and orientation of these canals. Humans have three canals oriented in the three planes, which allow us to experience three-dimensional space. Other animals have only two canals and experimental evidence suggests that they orient themselves in a two-dimensional space (de Cyon, 1901, cited in Kern, 1983: 136).

De Cyon's work was later incorporated into von Uexküll's (Mihkli, 1864–1944) *Umwelt und Inenwelt der Tiere* (1909). His proposals that organisms with different levels of development of spatial sense suggested that

> there [may be] ... complete worlds with distinctive spatial orientations scattered all along the phylogenetic scale ... [which challenges] the ego-centrism of man ... Among the throng of worlds and living spaces ... there may be higher worlds of greater dimensions that we are unable to see, as the amoeba is unable to see the stars in our sky. (Kern, 1983: 137)

For Mach, De Cyon and most famously von Uexküll, one's sense of space is not an *a priori* of the mind (cf. Kant) but an *a priori* of a body that is socialised as well as being physically configured (see von Uexküll, 2011).

Consider the constricted world or environment (*Umwelt*) of a tick, a blind, bloodsucking insect sensitive to the odour of butyric acid in hair follicles and the specific temperature of 37°C – the median body temperature of mammals. It relies on touch to climb, fall and bury itself into the skin of its host (see von Uexküll, 2011; see also Agamben, 2004). However, such a multiplication of spaces was deeply disturbing to the commonsense mind of late nineteenth-century Europe. The response was predictable. Implied subjectivity and relativism threatened the stability of objective reality, of what could be taken for granted as truth, and hence, what could be claimed to be the 'right way to act'. Familiar themes? Perhaps. The cat has been 'out of the bag' for nearly a century and the transformative effects of this new space are still being felt.

Lenin (Geneva, St Petersburg 1870–1924), in *Materialism and Empirio-Criticism,* devotes a chapter to 'Space and Time' (Lenin, 1908: 176–89), in which he attempts to defend the objective material world in terms of absolute space and time. Such an objective reality in which matter moves in space and time independent of any intervention of the human mind, he believed to be essential to the materialist position and to the authority of truth claims. Space and time were realities, not even the Kantian compromise of 'forms of understanding', or 'outer intuition'. According to Lenin, Mach's spaces were 'absurd', 'palpable idealist nonsense', and Poincaré – an entrenched representative of the imperial institutions of the turn of the twentieth century – was rotten and hypocritical (Lenin, 1908). The fierceness of Lenin's polemic is due to his belief that the reputation and political effectiveness of the Bolshevik Party were at stake. When an article appeared in *Die Neue Zeit* (1907, cited in Kern, 1983: 135) about certain Bolsheviks who had embraced a Machist philosophy, Lenin attacked to publicly define the Bolshevik position:

> Machism was simply ... one manifestation of a general disease of doubting material reality ... Lenin singled out the prominent Bolshevik philosopher A. Bogdanov, who had argued for the social relativity of all categories of experience in *Empirio-monism* (1904–1906). Such relativistic idealism undermined belief in one and only one real framework of time and space in which the events of all cultures take place. ... The reference to a plurality of spaces challenged the universality of a single space, and the suggestion that these various forms of space and time 'adapt' to man's experience identified Bogdanov with the genetic epistemology of both Mach and Poincaré. (Kern, 1983: 134–5)

Our argument in the following chapters will be that a nuanced appreciation of peoples' different temporal and spatial sensoria, and of the time-spaces of disparate processes that converge in places, is essential to cultural and political action. Without this, one is hostage to fortune, to the vagaries of the compounding effects of compossible[2] processes and actions. It is not so much that we face problems – risks – of 'tipping points' that popular commentators see in the non-linear dynamics of specific trends. We can specify actual and present dangers of compounding trends that produce not just *catastrophe points* as systems veer out of equilibrium and situations transgress 'norms' and limits. They also produce *singularities*, specific spikes or eruptions that reliably appear but cannot be predicted.

While Lenin was attempting to refute Poincaré's (Paris, 1854–1912; see Chapter 6) famous anticipation of relativity, Einstein had already published his 'Special Theory of General Relativity' in 1905. 'With the general theory of relativity, the number of spaces increased beyond calculation to equal the number of moving reference systems of all the gravitational fields generated by all of the matter in the universe' (Kern, 1983: 139). 'There is an infinite number of spaces, which are in motion with respect to each other' (Einstein, 1961: 139). Einstein was referring to multiple physical and physiological spaces, but it was not long before Bogdanov's (Moscow, 1873–1928) Machian hypothesis was followed by a plethora of suggestions for culturally-specific social spaces. Einstein's work contributed to changing the social spatialisation in which we live towards a topological understanding by questioning the absolute nature of time and space. Spaces could become relative, just as Einsteinian time was. Since Newton, an absolute, teleological conception of time (the arrow of progress) had been the preserve of the course of divine will (see Chapter 3). Replacing this with a multiplicity of time-spaces, determined by changing dimensions depending on one's speed, questioned the certainties of the Enlightenment sensorium. Einstein and Poincaré's time has been called the time of confinements, of separate workplaces and time-zones that had to be coordinated, worlds apart (see also Galison, 2003). Continuity and linkage between such discrete objects and spaces was the challenge. There were space-time localities whose positions relative to each other were of vital importance for the operation of capitalist modernity.

> In retrospect, the disciplinary society at its apex seems rather likely to have propelled the emergence of a notion of time as 'being kept' in little space-time containers. From such an historical perspective, then, the re-emergence of Bergson's critique of extensity is today far from surprising. It coincides with the completion of the long durée of capitalist extension ... followed by an accelerated intensification that Negri, Lazzarato and others have begun to describe. This is not to say – as some do – that space disappears. It only disappears as pure quantity in order to re-emerge as a problem, as something that is suddenly invested with time/quality but not as a succession of concrete, confined blocs but as virtual flow. (Olma, 2004, online)

Hence the importance of flows and virtualities that combine space with time in fluid topologies rather than the step-wise succession of moments. These flows involve the 'smearing out' of monadic, defined and self-contained time-spaces into topological neighbourhoods and manifolds in which time becomes qualitative duration.

Notes

1   Sent as Ambassador from Syracuse to Athens, he taught and popularised the practice of rhetoric and performances of oratory, establishing this not only in theatre but as one of the key features for which the political life of classical Athens is still looked to. Gorgias brought Sophist rhetoric to the Greeks, becoming a teacher of Alcibiades, and confidant of Pericles and Thucydides.

2   In Leibniz' sense of a collection of finite elements that combine to create multiple possibility (in the sense of concrete but future states and as probabilities), or as Deleuze reads it in *Cinema* (Deleuze, 1989), potential capabilities (virtualities – unfortunately we are not able to pursue this here). (See 'On the Ultimate Origination of Things', Leibniz and Holz, 1986: VII, 302.)

4

the socialness of space

Time, and Space, are 'forms of social coordination of the experiences of different people' said Bogdanov (1904–1906). Non-Euclidean mathematical spaces in physics and cosmology set the stage for a re-appreciation of the socialness of space. The Einsteinian shift in physics envisioned an infinite number of spaces in motion with respect to each other. This opened up a relativist plurality of spaces and helped legitimate the possibility that the history of the earth and its discoveries might be construed differently in different sociocultural spaces. As the previous chapter showed, it was not long before Bogdanov's hypothesis that spatiality and temporality were not universals but somehow grounded in human physiology was followed by more suggestions for physiologically-specific and culturally-specific spatialisations.

What does it mean to speak of an environment as a 'social space'? This relatively recent conception of community and social interaction appears to date only from the time of the mid-nineteenth century growth of the large metropolis. It raises a number of methodological problems: how are social spaces to be detected and delimited or mapped? How can we avoid allowing the spatial metaphor to confuse analysis of a professional network or association? These too are social spaces or milieux. Can we avoid confusing the social space of a local neighbourhood childrens' playground with the tendency to refer to all such public spaces as the 'social spaces' of a city? It is essential to distinguish actual areas set aside for congregation or social interaction – which can be named as 'social spaces' or public spaces – from social space as either a quality of an actual place or of a set of places. Both are real; both are empirical. However, the former is a category of tangible places, while the latter is an intangible quality, a spatialisation – casting a site as a place for this or for that and always with reference to other places or regions.

Adventurers and scholars had long sailed about the earth and dug into its crust to find out about other societies, but they always reconstructed them in the uniform space of the modern Western world, never imagining that space itself might vary from one society to another as much as did kinship patterns and puberty rites. (Kern, 1983: 137)

There are several examples of sociological treatments of space which deserve mention (see Kolaja, 1969 for a survey of post-World War II sociological approaches that generally allocate space to the status of void rather than spatialisation). The most noteworthy precedents in which aspects of social spatialisation play an important role include Marx and Engels, Simmel and others.

Recognising Spatialisation

Space, bounded territory, indefinite terrain, and discrete places are central mnemonic figures, and one must wonder what influence their metaphoric pre-dispositions, hidden deep in linguistic structures and etymological roots, has on the directions taken by philosophy – what liaisons and connotations; which 'connections' are made based only on metaphor and metonymy? Not surprisingly, such core spatio-temporal allusions are precisely what appear to be used most in slogans, theoretical description and ideological diatribes because they place us *in situ* in innumerable, politicised, socio-spatial/socio-temporal contexts and in partisan relationships to other groups, individuals, objects, social processes and ideas, without necessitating the explicit enunciation of this partisan relationship. 'Space' evidently plays an important role in defining the world of ideas, as well as the physical world. These metaphors reveal the deep penetration of space into our conscious and unconscious mental processes. Unexamined notions of 'space' ground the philosophical territory of conceptual terrains – the bordered 'space of reality'. It has been argued that the exploration of boundaries and spaces is the essence of philosophy (Le Doeuff, 1980).

These usages of the word 'space' to designate the reservoir of nature on and in which agents act (what Lefebvre calls '*materiaux*', materials (Lefebvre, 1981b: 19ff.)) are complementary and coextensive with the empirical uses of the word, as in 'lived space'. The argument to be presented here is that the full range of 'space' (i.e. social spatialisation) must be admitted to the debate before a complete argument regarding the cultural stature of 'space' as a term, operator, and concept can ever be fully formulated. One reaction was Einstein's: to 'shun the vague word "space", of which, we must honestly acknowledge, we cannot form the slightest conception and we replace it by "motion relative to a practically rigid body of reference"' (Einstein, 1961: 9). This displaces 'space' as a static neutral void in which objects acted without reference to context.

As discussed in the previous chapter, Lenin attempted to maintain a classical, non-relativistic model of space, which underpinned his project of a new and stable social geometry based on popular ownership of the means of production (Lenin, 1908). This informed the position of the Soviet Union and the Communist International for over 70 years. There was no advantage for the Bolsheviks to be gained from developing a non-economic definition of social space that was anything other than an input to production processes; that is, a use-value. Ironically, this precluded truly dialectical approaches to social space that only came to the fore by the end of the twentieth century with the work of Henri Lefebvre and David Harvey. Far from recoiling from the many metaphoric appropriations of 'space', as Einstein, Lenin and even Lefebvre do (Lefebvre, 1981b: 12–16), it is important to recognise the metaphoric relation all discourse has to a spatial reality.

Marx: The Economics of Land

In the nineteenth-century context, 'space' for Marx and Engels meant land and property first and foremost. Cohen put it well when he argued that '[s]pace deserves membership in the set of productive forces. Ownership ... confirms a position in the economic structure ... He who owns a hole, even exclusive of its material envelope, is a man to reckon with if you must reach the far side of the hole and cannot feasibly tunnel beneath it, fly above it, or make your way round it' (Cohen, 1978: 51). Only with later theorists of the nation, such as Ernest Renan, Elysée Reclus and Friedrich Ratzel (Bhabha, 1991; Ratzel, 1903), did space come to be understood as primarily the natural territory of an ethnic group or republic. However, human, economic and social geography can be easily read into the work of Marx as well as being clear in Engels' description of the *Conditions of the Working Class* (Engels, 1973). Marx's conception of society is argued to be innately spatial given his stress on social and economic relations and his recognition of the importance of land and of urbanisation in the transition from Feudalism to Capitalism.[1]

> Capital by its nature drives beyond every spatial barrier. Thus the creation of the physical conditions of exchange – of the means of communication and transport – the annihilation of space by time – becomes an extraordinary necessity ... to tear down every spatial barrier to intercourse, i.e. to exchange, and conquer the whole earth for its market, it strives on the other side to annihilate this space with time, i.e. to reduce to a minimum the time spent in motion from one place to another. (Marx, 1973a: 539–40)

Note the linkage of space and time in this quote. There is no doubt that Marx was well aware of Greek conceptions of space and the void from his 1841 doctoral thesis on Democritean and Epicurean philosophies of nature. However, Marx rarely stresses capitalism as a spatialisation. He notes that, 'Poverty robs the worker of the conditions most essential to his labour, of space, light and ventilation ... ' (Marx, 1976: 591). It is a quantifiable volume essential to be apportioned to labourers (Marx, 1976: 613).

Under capitalism, Marx argues that the wage labour system requires that land be held as private property and worked as a commodity, driving those who formed the peasantry in earlier modes of production off the land and into cities as potential wage labourers, thereby creating an industrial proletariat. For capitalist social relations to dominate, this transformation of the holding of land and its economic and social position was essential.

> The inner construction of modern society, or capital in the totality of its relations, is ... posited in the economic relations of modern landed property ... It is already given in the fact that landed property is the product of capital ... [W]herever landed property is transformed into money rent through the reaction of capital on the older forms of landed property ... there the cottiers, serfs, bondsmen ... become day labourers ... i.e., that wage labour in its totality is initially created by the action of capital on landed property ... (Marx, 1973a: 276)

Modern landed property also reproduces wage labourers by blocking the return to the land except by its purchase: 'landed property leads back to wage labour. In one regard, it is nothing more than the extension of wage labour, from the cities to the countryside, i.e., wage labour distributed over the entire surface of the society' (Marx, 1973a: 277). Indeed, private property, as the *form* of the insistent cultural connection of one family, one house, and one lot grounds the patriarchal family and structures the practice of dwelling as a family, and most recently, as a nuclear family of parents and children, into the *doxos* of capitalist modernity (Ardener, 1983):

> Economically considered, the spatial condition, the bringing of the product to the market, belongs to the production process itself ... The movement through which it gets there belongs still with the cost of making it ... [T]his spatial moment is important in so far as the expansion of the market and the exchangeability of the product are connected with it. The reduction of the costs of this *real circulation* (in space) belongs to the development of the forces of production. (Marx, 1973a: 534)

Harvey clarifies the different aspects and functions of space within capitalism in a way that helps make clear the intersection between the cultural and economic in spatialisation: space is fixed capital as an element in production; fixed capital in the form of a production site or framework – something to be consumed and a site or framework for consumption. It is commodified but each of these aspects has different working periods and rhythms of circulation (Harvey, 1989: 64) and contributes to or frames different circuits of capital – commodities, finance, land and the like. Space (and place) is also an experience and a framework for experience, for consciousness. Critical of the tendency in more recent Marxist geography to disconnect this political economy from space (or social spatialisation) as an overall symbolic system for consciousness, Landzelius adds that

> much discussion of capitalist space with regard to built form has been through the lens of a sort of commodity aesthetics, e.g. in the critiques and analyses of postmodernism by Harvey (1988) and Jameson (1984), with too little attention paid to the reifying aspects of *capitalist space understood as (dis)configured totality.* (Landzelius, 2009: 48, emphasis added; cf. also Gottdiener and Lagopoulos, 1986, on urban semiotics and capitalism)

When the stability of our intimate lives is so thoroughly rooted in capitalist practice, it is not surprising that there is little willingness to support initiatives for change amongst the majority, which are those in families (Petchevsky, 1981). In *Poverty of Philosophy*, Marx writes, '[i]n each historical epoch, property has developed differently and under a set of entirely different social relations' (Marx, 1973a: 265). Paraphrasing, Harvey spatialises Marx, saying, 'The rise of capitalism entailed the "dissolution of the old economic relations of landed property" and their conversion to a form compatible with sustained accumulation' (Harvey, 1982: 343).

> The history of landed property, which would demonstrate the gradual transformation of the feudal landlord into the landowner, of the hereditary, semi-tributary and often unfree tenant for life into the modern farmer, and of the resident serfs, bondsmen and villains who belonged to the property into agricultural day labourers, would indeed be the history of the formation of modern capital. (Marx, 1973b: 252)

Later Marxist theorists of the relation of land and capital argue that the preservation of private property in land performs an ideological and legitimising function for all forms of private property (Harvey, 1982: 360), maintaining its status as inviolable. These juridical and ideological aspects appear more important, in Harvey's eyes, than the ground rent function of landed property. Private property appears as a concrete capitalist spatial practice: a commodification of space itself, and as the single-family house and lot, a commodification of the family too. It is from this ideological perspective which Lefebvre, in *La Production de l'Espace*, considers the importance of private property not as a general principle or right, but as a practice of individuals and families across the spectrum of social classes. The *mythology* of the private 'lot', as he refers to it, stands opposed to not only the 'truth' of the lot itself as a unit of speculation, but also to the essential reality of the urban which is that of the collectivity (see below).

Lefebvre argues that the spatial property circuit can be considered a site of capital formation because savings in transportation costs – the spatial movement of goods – can be considered to have a role in the formation of surplus value. Although this argument is criticised by Gottdiener (1985: 186–190) as being inadequately supported by Lefebvre (Lefebvre, 1974; 1979: 293). Private property forms one of the bedrock elements of the modern spatialisation. As a spatial element and a clearly demarcated territory, it demonstrates the phenomenon of rendering space tangible, and in particular, visible. This rational and visual bias, which reduces space to a void or a 'space of possibilities' between boundaries, is a clear trend under the regime of Abstract Space which Lefebvre analyses at length (1981b: 384ff.; 1991a). In this approach, the character of the space is implicitly defined as the set of possibilities (enterprises, moods, etc.) allowable or most obviously achievable within the space. Limitations on these are set in turn by the influence of the boundaries or the character of the neighbouring spatial elements: for example, in an area with other single family dwelling lots all around, any given empty lot takes on the definition of those by which it is surrounded.

Marx's approach to social space is bound up with his understanding of location as economic advantage or disadvantage: 'the relation to the earth as property is always mediated through occupation of the land and soil, peacefully or violently' (Marx, 1973b: 485 and online). As land – soil and subterranean resources – space is an input into production processes. As a location, any 'place' is anchored within the circulation of goods and capital. It is near or far from markets and sites of production. But space is fundamentally stable in the sense of the Earth being a datum on which economic processes unfold. Rather than a Cartesian *extensio*, this space is the *terra firma* of land and coastlines, the empty expanse of the sea and the positional battlefield of military manoeuvre and march. The tyranny of distance – associated with the fixity of land – is circumvented by technologies that reduce travel time in the interest of capital.

Lefebvre discerns a gap between global processes of urbanisation and the decay of those older forms in which that process traditionally developed. Lefebvre suggests that, for historical reasons, Marx does not sufficiently insist on this identity between industrialisation and urbanisation (Lefebvre, 1973). In our time, the recognition that the 'urban' is the meaning and truth of industrialisation is politically essential. The crisis of the urban cannot be resolved by 'urbanistic' means; the problem is socio-ideological, not rational-technical.

Engels: Inequality and the Built Environment

By contrast, Engels goes beyond crowding or density to detailed observations on the relations brought about in the new industrial cities by patterns of development in time and space. Manchester appears 'peculiarly built' in ways that accommodate but mask the true relationship between the great new metropolises and industrial capitalism:

a person may live in it [Manchester] for years and go in and out daily without coming into contact with a working-people's quarter or even with workers, that is, so long as he confines himself to his business or to pleasure walks. This arises chiefly from the fact, that by unconscious tacit agreement, as well as with out-spoken conscious determination, the working people's quarters are sharply separated ... all Manchester proper ... are all unmixed working peoples' quarters, stretching like a girdle, averaging a mile and half in breadth, around the commercial district. Outside, beyond this girdle, lives the upper and middle bourgeoisie ... in free, wholesome country air, in fine, comfortable homes, passed once every half or quarter hour by omnibuses going into the city. And the finest part of the arrangement is this, that the members of this money aristocracy can take the shortest road through the middle of all the labouring districts to their places of business, without ever seeing that they are in the midst of the grimy misery that lurks to the right and to the left. For the thoroughfares leading from the Exchange (commercial district) in all directions out of the city are lined, on both sides, with an almost unbroken series of shops, and are so kept in the hands of the middle and lower bourgeoisie, which out of self-interest cares for the decent and cleanly external appearance ... [T]hey suffice to conceal from the eyes of the wealthy men and women of strong stomachs and weak nerves the misery and grime which form the complement of their wealth. (Engels and Kelley, 1892: Part 2, 79–80 and online)

Zieleniec observes that 'What Engels describes here is the structuring of space to reflect not only its role in particular functions ... but also an associated aestheticisation that encourages the socio-spatial divisions' (2007: 25). It is not just a matter of objects in space, but the city as a designed and divided space articulated by a diurnal rhythm of temporal divisions and routines.

A geographical sensitivity is found in Engels' writing and letters: 'The great geographical discoverers and the colonisation following upon them multiplied markets and quickened the transformation of handicraft into manufacture' notably in cities (Engels, 1970: Ch. 3 online). He attributes part of the expansion of scientific and technical knowledge to the expanded information on the natural world that was brought back from European voyages of discovery (Engels, 1974: online).

There is a risk that commentators' interest in a spatialised Marx imputes a modern geographical consciousness to his work. They discern spatialisation in these points, but his is fundamentally an agricultural and geological space of resources fixed in a location, and is concerned with crowded bodies engaged in tasks and tending factory machines. It is a functional not a qualitative field, where places take on an identity themselves that then influences economic processes.

Much of the geographical work of the late nineteenth century presents various forms of environmental determinism, where ecology, territory and climate determine social activities and then social action, in turn, altering the landscape. An early exemplar of this bioregionalism is the multi-volume work of Elisé Reclus (1830–1905), the French geographer who worked from exile in Switzerland due to his anarchist views and involvement in the Paris Commune. As early as 1868, Reclus advocated a united Europe against the imposed political divisions and structures of the nineteenth-century monarchies. His particular interest was in topography and the implications of mountains and rivers on human settlement. He saw in environmental determinism an alternative to centralised political administration across diverse topographies (Reclus, 1892).

Simmel: Spatial Projections of Social Forms

> Out of all the potentialities of life, space is generally the impartiality that has become visible; almost all other contents and forms of our environment, through their specific properties, somehow have other meanings and opportunities for one or the other person or party, and only space reveals itself to every existence without any prejudice. Often, the uninhabited terrain belonging to no one, which is simply, so to speak, pure space and nothing more, generally nourishes this neutrality of space for practical utilisations. (Simmel, 2009: 618–19)

Georg Simmel's (1858–1918) essays on 'The Sociology of Space' and 'On the Spatial Projections of Social Forms'[2] written in 1903, mark a key shift by integrating and extending understandings of the social shaping of environments, the drawing of boundaries, the designation of regions, and the casting of them as spaces for certain types of activity. As opposed to Engels' urban geography that focuses on the built form of the city as a type of infrastructure for capitalist production and social reproduction, Simmel considers space itself as a shared social construction:

> people cannot be near to or far from one another without space lending its form to it, any more than those processes that one attributes to time can occur outside of time. But the contents of these forms still take on the distinctive feature of their fates only through other *contents*; space remains always the form. ...

> In spite of these facts the emphasis on the spatial importance of things and processes is not unjustified. This is so because these often actually

take their course in such a way that the formal, positive or negative condition of the spatiality comes up especially *for consideration* and we possess the clearest documentation of real forces in it ... Social interaction among human beings is – apart from everything else it is – also experienced as a realisation of space. (Simmel, 2009: 543–5)

In theory, this research could include wolf packs, herds and animal territoriality. Forms of association are distinctively institutionalised depending on their spatial and temporal qualities. If Simmel's focus is on content – that is, human social interaction – space is a necessary material force in organising and permitting what interactions are possible, 'the course of which stands in relationship to its spatial form in principle no differently than a battle or a telephone conversation to that of theirs – thus doubtlessly these processes too can be realized then only under quite specific spatial conditions' (Simmel, 2009: 544). Space is 'form', that is, arrangements and relations to other arrangements. There is a double sense to the space between entities. In terms of relationship

[the] betweenness as a merely functional reciprocity, whose content continues in each of its personal bearers, is also actually realized here as a claim of the space existing between these two; it always takes place actually *between* both points of space ... Kant defines space simply as 'the possibility of being together' – this then is sociological; interaction makes the formerly empty and null into something *for us*; it fills it. (Simmel, 2009: 545)

One online summary of Simmel's chapter on space gives a good indication of its muted reception in the bounded rationality of twentieth-century social science,

[t]he chapter centers around spatial themes including (a) the socially relevant aspects of space, (b) the effect of spatial conditions upon social interaction, and (c) upon forms of social, physical, and psychological distance. As typical of his writing, however, Simmel did not present an organized theory of space. Rather, his interweaving of concepts, historically oriented examples and context, and occasional tangential discussions, provide heuristic tools for a sociological approach to space.

Simmel's approach to spatial analysis, especially in 'The Sociology of Space' was, in part, a continuation of his uncompleted [sic] project to express the preconditions of human sociation by formal categories of time, mass, and number, which he called 'social geometry.' What the philosopher Kant had approached in the abstract, Simmel would attempt to catalog as the spatial reality of social life ... (Fearon, 2001: online)

Simmel's thoughts on the relation of space to the social world did not, at first, leave a legacy. This was in part because he offered mainly a collection of ideas and insights, rather than a theory or method that others might adopt. Simmel, however, clearly showed his readers the relevance of space to sociological thinking and analysis, which has only recently been rediscovered (Fearon, 2001: online). Some mistakenly believe that Simmel argued that social interaction 'produces various spatial effects and forms' (Fearon, 2001: online), when, in fact, his seminal insight is that these forms are cultural categories that rebound to guide support or frustrate particular forms of interaction and association. 'It is rarely made clear how wondrously now the extensity of space accommodates the intensity of the sociological relationships, how the continuity of space, precisely because it contains subjectively no absolute boundary of any kind, simply allows then such a subjectivity to prevail' (Simmel, 2009: 549).

Simmel's method is to present illustrations as exemplars of social constants in order to show social forms *sub speciae aeternitatis*. He is primarily concerned with establishing principles not laws, a process which involves building theory based on empirical observation of necessity by looking for exceptions to the rules or everyday consistency in social interaction. He then describes and elevates these exceptions to the level of principle. An example would be his use of figures such as the Stranger to illustrate the often anomalous status of migrants who maintain (and cannot shake) their foreign-ness as newcomers, while developing an intimacy with local culture and communities. They introduce otherness into social settings that are often stereotyped as homogeneous. The exception to this case would be the manner in which contemporary societies integrate diversity by reducing their stress of particular markers of diversity, overlooking or rendering irrelevant distinctions between members that elsewhere may have an exaggerated importance as indicators of membership. Racism – based on skin colour, physiognomy and/or body type – is an example of how pernicious this can be. In *Gulliver's Travels*, for example, Jonathan Swift describes the sailor's encounter with the 'Lilliputians and Blefuscans' whose parodic obsession with the end on which boiled eggs were broken lampooned the xenophobias of British society.

Simmel also finds in shared places and areas (neighbourhoods and regions) an antidote to clan-based divisions that allows societies to grow beyond tribal organisation and to be rationalised around non-biological relationships that become progressively more abstract under political forms of representative democracy, monetary exchange relationships and citizenship in large states (Simmel, 2009: 563):

> space as a basis of organisation possesses that impartiality and regularity of behavior that makes it a correlate of governmental power ... The most important example is the reform under Kleisthenes; it succeeded

in breaking up the particularistic influence of the aristocratic families in that it divided the whole Attic nation into spatially demarcated *phylae* and *demes* as bases of self-administration. (Simmel, 2009: 606)

Castoriadis and historians, such as Lévêque and Vidal-Naquet, emphasise the importance of this spatial reorganisation, which marks a shift away from not only kinship but the calendar of rites at religious sites as the foundational time-space of Athenian democracy (Lévêque and Vidal-Naquet, 1996).

Although Simmel generates maxims, he is not aphoristic. It is incorrect to argue, as many late twentieth-century sociologists did, that his process of deriving principles from empirical necessity is atheoretical. A given institution or occupation is abstracted into a place on a continuum of organisational forms or of relations with a determining variable. In the case of space Simmel identifies the spatial properties of the forms of social interaction: *exclusivity, boundaries or subdivisions, localising interaction in place, proximity and mobility*, and *emptiness*. The argument that Simmel does not present a theory of space or of society is in part a result of piecemeal translations of the illustrative *excurses* of his work, which lack the theoretical skeleton. This is a damning reflection on the lack of depth and the unsystematic craft of subsequent social science.

1. The exclusivity of space is illustrated by the dependence of some institutions such as the territorial nation state on exclusive occupation of a territory, whereas others such as a community, labour organisation or the Catholic church can coexist with other churches in the same region. Simmel extracts the principle of exclusivity and the effect of variety:

Just as there is only one single universal space, of which all individual spaces are portions, so each portion of space has a kind of uniqueness for which there is hardly an analogy. To think of a specifically located portion of space in the plural is complete nonsense, and yet this makes it possible for a plurality of fully identical exemplars to be constituted simultaneously from *different* objects ... there is indeed *variety*, although their properties are absolutely indistinguishable. (Simmel, 2009: 545–6)

Thus – 'A baseball there, another baseball here', usually means that there are two identical but separate baseballs, a variety, each the same regulation ball but in their own locations. Although coded as geometrical, Simmel's point is topological. The basic features of three-dimensionality are constitutive of social interactions. If the state and churches are poles,

[t]o a certain extent the municipality has the same character: within the boundaries of a city there can be only that city, and if by chance a second nevertheless arises inside the same boundaries, there are not two cities on the same ground and soil but on two territories, formerly united but

now separate. However, this exclusivity is not as absolute [nor as clear] as that of the state. The significant and functional area of a city – inside a state – ends though not at its geographical boundary, but, more or less noticeably, it extends out ripple-like over the whole land with cultural, economic, political currents ... From this perspective the community loses its exclusive character and expands functionally over the whole state in such a way that this is the common sphere of influence for the, so to speak, ideal. (Simmel, 2009: 546)

Not only cities, but guilds and communities lie between these poles of spatial dependence:

there could exist side by side on the territory of a city any number of sociologically quite similarly produced guilds. Each was indeed the guild of the entire city; they did not divide the given expanse quantitatively, but functionally; they did not collide spatially because they were not, as sociological formations, spatial, even though determined *by locality*. (Simmel, 2009: 547)

To this, Simmel brilliantly adds another level of abstraction that is not noted by commentators and is almost unexplored in the century since: he compares and contrasts the structure of everyday spatiality with that of time, specifically the relative dependence on spatiality or temporality implied in our conceptions of social institutions, a move played out a second time later in the century by Castoriadis (1987). Whereas time may flow, have instants, be divided into past, present and future, or may be eternal or timeless (and therefore 'accessible and current' any time), space can be distinguished by its expanse, points, and regions. Some universal institutions have 'an equable relationship to all individual points ... as generically real and essential solidarity with the space. The purest type of the temporal example is religion, and of the spatial example, the state' (Simmel, 2009: 548).

2. *The boundary form*, in Simmel's view, is a frame that acts to define as well as function as an interface. While he insists that boundary lines are not natural occurrences, specifically 'sociological boundaries' are cases of mutual limitation. Spatial division, then, can be a form of reciprocity: 'one sets the boundary for the other, but the content of this influence is simply the qualification beyond this boundary, still *not* in general *meant to or able to affect the other*' (Simmel, 2009: 551). Codes differ between different zones and within boundaries themselves as interfaces.

The boundary is not a spatial fact with sociological effects, but a sociological reality that is formed spatially. The idealistic principle that space is our conception – more precisely, that it is realized through our synthesizing activity by which we shape sense material – is specified here in such a way that the spatial formation that we call a boundary is a sociological function. If indeed at first it had become a spatial-sensual formation that we write into nature independent of its sociological-practical sense, then it has strong repercussions for the consciousness of the relationship of parties. While this line marks only the differentiation of relationship between the elements of a sphere among one another and between them and the elements of another, it becomes then, nevertheless, a living energy that drives them towards one another and does not leave them out of its unity and moves, as a physical force that radiates repulsions from both perspectives, between both. (Simmel, 2009: 551)

Simmel repeats his point in terms of 'embodying', 'making concrete' or giving 'tangible form' to something intangible (*Verräumlichung*). Frisby and Featherstone translate this using the contemporary notion of 'spatialisation' (Shields, 1989), rather than 'realisation' (although elsewhere '*räumliche Verwirklichung*' has been translated as 'spatial realisation' (compare the original Simmel, 1908: 474 with Simmel, 2009: 560)). This shift in translation recodes the Simmel of 1903 in the language of eight decades later, making it hard to discern the origins of this discourse on space without reference to the original German. 'Spatialisation' has the effect of stressing the '*räumliche*' of Simmel's term with an eye to French and Italian (*spazializzazione*) terminology analysed earlier in this book.

I have here touched again on this matter, rather far from the issue of space, in order to clarify in it the incomparable solidity and lucidity that the processes of social boundary-making obtain through their *spatialisation* [*Verräumlichung*]. Every boundary is a mental, more exactly, a sociological occurrence; however, by its investment in a border in space the mutual relationship acquires, from its positive and negative sides, a clarity and security – indeed also often a rigidity – that tends to remain denied to it as long as the encountering and partitioning of powers and rights is not yet projected into a physical form, and thus always persists, so to speak, in the *status nascens* [sic]. (Simmel, 2009: 552, emphasis added)

This notion is found in later urban planning literature as perceived and symbolic 'edges' that are the zones of transition between different neighbourhoods and functional zones (Lynch, 1956).

3. Fixed Points or Pivots localise social activities, stabilising and helping to reproduce them by concretising specific modes of interaction. From medieval times in Europe, a customs house embodied authority and symbolises a border and may facilitate commercial interaction and trade in a hall built for this purpose. A stadium establishes clear divisions between the stands and the pitch that spectators are expected to respect, while the facility may anchor a home team to a community. Simmel's greater point is that presence and proximity are often powerfully localised in specific gathering places, including cities such as Jerusalem and Rome (Simmel, 2009: 560, 564–5, anticipates Serres, 1991). Latour gives the example of North European outdoor meeting places – *Ding* – as the geographical root of the notion of specificity and particularity of any object or thing. The early etymology of 'thing' derives from 'place' and specifically a 'gathering place' for judicial and political decisions in rural communities such as Iceland's '*Thingveillir*' where the Althingi, the oldest continuous parliament, first met in 930 CE.

> The importance of a sociological relationship as pivot attaches to the fixed locality especially where the contact or assembly can occur only at a particular place for elements otherwise independent of one another ... For churches in a situation of diaspora it is an extremely wise policy, especially where only the smallest number of adherents lives in a district, to immediately erect a chapel... a pivotal point for the relationships and the solidarity of the faithful. (Simmel, 2009: 559)

Pivots are reference points that social interaction may be structured in relation to places set apart for certain activities; they are sites visited on a seasonal basis for specific activities (vacations, hunting, seasonal pastures), or *axis mundi* that are cultural or sacred global reference points for entire societies. This contrasts with the linear organisation of activities in time via historicising and biographical narratives. For example, using a grid of coordinates or numbered addresses, location may be individualised as named places. The power of place is that it can be associated with events and interactions, and 'thereafter remains the pivot around which memory then spins the individuals into an increasingly idealized correlation' (Simmel, 2009: 551). The spatial concentration or dispersion of key centres of authority are corollaries of relations of governance, congealing sociological forms into clear formations (Simmel, 2009: 611). The critical question is whether or not all the qualitative memories remain understood as parts of a single spatialisation or whether they are seen to spring into their unique dimensions that could vary between groups. Space could be understood either according to the flat planes of Euclid's geometry and Descartes' grid, or 'topologically' to have variable, affective, cultural dimensions. But we are getting ahead of ourselves.

4. *Proximity* and direct, embodied contact is a characteristic of some social interactions, but even intimacy can be felt in an epistolary relationship, despite infrequent visits. If associations can be abstracted, tensions can be managed. Many different interactions can be conducted at a distance, including 'economic or scientific transactions because their contents are expressible in logical forms ... [or] religious and some unions of the heart,

because the force of imagination and the submission of feeling often enough overcome the conditions of time and space' (Simmel, 2009: 566). By contrast, nearness implies affect of one kind or another for Simmel. Hostile or friendly, 'mutual indifference tends to be excluded to the extent of spatial closeness' (Simmel, 2009: 568). Unnecessary nearness can generate extraneous conflicts that undermine the relationship; these have to be managed through reserve, a specific skill for navigating the density of urban social life: 'It belongs to the finest social task of the art of life to preserve in a close relationship the values and sensitivities that develop between persons in a certain distance relative to the rarity of togetherness (Simmel, 2009: 583).

5. *Mobility* is illustrated by nomads and migrants, Simmel's notably famous Excursis 'The Stranger' (2009) presents cases of mobile labourers and craftspeople, where often mobility is in relation to a specific centre or home pivot. He explores the questions, 'Which forms of social interaction are established in a wandering group [nomads, travel acquaintances], as opposed to a spatially fixed one? And: 'Which forms emerge for the group itself and for wandering persons if in fact no one group wanders as a whole but certain members of it do' – that is, immigrants (Simmel, 2009: 587)? What are the implications of mobile populations for sedentary, territorial authority and city life? Mobility raises the question of sovereignty.

6. '*Empty space* gains a significance as something more empty, in which particular sociological relationships of a negative as well as positive kind are expressed' (Simmel, 2009: 615, emphasis added). The maintenance of neutral zones, empty 'marchlands' and deserted territory can be not only the result of natural conditions but a political effort to manage conflict or avoid interaction while preparing for any eventuality. This section of Simmel's text is often neglected by commentators, but demonstrates how even empty space is a vehicle and expression of a type of interaction (Simmel, 2009: 620). Simmel presents the European colonial expectation that any empty space is common, but is also at risk of being seized (Simmel, 2009: 617).

   In short, Simmel provides a first social geometry, postulating the importance of a common territory; the social quality of boundaries that create insiders and outsiders and thus membership; the power of social landmarks or pivots; the significance of distance but also the socially constructed quality of nearness, the contrast that mobile nomadism has with sedentary society; and finally, the deliberate construction of empty zones to separate groups.

Cultural Understandings of Space: Emile Durkheim

Both Simmel and Durkheim (1858–1917) were negatively affected by the First World War, which disrupted personal lives and devastated their students. Emile Durkheim is often overlooked, but is one of the first to argue that spatiality varies between cultures. He proposed a correspondence between social structure and a society's notion of space, thereby laying the groundwork for structural anthropological studies. Strongly influenced by Mauss' symbolic anthropology, Durkheim draws on the example of the Zuñi Indians, concluding that their space was nothing else than, 'the site of the tribe, only indefinitely extended beyond its real limits' (Durkheim and Mauss, 1963: 12).

> There are societies in Australia and North America where space is conceived in the form of an immense circle, because the camp has a circular form; and this spatial circle is divided up exactly like the tribal circle, and is in its image. There are as many regions distinguished as there are clans in the tribe, and it is the place occupied by the clans inside the encampment which has determined the orientation of these regions. (Durkheim, 1976: 11–12)

One could venture from such Aboriginal conceptions of space (and time) as the 'Dreamtime' that landscape is not merely sedimented traces but a historiography, read through embodied presence, peregrination and pilgrimage. This view of social space is topological in that it emphasises its qualitative heterogeneity, varying not only from place to place, region to region (some being perhaps sacred, others profane). It is not locked within one spatialisation, however, as space – since the mid-1950s – is argued to be contested within and between societies. If there is an overarching, 'collective sense of these unique 'spaces', shared by all members of a society', then this heterogenous space made up of multiple 'spaces' must be produced incrementally as a cultural artefact, while action takes place in this same historical space. The production of social space, spatialisation is intrinsically wedded to the performative quality of community, culture and national identity. There is no reason why this cannot be extended to a global scale with a transnational social space of cosmopolitan institutions and cultures, which could co-exist alongside of intensely local or intimately clannish regional social spaces (cf. Urry, 2000).

Although Durkheim affirms that something must objectively exist, broadly corresponding to perceptions that were widely held across societies, his proposal has been roundly critiqued from a neo-Kantian perspective. Space, it was argued, must 'exist before social groups can be perceived to exhibit in their disposition any spatial relations which may then be applied to the universe; the categories of quantity have to exist in order that an individual mind shall ever recognize one, the many, and the totality of the division of his society' (R. Needham, 'Preface', in Durkheim and Mauss, 1963: xxvii). Such opinions arose from attempts to perfectly align social science with the natural sciences (to re-achieve the lost Kantian orthodoxy of one Euclidean or Cartesian space: an alignment such that 'social space' can be derived from or read from one single 'physical space'), and dominated the subsequent sociological literature in English. Whether Functionalist or Marxist, mid-twentieth-century schools of sociology, in particular, confused quality and quantity. The irony is that this deprives social science of an important area of research. Durkheim's argument ultimately draws on Poincaré and topology:

> [S]pace is not the vague and indeterminate medium that Kant imagined; if purely and absolutely homogeneous, it would be of no use, and could not be grasped by the mind. Spatial representation consists essentially in a primary co-ordination of the data of sensuous experience. But this co-ordination would be impossible if the parts of space were qualitatively equivalent and if they were really interchangeable. To dispose things spatially there must be a possibility of placing them differently, of putting some at the right, others at the left, these above, those below, at the north of or at the south of, east or west of, etc., etc., just as to dispose states of consciousness temporally there must be a possibility of localizing them at determined dates. That is to say that space could not be what it is if it were not, like time, divided and differentiated. But whence come these divisions which are so essential? By themselves, they are neither right nor left, up nor down, north nor south, etc. All these distinctions evidently come from the fact that different affective values have been attributed to regions. As all the men of a single civilisation represent space in the same way, it is clearly necessary that these affective values and the distinctions which depend upon them would be equally shared, and that almost necessarily implies that they are of a social origin. (Emile Durkheim, 1912: 19, author's translation, cf. Durkheim, 1976: 11)

Kern, reading Durkheim, says 'logical categories derive from social categories, space being one of them' (Kern, 1983: 138). Returning to the example of the Zuñi Indians:

> [T]he pueblo contains seven quarters; each of these is a group of clans which has a unity ... their space also contains seven quarters, and each of these seven quarters of the world is in intimate connection with a quarter of the pueblo, that is to say with a group of clans ... each quarter of the pueblo has its characteristic colour, which symbolizes it; each region has its colour which is exactly the same as that of the corresponding quarter. (Cushing, 1896: 367ff., cited in Durkheim, 1976: 12)

The heterogeneity of social space – the manner in which it becomes multiple, subsidiary social spaces – is in turn used to coordinate sense data into basic categories. In every society, there is a collective sense of these cultural sub-spaces, places where spatial norms shift, are inverted or are lifted. This is shared across members of a society (Kern, 1983: 138), despite variations in felicity and familiarity with them. A heterogenous space made up of multiple 'spaces' must have a social origin. In a footnote, Durkheim adds that, if this were not so,

> it would be necessary to admit that all individuals, in virtue of their organo-physical constitution, are spontaneously affected in the same manner by the different parts of space: which is more improbable, especially as in themselves, the different regions are sympathetically indifferent. Also, the divisions of space vary with different societies, which is a proof that they are not founded exclusively upon the congenital nature of man. (Durkheim, 1976: 11, n. 3)

Further, Durkheim suggests that the classification of space into 'spaces' – the spatialisation of the world as more than just terrain but also landscape with all of its cultural nuance and value-laden qualities – is structurally similar to the social form of the society:

> In the course of history the number of the fundamental regions of space has varied with them. Thus the social organisation has been the model for the spatial organisation and a reproduction of it. It is thus even up to the distinction between right and left which, far from being inherent in the nature of man in general, is very probably the product of representations which are religious and therefore collective. (Durkheim, 1976: 12)

Against *a priori* space, Durkheim's understanding of these representations of space and their relation to the form of the group, derive from Ratzel's (1844–1904) *Political Geography*, in opposition to Simmel's emphasis on the shared commonality of social space which Durkheim explicitly critiqued on this point (Ratzel, 1903). Similarly, Spengler suggests that different cultures have a unique sense of space manifested in symbolic systems. Space is the 'prime symbol' of a culture, never conceptualised directly, but inherent in political institutions, religious myths, and interpreted and expressed through ethical ideals, science, and art forms (Spengler, 1926–28).

Positivist objections do not affect the integrity of Durkheim's suggestion. They merely assert the need to provide room for the 'pre-cultural' experience of space as in the conception of 'up' and 'down' which, in the sense that 'up' and 'down' are the human experience of gravitational forces, transcend the more specifically cultural definitions of space, such as 'right' and 'left'. Durkheim could easily have admitted a pure and homogeneous 'physical space' (what I have called 'pure space', above) while preserving a 'social space' (social spatialisation). Durkheim, I believe, intended to acknowledge this difference between the brute perception of space and its cognition as a concept and representation as 'space'. In his Conclusion, he comments: 'the space which I know by my senses, of which I am the centre and where everything is disposed in relation to me, could not be space in general, which contains all extensions and where these are co-ordinated ... ' (Durkheim, 1976: 441).

A number of sociological treatments of space as a symbolic classification or as representation, rather than behaviour or territoriality, were produced in the mid-twentieth century. One year after Needham's prefatory mid-60s critique of Durkheim, Piaget's (Piaget et al., 1964) developmental psychology, challenging the Kantian assertion that space and time are *a priori* modes of conception, was translated into English. After the Second World War, Maurice Halbwachs extended Durkheim's work as a theory of different social spaces that coordinated their members' perceptions and actions (Halbwachs and Coser, 1992; see also Kolaja, 1969) much like Simmel's 'pivots'. Sorokin differentiated 'sociocultural space' from actual space-time on epistemological grounds. Social space involves the symbolic, media (such as sound or light) and agents who produce and receive meaning which is not located in physical space but in a discursive universe defined epistemologically and by social categories and status (Sorokin, 1943). The relativism in the way a social time-space relates to the materiality of the physical world led to accusations of idealism because social position could well determine an inaccurate outlook on the natural world, according to Sorokin's theory. While the anthropological evidence supported this, commentators such as Kolaja illustrate how little room there was in twentieth-century positivistic social science for discussions of anomalies and variation between social perceptions and natural phenomena (Kolaja, 1969: 24–7). Social construction theories from the late 1960s through to the end of the twentieth century gained in credibility but continued to face the accusation of Platonic idealism because of the lack of a sophisticated ontology that would admit real but intangible objects and instead embraced only ideas or material objects. This led to the marginalisation of theories such as Kurt Lesin's: his approach to topological or phase space mapped natural phenomena onto a simultaneous sociocultural plane or field. In his *Field Theory*, this is as real as actual space but clearly also virtual, rather than simply ideational (Lewin, 1964: 151). The field is the totality of everything affecting behaviour at a given time to assess our psychological sense of social proximity or alienation (Lewin, 1964: 241).

The overarching problem for English-language scholars is the reception of these key works in the form of critiques rather than translations of the original texts. Introductions consistently framed approaches to social space as inadequate or non-scientific without offering strong theories of social space, but rather repetitive assertions of Cartesian conceptions of space as an objective void in which physical objects stand and can be unproblematically detected and analysed. This is also part of a geography of the hostile reception and translation of European social science in North America in the post-Second World War era, which was broken with a veritable paradigm shift to Marxist theory mediated first through British scholarship in the late 1960s and early 1970s, and then through the American university Left in the 1970s and 1980s.

We may also note that Merleau-Ponty produced a strong argument against any sort of *a priori* space. In his *Phenomenology of Perception* (Merleau-Ponty, 1962), he asserts that space is created by the pre-reflective activity of the subject. In visual terms, prior to having a spatial field, one has access to a 'pre-spatial field' of colour and lighting, which is then structured into a lived spatial field by the interaction of the body with objects and the interrelation of things. Before the first perception of space, one is 'already at work in a world' and spatiality is 'already required' (Merleau-Ponty, 1962: 293). In a similar manner, social space is permeated by otherness and requires the mediation of the body in order to be constituted as a spatial field which unites the body and the world of objects (cf. 'I am now identical with my presence in the world' (Merleau-Ponty, 1962: 340).

In 'Origins of Geometry', Husserl argues that conceptions of space are founded in human corporeality (Husserl, 1962; see Derrida, 1975). *Dasein* ('Being-ness') has the property of 'Being-in Space' on the basis of its 'Being-in-the-World' (Heidegger, 1962: 82). Our own personal experience of orienting ourselves against gravity and relative to static and dynamic objects and beings in space grounds the philosophical postulation of the character of space. Heidegger comments that 'spaces receive their being from locations and not from "space"' (Heidegger, 1971: 155). Here, a multitudinous diversity of spaces replaces the more cerebral notion of 'pure space'. In fact, this is so much so, that these spaces become simply 'places' in some texts. Norberg-Schultz breaks up territories the size of nations into 'places', each with a particular spirit or *genus loci* (Norberg-Schulz, 1980: 10). This, however, would be somewhat counterintuitive for a Canadian who would be perhaps more sympathetic with Lefebvre's opposite quirk of collapsing specific 'places' into the general characteristics of regional 'spaces'.

The linking of the definition of 'space' to corporeal practice (*hexis*) may also be found in Marx who links time to space and space to agricultural labour in his footnote on 'the temporal concept of *Tagwerk* (*tagwanne*, from *terra jurnalis, jurnale*) – "the measure of land which could be tilled in a day"' (Marx, 1976: 55). The point is not to decide on the temporal or logical priority of society or space, but to examine the dialectical process of producing social definitions of space and the spatialisation of social action (including the reservation of spaces for specific social functions and rituals). Soja, and Lefebvre before him, argued this was crucial to the achievement of an appropriate (homogenous) spatialisation allowing and legitimating the power practices of an expansive global capitalism (Lefebvre, 1974; see also how this is taken up in translation in Soja, 1980: 204ff.).

Land Use Planning, Spatialisation and Spatial Semantics

According to Hillier and Hanson (1984) social science research on space in the last half of the twentieth century could be characterised as falling under a number of generic headings. Anthropological studies, such as those of Durkheim and Mauss (cf. Levi-Strauss, 1966); 'territoriality' (cf. Hall, 1966); cognitive mapping (Downs and Shea, 1977; Lynch, 1956); descriptive and empirical environmental discourses (cf. Jackson and Zube, 1984); and semiotics (cf. Preziosi, 1979) are all approaches that planners and geographers criticise for de-emphasising or reducing the space of the built environment to other social, biological or environmental factors (Hillier and Hanson, 1984: 4). For example, semiotics produces a 'systematics of appearances', or a 'semantics' (Hillier and Hanson, 1984: 8), when what is required is a demonstration of how spatial configurations of architecture, or the 'syntax' of the urban fabric, helps constitute a society through the way in which their configurations organise and present space.

Hillier and Hanson embark on a search for a 'theory of space'. Unfortunately, their point of analysis – the built environment – does not allow them to produce a theory of space either. Seeking independence from psychological and spatial determinants, they are limited to the physical-morphological space of settlements. This is only a small segment at one scale of the spectrum of the spatialisation, which I have discussed in this and previous chapters. The analysis degenerates into a mathematical model of a theory of urban clustering and the geometric rules of aggregation of close-packed cell structures – spatial syntax in which 'spatial structure [is] reduced to a graph'. That is, social communities are reduced to 'house cells and continuous [external] spaces' separated by boundaries of varying 'permeability'. 'Social meaning is ... expressed in terms of relations of physical configuration' (Hillier and Hanson, 1984: 15–16). Even in its own mathematical terms, such a system is unable to account for the ordering of the general landscape which extends beyond the settlement – as most scholarship would insist is essential (compare another late twentieth-century account by Jackson and Zube, 1984). 'Space' is, in effect, purely physical in Hillier and Hanson's computer models; it must be separated or articulated by physical barriers (walls, buildings).

Semantic approaches analyse the potential circulation patterns within the spatial morphology of urban streets and properties, as well as the interior arrangement of rooms in a building. They fit well within expansionary development cycles, where builders and entrepreneurs want to maximise the exposure of their business and expand the rentable frontage of new developments. By way of mapping plans or street grids as mazes or networks, this analysis yields more or less accessible points, and more or less frequented routes. It is possible to include one-way streets as limits within these routes or prohibited areas. But this functional approach assumes the homogeneity of urban and architectural space: there are no qualitative differences between south and north exposure, and inhabitants are assumed to only travel the most direct routes all the time. However, inhabitants, of course, do not always walk on the sunny side of the street in winter, or the shady side in tropical cities. These assumptions are also coded into way-finding devices such as GPS navigation systems. People are assumed to not be tempted to detour in urban dérives, nor to get lost by taking a wrong turn. As Hillier and Hanson's critique of conceptual mapping makes clear, people's preferences are excluded from analysis. This approach attempts to find the most efficient routes and reads 'privacy' from the lowest ease of access. It universalises these median routes, often enforcing them through the imposition of regulations and physical barriers, or reinforcing them by locating services only along these selected routes or at the intersections of what are predicted to be the highest traffic routes. It responds poorly to social and historical change and tends to justify investments regardless of cultural attitudes or any factors that are not easily located on plans and maps.

Zoning and physical planning approaches follow from these assumptions, and naturally privilege physical interventions because social space is collapsed into physical space. Borders quickly become walls because only physical barriers are taken into consideration despite the variety of flows, tangible and intangible. Within cities and broader regional landscapes, Perrin suggests that zoning which proceeds in this manner is a mechanism by which social reality is defined and negotiated on an ongoing basis (the possible uses of various classes of objectified 'space' are established). Newcomers with alternate ideas are held off through exclusionary tactics which homogenise the use of land over broad areas (Perrin, 1977). For example, it becomes difficult to discern why groups struggle over the meaning of space and how this might factor in debates over procession routes, merely describing the directions routes take.

This approach to physical space is reinforced in a complex mesh of bureaucratic zoning restrictions and plans, which have as their object the stabilisation of the set of possible 'land uses' for a given 'piece' of property (lot). The North American imposition of zoning in the early decades of this century turned the uncertain and fluctuating nature of real estate investment into a conservative and predictably increasing investment by making the physical-spatial ordering highly predictable and subject to social control at the local level. The extension of commodification to space marked a great victory for the consolidation of capitalism. Zoning was an attempt to replace the unpredictable and expensive process of nuisance litigation:

> Subjection of a tradition to modification in the interests of making real estate a commodity, such is apparent throughout the movement for zoning ... Sentiment has been taken from the notion of individual

property rights and added to a new definition of the rights of the community. The dealers in the commodity affected have played the part of heralds ... The trader is he who would make all values economic ... he is a revolutionary in relation to his own commodity ... (Hughes, 1928: 340–2)

To what extent do the rules of this economic model condition the abstract concept of space adopted? How could power relations expressed in the 'right' of control over territory be assessed? The production of space as homogeneous and continuous as opposed to stratified and heterogeneous is masked. This is not to mention the issue that space is often conceptually divided: being 'from the North' in England has clear social meanings for any person who has lived in Britain. What is the relationship between the perceived qualitative aspects of space – of a particular place – and the manner in which it is incorporated into a built environment to serve a particular social function (cf. Norberg-Schulz, 1980)?

In Lefebvre's analysis the power practices (i.e. of the planners) and the ideologies of capitalism are all to be seen as part of a global strategy (rather than a system) which aims to appropriate the function of the urban while destroying its form. Such a strategy can be detected in its various aims and features: segregation; systematicity (of control); integration, even participation, as a way of securing the consent of its subjects. A 'spectral analysis' of the urban needs to recover the vision of some ideal and new, original, urban life implicit in the degraded urban life of today, but nowhere empirically visible. Only this vision would allow the development of a counter-strategy to that of capital.

> The urban is a highly complex field of tensions, a *virtuality*, a possible-impossible that attracts the accomplished, an ever-renewed and always demanding presence-absence. Blindness consists in the fact that we cannot see the shape of the urban, the vectors and tensions inherent in this field, its logic and dialectic movement, its immanent demands. We see only things, operations, objects ... With respect to the urban, there is a twofold blindness, whose emptiness and virtuality are masked by plenitude. The fact that this plenitude is called urbanism only serves to more cruelly illuminate the blind. Moreover, this plenitude borrows the objects and products, the industrial operations and technologies of the previous epoch of industrialisation. The urban is veiled; it flees thought, which blinds itself and becomes fixated only on a clarity that is in retreat from the actual. (Lefebvre, 2003: 40–1, emphasis added)

Urban planning presents one of the great realms of the generalised discourse on space, closely linked to that of architecture. Lefebvre argued that the present-day myopia towards social spatialisations as a topic for investigation and a medium of action and social reform stems partly from the 'scientism' of urban planning practice (Lefebvre, 1976). In urban and land use planning – the profession which, since the Second World War, sought to unify the various discourses on 'space' and the 'environment' into a single professional domain – discussion centred around the issue of 'patterns' of use in space (Lefebvre, 1974: 30) until the 1970s. In their zeal to secure for their profession the positivist legitimation of a science, urban planners argued that urban planning was a methodologically and epistemologically mature discipline, along the same lines as such established disciplines as economics. It was hoped that this would render the urban planning process wholly objective and apolitical. In planning, the crucial body of professional knowledge comprises a 'science of space'. This science could be practised at the micro scale (housing) and the macro scale (community planning). This rarely questioned attitude was based on the implicit assumption that,

> urban space ... appeared as a given ... and it was primarily discussed in connection with high-level [non-spatial] decision-making and only secondarily with social needs which were considered to be localized ... planned space was objective and 'pure'; it was a scientific object and hence had a neutral character. Space in this sense passes as being innocent or, in other words, apolitical. (Lefebvre, 1976: 30)

However, while it might be possible to argue that epistemologically sound methods and techniques exist for the manipulation of such a pure and Abstract Space, no guarantee exists that the inhabitants of the planned spaces – of the modern spatialisation – will be able to live without having to adversely modify their lifestyles. Indeed, it is this human, ontological dimension which renders the epistemology of geometry inappropriate to planning, where space cannot be said to be a neutral 'void' but must be treated as a produced, planned spatialisation. The necessity to take into account human and social needs and 'wants' (from personal whims to the generalised desire of the ideologies and discourses of cultural progress) involves prioritising and adjudicating between values, between needs, and between desires. Planning-as-science is far from being value-neutral. Professional planners have never been able to escape the fact that their practice is political in that it involves the insertion of society into the 'planned spatialisation' of modernism and, the maintenance of this state, within contemporary political and economic conditions.

Another Marxist philosopher of Lefebvre's generation, Carlos Castoriadis, emphasises the separation of space from time or temporalisation: first to create Euclid's geometric space and ultimately to found what Lefebvre calls modernity's 'Abstract Space' of rational calculation. 'Space is the possibility of the difference of the same from the same, without which there is nothing at all' (Castoriadis, 1987: 194). Modern capitalist logic requires that

> [t]o think, we must be able to grasp the same as different and vice versa ... This is the possibility that 'pure' space provides, the possibility for the 'same' point to be different if it is placed *somewhere else*; and in this sense, reflexively, space exists prior to the figure as its *a priori* condition. There is nothing like this in the case of time ... An 'empty' space is a logical and physical *problem*; an 'empty' time is an absurdity – or else, it is simply a certain name given ... to a spatial dimension ... (Castoriadis, 1987: 193)

This is a stark challenge to the broadly accepted position that accords critical privilege to temporalisation. Identity is understood as a form of the instant, the *punctum*, as a singularity that negates undifferentiated space with the temporal point. Generally this point is treated as a founding, singular presence in contrast to the void nothingness of space. But '"Pure" space is the possibility of difference insofar as it is the condition of the repetition of the same as different, that is to say, as *iteration* – atemporal repetition, in the *forever*, *aei*, of spatiality or of coexistence, or of composition ... As such, it is ... presupposed by logic and mathematics' (Castoriadis, 1987: 194). He also argues that 'It serves no purpose to criticize the "spatialisation" of time ... once being has been thought of as determinacy, it has also, necessarily been thought of as atemporality' (Castoriadis, 1987: 192). That is, not as a singularity such as an instant of time but as a (spatial) entity that can enter into relations. Castoriadis' emphasis is instead on the importance of space as the possibility of two identities being with each other and establishing difference on the basis of comparison and contrast (Castoriadis, 1987: 189).[3]

> Plato posits a *chora*, a 'space', as separable-inseparable from what unfolds 'there'. This *chora*, itself an *eidos* [entity], being always, incorruptible, other than the genesis it 'receives' is referred by Plato here only to sensible becoming, to actual genesis ... ' ... what is neither in heaven nor in earth has no existence.' ... Being an *eidos* necessarily implies being 'with', 'before ... ', 'opposed to ... ' some other *eidos*; and the *topos*, the place, whether it be ... 'ideal' is being-in-a-relation-to ... being *syn-*: 'space' and 'place', the *chora* and the *topos*, these are the *co-* in the order of coexistences ... Can there be intelligibility except in and through the order of coexistence? A 'space', a 'dimensionality' is necessary if the *eide* are to be able to be together, at once, *ama* – and they have to be able to exist in this way for they cannot exist without one another. ... The *topos* is necessarily implied as soon as there is more than One – regardless of the nature, substance or consistence ... The *topos* or *chora* is the first possibility of the Plural (... thought of the One must exclude the *topos*: Parmenides) ... since it founds the final co-belonging of all that is different ... to differ (*dia-perho*) is to *displace*, to *trans-port*; to differ is still to relate to ..., to-be-place, to-be-posited or to-be-taken ... *together*, hence in the unity of a spacing of a gap. (Plato, 1925: 52 b cited in Castoriadis, 1987: 190–1)

Spatial Struggles

The approaches that privilege physical space tend to derive social space entirely from forms of social solidarity, disregarding dissent where multiple understandings of a space or architectural form are in conflict. This can lead to rendering the social epiphenomenal or discarding space as an inconsequential void. These reductions eliminate the possibility of understanding the production of 'counter-spaces' of resistance and refusal to acquiesce to the dominant spatial order and codes of societies. Confining the notion of 'conceptual mapping' to the physical landscape of geography ignores the intuitive evidence that conceptual maps are more than maps of the physical world. They are also surely matrixes which function as 'mappings' of the social cosmos (Dreyfus and Rabinow, 1982: 45); people are located not only 'in space' but 'in society'. Knowledges of 'space' are part of social and cultural processes; that is, they are part and parcel of social spatialisation. This spells the demise of the Cartesian man-environment separation such that a subject's 'location' and 'spacing' with respect to a broader ordering of space or 'spatialisation' forms an integral part of their perception, character and possibilities of action.

1. *Conceptual Mapping:* Hillier and Hanson's arguments illustrate the contrast that planning and architectural disciplines' approach to physical space presents. They argue that theories of conceptual mapping do not constitute true 'theories of space' because the order they seek to explicate is mental. The spatial system of the built environment and historical landscapes in which people live is taken as a given and its reproduction is not questioned. To these approaches, the Social Ecology theories of the Chicago School must be added, which also suffer from a lack of examination of the term 'social space'. In ecological approaches, which commonly utilize a biological analogy to assess the relationships between spatial areas, space is implicitly considered under the banner of 'area'. Rather than probe the meaning of 'space', however, spatial distinctions are used to 'explain' social differences (with the result of the accusation of espousing an 'ecological fallacy'; see Jackson and Smith, 1984).

From the late 1950s to the 1960s, ecological approaches or interdisciplinary social science approaches in planning and urban geography began to unify around particular problems of scales of phenomena. At the urban scale, Kevin Lynch's work on conceptual mapping laid the basis for work on the cognitive images people have of their environment by which they orient themselves to their surrounding 'environment' of objects, landmarks and edges in the landscape. These cognitions are inaccurate and incomplete because they are based on selective discriminations of the 'world', 'space', or 'environment in which people find themselves. Again, however, the Cartesian *res extensa* dominates, with a focus placed on objects and faulty mental cognition rather than space by these geographers and planners. Difference and struggles over the meaning of, and proper relationships between, objects, places or zones is pathologized in favour of an imposed, dominant mapping.

2. *Zoning and division of space:* Once social space is recognised as differentiated and heterogeneous, we must recognise that there is a politics of space. The meaning of social space itself could be an object of struggle along with the ordering within space. The function of spatial metaphors to obfuscate real conditions is a central issue for cultural production, ideology and the politics of representation.

As a spatial practice, the private property of the individuated lot serves to ensure the commodification of space. Further, the individual citizen – either bourgeois or proletarian – is made a player in the bourgeois game of accumulation-in-space and the consumption of space. If not landowners, all are potential landowners. As a doctrine and a 'representation of space', it allows the grounding of a whole rational, bureaucratic system of spatial definitions: look, you can see it right in your own home! Legal doctrine is mapped onto space and social codes of propriety are prescribed through zoning laws.

The notion of private property, expressed in the real estate lot, demonstrates the movement from the use value of land to the exchange value of property (Lefebvre, 1981b: 114ff; 1991a; Harvey, 1982). At the conceptual-symbolic level, private property in space, as the 'lot', not only grounds the whole realm of 'private property' in real articles, but also draws individuals into the property structure of capital (every person has at least some capital, a vested interest). This, in turn, induces the homogenisation of space for exchange, where consumption acts as a discourse of space. Every homeowner's plot is a 'space of representation' – to use Lefebvre's terminology – which condenses the essence of 'property', or of a spatialisation, whereby 'space' is abstract, homogenous, and can be broken up into parcels that are exchangeable. All of the contradictions of an Abstract Spatialisation can be found in the exemplar of private property which furnishes a paradigmatic summation. The inducement of lack, in terms of quantity and quality of space, is explicitly incorporated into the operation and rhetoric of private home/lot sales: quality is made a rarity for which economic compensation is demanded. This later manifests itself in the 'consumption' of Leisure Space as a compensatory mechanism.

The mythology of the 'lot' as being the true representation of the spatialisation to its owner aptly demonstrates the schism between the global and the local. The lived reality is radically separated from the contradictory flows of the global spatialisation. In forming the 'space of representation', the private lot becomes a paradigm for all relations in space. A key issue that this book cannot fully address is the legal and legislative production of spatialisation by the State in the form of a zoned and regulated territory.

Blomley argues that property involves boundary-work via physical and legal procedures, dividing and relating objects, subjects and areas:

> Our conceptions are premised on the drawing of bright lines, marking off one individual interest or estate from another. At work here is a particularly sharp logic of Euclidean spatialisation, in which categories are detached, bounded and contained, and imagined as individuated spaces. The production of property thus requires categorical cuts, in which "belonging is... given a boundary." (Strathern, 1996: 525 cited in Blomley, 2010: 205)

Property requires that subject and object are separated and individuated by physical and symbolic divisions in an 'ethic of inter-subjective separability' (Blomley, 2010: 216); that territories are divided rather than being understood as connected, despite the constant boundary-crossing that everyday life entails. Legal discourses of property rights are part and parcel of a specific form of Abstract Space, a spatialisation that parses space into territorial units thereby regulating social relations and promoting the autonomy of the individual.

3. Territoriality originates in psychological studies: a culturally-modified sense of spatiality and territory is accounted for by biological impulses. A territorial principle may be extended from the level of the individual outward from the body through a zone of personal space and further to inter-personal interaction at specific distances ('proxemics') to provide an argument for the biological necessity of 'social territory'. However, the correspondences between social groups and distinct spatial domains become more and more vague the higher one goes in this progression of scale. However, as Simmel demonstrates, there is a variety of cases: the supposed law of spatial integration of groups with a specific territory is not univocal; the social identity of migrants, diasporic communities or nomads may not be directly linked to a territory. Finally, territoriality also obscures the reproduction and change of specific spatial behaviours and of the production of social communities with specific spatial forms (i.e. urban morphology, function) behind a mask of functional necessity.

Social Space has been only implicit in most social science research. Sociologists influenced by Anthony Giddens' work developed Marx's notion of the annihilation of space by time as the 'space-time structuration' of society, which was similar to but without the benefit of Simmel's earlier sociology of space or Lefebvre's critical approach to social spatialisation. The projects of Lefebvre and Giddens differ significantly, despite the many parallels, especially at the superficial level of issuing the rallying cry of 'Space!' in the social sciences. Giddens concentrates on the spatial variables of distance and division of territory into symbolically coded regions or places. Both of these variables are subsumed under 'space'. This is reminiscent of the positivist model-building projects of territoriality and even space syntax.

Giddens comments that the development of an increasing reliance on non-'face-to-face' interactions poses problems for social integration. But such observations are of only superficial use; Simmel in 1903 notes that social integration can be accomplished *technically* using media that have the effect of negating distance, separation, and the isolation of individuals. The community festivals pictured in Breugel's seventeenth-century artworks are simply not the norm, nor could they be, given the predominantly non-contiguous communities (characterised by temporal and spatial absences as Giddens would say) (Giddens, 1979: 203), which exist, like Russian matryoshka dolls, as societies within societies. Resorting to a communication model, Giddens points out that these absences are ones of 'distanciation', and are greatly extended by writing and other communications technologies (radio, TV, etc.). Writing before the advent of social media, such as Twitter – which blur one-to-one messaging with one-to-many broadcasting of short comments – Giddens argues that micro-sociological interactions are 'face-to-face' as opposed to macro-sociological interaction. While differentiating between face-to-face and relations 'at a distance', the continuities in the characteristics of long-distance telephone calls and face-to-face conversation are surely not to be overlooked. Nor can these properly inter-personal but technology-assisted communications be removed from their essential character as *micro-social* interactions. Nonetheless, Giddens' point that these new forms of interaction overcome 'distanciation' suggests changes at the level of macrosociological interaction. In such a spatialisation of the environment and world, alternative, possible 'politics of arrangements' are masked. We need to know how space is not just about relations and distance between elements, but is a socially produced order of difference and a technology of differentiation. That is to say, it is a topology kneaded, recast and wielded by active social agents in the context of everyday manoeuvres for status and tactical advantage that attempt to leverage spatialities as cast and caught in the moment.

Discourses on Space

These 'discourses on space' (Lefebvre, 1974, generally translated as 'representations of space' (see the extended discussions in Shields, 1991, 1999), lead to the conclusion that attempts to consider 'space' critically as a socially produced concept or representation have been lacking. A modification of Kant's notion of 'synthetic judgements' was dismissed, often without investigation, in favour of (implicit or explicit) attitudes to space as an absolute and homogeneous *a priori*, where space is just the expanse 'out there'. Initiatives to further investigate the 'nature of space' in social science have been frustrated by this Cartesian dogma and abstract spatialisation that combines an absoluteness with an abstracted spatiality. This assertion and assumption of the *a priori* nature of space, as an extra-social meta-category dominates most sociological investigation which utilizes the concept. Hence, E.T. Hall's classic study of human 'territoriality' and interpersonal 'spacing' would scarcely bother to ask the question 'what is space?' (Hall, 1966). It is simply the 'space between' social actors, in other words, their separation or non-contiguity.

In general, space has been considered as an abstract, ineffable and purely empirical ... an empirical what? Our accepted terminologies do not accord space the status of 'object'. Space is only what architects referred to as the 'void'. Space has been allowed to remain as simply a medium of objects and social action, written off the sociological agenda and relegated to the cartographic 'terrain' of the geographer (see Znaniekci, 1950: 133, cited in Kolaja, 1969: 19). In this status, 'space' has found its usage as the designator of the environmental continuum – something every properly bred sociologist knew had thoroughly neutral characteristics and attributes (Teymur, 1980). This continuum is a framework that is conceptual and practical. Besides the substantive concept and entity, the linguistic aspect of 'space' – at one moment 'itself' but at another moment a metaphor or analogy – is the most ineffable of intangibles and virtualities.

There is a sublime affect involved in this attitude: 'Behold, "space"!' it proclaims (on affect see Davidson et al., 2011). This empty space is sublime in its expansiveness, and awesome in its ineffable unknowability. We cannot grasp it, the mind reels and turns to easier topics. What lies in front of our faces is simply the distance that ensures the separation of the analytical Cartesian mind from the objects to be arranged and dissected. This 'void' or spacing is the framework of the subject-object split. It ensures a pragmatic attitude to the world and a self-understanding as a monad in a world which is readily at hand and available – 'there', 'just for us', to be colonised and dominated as we see fit, according to affect and whim. This view is the romantic heart of the scientific stance of disengagement and value-neutrality.

The intervention of the mathematics of relativity and quantum physics in the twentieth century with the discovery of non-Euclidean spaces and Riemannian geometries (Câpek, 1961) ironically resulted in the recasting of space into a domain of pure science even as relativistic space and time were being theorised. The art of Escher ably summarises the paradoxes of projecting everyday life into these purely logical spaces. 'Les mathématiciens *s'emparent* de l'espace ... ', says Lefebvre (Lefebvre, 1981b: 8, emphasis added; 1991a), likening mathematics to a hijacking or kidnap scene. The radical separation of these 'pure spaces' from the lived space of social reality aggravated all the problems of 'knowing' the truth of social space. 'Social Space' has been allowed to remain unchallenged by the (de-stabilising) relative spaces of science and philosophy. These invented spaces, bearing no relation to lived space, were bequeathed to modern philosophy to find some means of reconstructing the Kantian project of a natural philosophy (i.e. cosmology). The epistemological question, 'how can a theoretically consistent leap be made from these mathematical spaces of logic to the spaces of society?', or in the conventional formulation, 'how to move from theory to practice?' becomes of prime interest during this time.

Lefebvre notes that the diversification of mathematical and logico-epistemological spaces has been mirrored by the proliferation of a variety of thematic, conceptual, pseudo-spaces, ('l'espace mentale', corresponding also, in English, to the colloquial 'head space' and more formally to 'problem space'). Literary spaces (Blanchot, 1968), ideological spaces, and dream spaces all compete as discourses on space which mask a lack of fundamental investigation and an acceptance of the notion of space as an *a priori*, necessary concept which describes a 'posture' or logical set of arguments and orientations to a particular problem or activity.

The absence of an examination of possible limits to the elasticity of the term 'space' – in any precise sense of the term – found in these discourses underscores what Lefebvre sees as the epistemological shallowness of these approaches. It must be noted, in all fairness, that the conflation of a theoretical posture, or problematic, with the concept of a 'problem space' does have a foundation in the Hegelian definition of space as the negation or inverse of the single point, instance or moment (read 'Time'). A totalising set of theoretical 'points' forms a particular 'space', or theoretical domain, of propositions. Nonetheless, the metaphoric appropriation of 'space' is itself a highly significant component to the linguistic 'deformation' of the term 'space', and (hypothetically) a characteristic of a particular historical usage of the term. Philosophical advances on the 'perspectival' and relativistic nature of space have been relatively ignored, but resurface like repressed desires in the language of social discourse.

All of the above theoretical operations which depend on the concepts that the term 'Social Space' normally denotes, 'slide off' the topic of 'space' itself. This leaves the discourses which typically feature 'social space' as an operative concept full of undefined conceptual gaps when scrutinized closely from the angle of 'space' *per se*. 'Social space' is itself a term indelibly stamped by a particular tradition of usage: it is a structural part of a specific social spatialisation and must therefore be regarded with suspicion and rigorously problematised. Foucault notes the importance of discourses on space at the level of metaphor:

The recourse made in this text to spatial metaphors (field, terrain, space, site, situation, position, etc.) poses a theoretical problem: the problem of the validity of its *claim* to existence in a discourse with scientific pretensions ... Althusser thus presents recourse to spatial metaphors as necessary, but at the same time as regressive, non-rigourous.

Everything tends on the contrary to suggest that spatial metaphors, far from being reactionary, technocratic, unwarranted or illegitimate, are rather symptoms of a 'strategic' or 'combative' thought, one which poses the space of discourse as a terrain and an issue of political practices. (Fragment of questions posed to Foucault by the editors of *Hérodote*, cited in Foucault, 1980: 69)

At a deep level, the postulate of the bedrock importance of 'space' in epistemologies, and hence in any sort of discourse, must be considered. Not only are the above theories discourses *on* space but, unsuspectingly, they are discourses animated by a spatialisation. These discourses not only contain what can metaphorically be called interstitial voids, but are filled up with a particular notion (lived and thought) of 'space' that is implicated in every theoretical gesture. They are literally discourses *of* that space, spaces of representation or frameworks that ordain a specific stance and engagement with the world.

Notes

1 While his works are now easily searched systematically online, Elden suggests the following sources: on the circulation of capital, Marx (1973b: 52l, 618–23; 1976: 135; 225–9; 326–32; 1981: 164). On spatial scarcity, see Marx ('The Eighteenth Brumaire of Louis Napoleon', in Marx, 1973c, 1976: 442, 444, 596–8, 612; 1981: 185–90). On the relation of town and country, see Marx (1976: 848–9, 877; 1981: 789–90, 904–5), Marx and Engels (1964), and the 'Manifesto of the Communist Party' (Marx et al., 2006). See also Marx's geographical comments in *Neue Rheinische Zeitung* and 'The Class Struggles in France: 1848 to 1850', 'Agitation Against the Sunday Trading Bill', 'The British Rule in India' and 'Articles on the North American Civil War' (Marx, 1973c).

2 These were later revised and expanded with three appendices, including 'The Social Boundary' (Simmel, 2007 [1908]), 'The Sociology of the Senses', and 'The Stranger' (see Simmel et al., 1997), as Chapter 9 of his Soziologie, entitled 'Space and the Spatial Orders of Society' ('*Der Raum und die räumlichen Ordnungen der Gesellschaft*' in Simmel, 1908: 460–526; 2009).

3 'Could it [difference] exist in and through the "order of succession"? But, as the terms of a succession are by definition, not *com*possible, there could be no difference ... only to the extent that ... in the inspection of a "retentional spectator"... the Plural ... would have been *com*posited, *com*-prehended, *zusammengesetzt*. .... And, of course, conversely, "time" as the "order of succession" *seems* to be required – the "same" thing is never exactly the same ... for the very reason that it is in another time' (Castoriadis, 1987: 192).

> 'There is no essential time, no time that is irreducible to any sort of "spatiality", unless and to the very extent to which ... *what* emerges is not *in* what exists ... to the extent that it is not the actualisation of predetermined possibilities ... Time is the self-alteration of what is, which is only to the extent that it is *to-be*' (Castoriadis, 1987: 190).

5

topologies

This chapter[1] turns to the broader possibilities for an integrated approach to spatialisation and temporalisation by first considering the history of topology as developed in mathematics and in quantum mechanics as a mathematical language of space-time. This takes us from successive spatialisations in geographical space and from geometry to non-Euclidean topological spaces that speak to attempts to diagram power and to depict the multiple dimensions by which the local and social spaces are defined and understood. Supported by the Glossary at the end of this book that covers the italicized terms in this and other chapters, we will look at how topology has been developed. The next chapter will consider how this has been more generally received and applied, and will explore the critical implications of this approach in more detail. 'Topology' as a term is often loosely used to indicate the geographical organisation of a particular network (e.g. a mapping of submarine cables (O'Kelly and Grubesic, 2002) or the internet). It also features in discussions of whether linkages are organised in a hub and spoke pattern, a hierarchy or a more decentralised rhizomatic pattern. One recent article attempts to review and synthesise geographical aspects of communications research under the rubric of 'topology', contrasting studies that stress an absolute, 'physical space' of distances against those that emphasise the space-shrinking qualities of communication. But in the end, it says almost nothing about topology and does not grasp that it might be a method that allows these approaches to coexist (Adams, 2011). Our interest is in both the history of topology as a field and as a method, including its often incorrect and metaphoric appropriation in social science and cultural studies. We are interested in topology as 'the primary intellectual operation capable of revealing the modalities of surfaces, volumes, boundaries, contiguities, holds and above all the notions of *inside* and *outside*' (Morrissette, 1972: 47), and hence of the limits of the social and cultural flow of lines of causality, the interactions of groupings, categories and other figures of recognition, status and power.

'Another Kind of Analysis' – Beyond Geometry

Johann Benedict Listing (1808–82) introduced the term *'topologie'* (*topos*, 'place' and *logos*, 'saying', speaking or discourse) in 1847 (see Listing, 1848). It was only translated into English in 1883 – a fact that gives some sense of the newness of the field – a field whose tools became central to understanding quantum mechanics (see Timeline and Map, Figure 5.3 see also Figure 3.1) and relativistic approaches to time-space. Topology offers a rigorous method for working with multiple spatialities by focusing on connections, and fluid networks of relations (Blackwell, 2004). It offers theoretical spaces where each dimension represents a variable. Graphs are often two-dimensional topologies defined by x and y axes. They make it possible to diagrammatically pose questions in which the combinational is the focus, not just one of the variables (Kantor, 2005: online). Well-known examples of graphs would also be the presentations of information in the media – for example, a 3D histogram that charts the incidence of crime in the form of peaks and valleys, laid over the map of a city. Or, one might model a changing phenomenon as is often done in animated graphs, for example, a fluctuating 'crime topology' of a city. Some topologies simplify the number of dimensions to present a schematic *diagram* or *projection*. Others build in extra dimensions of a problem, showing the relationship between different factors in shaping an outcome. Mathematical topology contributes to modelling how complex processes unfold – sometimes maintaining an appearance of stability only to change catastrophically at a certain 'bifurcation point' in some of the dimensions. All of these involve topological spaces, but as the previous chapters have argued, 'space' is redundant. In these cases, 'topology' directly names the form and quality of any space and any locations in it – from schematic drawing to animated chart to 12-dimensional cosmos. As we will see, these spaces may be large or nanoscopic – or without any metric scale at all to their dimensions.

Because it models fields dynamically, one could imagine the utility of topology to being able to relate one group's spatialisation to an antagonistic group's appropriation of the same places (material or virtual). Struggles over the meaning of the built environment are also struggles over its use and meaning; over what is to be foregrounded as opposed to repressed into the background. The fluid and conflicting set of spatialisations surveyed in the case of Québec City (see Chapter 2) illustrate the need for a topological approach: rather than a succession of Lefebvrean spatial epochs, we want to capture the multiple, conflicting spatialisations that intersect, usually remaining separate but at certain times and places breaking in on each other. The neatness of historical periods is replaced by local 'neighbourhoods' of coherence which emerge in a broader, continuing temporal-spatial world as matrix. Topology is more appropriate at inconsistent margins, dis-organising moments and uncertain times. It privileges sense-making through understanding risk and variance rather than predictability and consistency.

Connectivity and Schematics

Topologies focus on connections. They can be translated across disciplines and operationalised in geographic information systems. A very common illustration to distinguish between geometry and topology is the example of the Tube maps of the London Underground which are diagrammatic rather than true to actual distances. Most Londoners engage in a kind of topological sensibility, by knowing that the well-known Tube maps are abstract diagrams. The maps show the virtual network of lines as a schematic rather than how the lines actually twist and intersect underground: 'Geometry can determine the distance from Piccadilly Square to King's Cross, while topology is more interested in how many different trains the trip will take' (Blackwell, 2004: online) – how are the two stations connected?

The schematic map of the London Underground, the Tube, was designed by Harry Beck in 1931 and included the bends of the River Thames in diagrammatic fashion as a point of reference to the Euclidean world of everyday life and also to the imagined world of London historically defined by the course of Thames. Later attempts at its removal to make the maps more systematic have been highly unpopular (e.g. debates in 2009). Beck's Tube map shows the relationships between stations in a network space: each station is a circle on a coloured line that represents one routing. All the routes are smoothed out, the detail of actual twists and turns underground is omitted in the schematic style. Though no actual timing information is given, one can guess graphically that an itinerary or route with two stops along a line will be faster than an itinerary with three stops, long spaces between the stops or that also requires a change of lines. These relationships are paramount rather than actual distances or the precise street locations. The topological approach uses a virtual rather than actual space; it creates an 'as if' map of London's Underground.

How do these connections or relations change as the field is deformed? Topology has also been called the 'science of self-varying deformation' in so far as it can map one stretched space or shape onto a shrunken one. The most basic deformation is a fold, but stretching is usually given in the most common examples. Folding this page 'bifurcates' the paper by creating an edge that cuts the plane of the page into two. But other deformations are possible: try making a trough to bring words on different parts of the page together with others to make unexpected associations of text. Imagine forming a cusp either as a 'z-fold' by first folding the paper over then making a second, aligned fold back again in the opposite direction. Bending the page back on itself in this manner makes a sort of 's-curve' if seen edge-on. Not creasing it forms a cusp that late-twentieth century topologists will model as a 'catastrophe'.

More complex foldings and warpings defy the two-dimensional limits of paper and stretch our ability to describe them adequately. As a further complex example, imagine one had a lump of bread dough with a triangle drawn on its surface. If we begin kneading it, the points of the triangle will be folded into the dough, but the points will still remain in some warped relation to each other that can actually be described topologically. Architecturally, design focused on similar moldings of the surfaces of roofs and the building envelope has been described as 'topological architecture' (see Perella, 1998: 10).

> [Topology] engulfs forms in their own variation. The variation is bounded by static forms that stand as its beginning and its end, and it can be stopped at any point to yield other still-standing forms. But it is what happens in-between that is the special province of topology ... When the focus shifts to continuity of variation, still-standing form appears as residue of a process of change ... The variation ... is the virtuality of that form's appearance (and of others with which it is deformationally linked). (Massumi, 1998: 16)

Geometry and Topology

Both geometry and topology concern figures and objects. However, a fundamental interest in geometry is with the congruence of figures as they are stretched or deformed, establishing the similarities and 'sameness' of triangles, for example. Congruence is demonstrated through an exact mapping of points. 'In this way, geometry is concerned only with manipulating the extrinsic properties of a figure, that is, with its variable properties' (Blackwell, 2004). For example, geometry is concerned with the value or 'kind' of round figures (elliptical, hyperbolic, circular, etc.); it distinguishes between them to arrive at quantitative differences. By contrast, topology would be concerned with qualitative similarities between all round figures: the nature of roundness provides the basis for narrower geometrical concepts such as circular or elliptical. It is the quality of 'roundness' that remains despite transformations of an ellipse into a circle. As a circle might be stretched into an ellipse, roundness is an example of an intrinsic spatial quality that remains constant across the transformation of these figures into each other.

Topology is concerned not only with figures but sets of figures, such as those that are round, those that exist in a given dimension or those that have a certain number of holes. Topology is the mathematics of context, connectivity and consistency. It includes several branches. Differential topology understands change through calculus, as distinct from algebraic topology's phase spaces and their transformations. For example, algebraic topology measures the degrees of connectivity mentioned in the examples above. Whereas geometry classifies by describing angles and sides, topology transforms the logical problem of consistency into the spatial concept of connectivity. Systems and networks are said to be 'consistent' if they have similar connectivity. They can be transformed – warped, stretched, shrunk – into each other without any tearing or gaps. A doughnut shape can be flatted into a circle or moulded into a mug with a handle (the doughnut hole becomes the handle while one side of the doughnut is shaped to make the concave part of the cup), but it cannot be turned into a figure-eight without punching another hole.[2]

The shift to connectivity is typical of topology and important because propositions or 'axiomatics' cannot logically prove their own consistency (this is Gödel's (1906–78) Second Theorem; see also Blackwell, 2004). In effect, propositions cannot be used to prove their own fundamental validity, which would be tautological. Euclid's Fifth Postulate states that for a given line, only one parallel line could be drawn through a given point in a given plane (see Chapter 3; Euclid, 1998; c.325–265 BCE Alexandria). However, this assumption could not be proven within the context of Euclid's own system. Nor could Euclid establish through logic alone that everyday spatiality was three-dimensional (see Schweikart's experimental demonstration, below).

> Euclidean geometry employs a metric understanding of space, in which a distance function is defined for every pair of points in the space. The Cartesian coordinates of Euclidean geometry allow location to be defined in terms of positions along intersecting axes. Euclidean space is thus topographical; it refers to mappable, graphable, measurable space. Yet this is not the only way that space works. (Blum and Secor, 2011: 1034)

Smirnov notes that topology has the advantage over metric-based, distance measurement approaches to geographical space based on location, distance and area (Beguin and Thisse, 1979). These approaches require separate methods to explain direction, coordinates and the clustering of activities in places and in patterns (Getis, 2008; Smirnov, 2010; Tobler, 2004). They cannot deal with non-point geographical objects like regions. Smirnov argues that 'The importance of topology in theoretical geography was expressed as early as the 1960s (e.g. Bunge, 1966; see Gatrell, 1983) ... Although ... the utilisation of topological constructs in theoretical geography never actually took place' (Smirnov, 2010: 1).

Euclid has deeply informed geographical space with little critical reflection on the part of geographers and cartographers. Rather than abide such a shameful lack of self-reflection, Smirnov suggests that this 'geographical space', a peculiar 'Abstract Space' or spatialisation characterised by sets of 'locations', cardinality and so on, be developed as only one type of topological space to construct a theoretical object of analysis which founds geography as a spatial and topological science rather than a descriptive positivist discipline about 'the Earth'. 'Geographical space' is a concept that is independent of any measurement framework or any representations of that space (Smirnov, 2010: 4–8).

For geographic space Euclid's geometric distance turns out to be unhelpful: the more detail given in the measurement of some irregular objects, such as the coastline of the United Kingdom, the longer their total length will be found to be. Mandelbrot (1924–2010) demonstrated the nature of fractals using exactly this example where, as the unit of measure shrinks, the longer the coastline extends (Mandelbrot, 1967). Problems such as this are of little importance until one begins to model geographical objects computationally as in contemporary Geographical Information Systems.

Topology has played a major role in the relativisation of space and time. In the 1730s, early proto-topologists, such as Euler (1707–83), followed Isaac Newton (see Chapter 3) in accepting the necessary existence of absolute space as a real substratum needed for the determination of absolute rest and motion and for a law of inertia. In this Enlightenment vision, space is a substance, an ether. Space is not just an imagined abstraction nor is it a virtual phenomenon of forces between relations among material substances (i.e. a set, see Jammer, 1969: 131ff.). However, topology allows us to work with multi-dimensional mathematical spaces, or *phase space*, that can contain an infinite number of incongruent, even contradictory propositions and dimensions. In 1914, Felix Hausdorff (1868–1942) first spatialised these as different '*neighbourhoods*' that could be related together in a type of patchwork (Hausdorff, 1957). Neighbourhoods are areas of relative consistency. However, changing variables radically shift the way phenomena work in different neighbourhoods of the same topology. Phase spaces are logically defined spaces similar to those which allow us to visualise data in graphs; they have x-y-z-... dimensions without a Euclidean sense of fixed distance (Kuratowsky, 1948).

In geographical space, sites are '*entourages*', assemblages or sets of elements or neighbourhoods in and of themselves. This space has a fractal quality but can be simplified by selecting the *scale* of locations – in practical terms, street addresses, census blocks, municipalities, watersheds could all be the key operational scale at which relations between these locations are considered. Smirnov argues that geographical space consists of a set of locations, a set of relations and a topology selected so as to be countable at a given scale (to be more precise (Smirnov, 2010)). This allows us to connect the abstract discussion of topology and its infinite possible locations to the practical operations of navigation, orientation and a sense of place which are the significant social aspects of geographical space.

It is crucial to recognise that this stance connects scale to not only pragmatic concern but to choice backed with power that becomes institutionalised as standard practice.

Let us trace out the map, real and imaginary, unique and double, ideal and false, virtual and utopian, rational, analytic, of a world where the Alps can change place with the Himalayas, such that their forms reply to each other, and that the callings from here correspond to the groanings of the excluded there. This map of tendering – as verb and adjective – displays and demonstrates morality, concrete, reasonable and true. (Serres, 1994: 262–3)

Schweikart (Marburg and Königsberg, 1780–1857), who published the first non-Euclidean geometry, demonstrated that the everyday 'actual space' of objects was Euclidean (Schweikart, 1818):[3]

> He tried to measure directly by an ordinary triangulation with survey-ing equipment whether the sum of the angles of a large triangle amounts to two right angles or not. Accordingly he surveyed a triangle formed by three mounts, the Brocken, the Hoher Hagen and the Inselbert with sides measuring 69, 85 and 107 km ... he did not detect any deviation from 180 degrees within the margin of error and thus concluded that the structure of actual space is Euclidean as far as experience can show. (Jammer, 1969: 147)

However, '[e]ach historical attempt to define space has only extended our understanding of the irreducible multiplicity of spatial concepts, each necessary for a comprehensive description of certain phenomena' (Blackwell, 2004: n. 16). By the early twentieth century, Poincaré (Paris, 1854–1912) could say, '[w]hoever speaks of absolute space uses a word devoid of meaning' (Poincaré, 1914: 93). He demonstrated the fallacy of any attempt to discover by experiment which of the mutually exclu-sive geometries applies to everyday physical space. Working on time, he showed that measurement is never of space itself but always of empirically given objects in that space. Experiments only tell us of the relations within a space. Experience can neither confirm nor refute geom-etry. Mathematical entities, such as topological spaces, are proven to exist through a demonstration that their definition does not lead to a logical contradiction (Poincaré, 1952). One classic illustration of the change in approach that he initiated is the shift from Newtonian empty space to the understanding of space as a field of stresses or forces which determine how any given entity manifests and behaves – like the Earth's magnetic field which changes the direction the compass needle points in its case when moved to different locations.

The Seven Bridges of Königsburg

Topology has existed as a mathematical discipline for less than one hun-dred years. However, as early as 1750, Euler discovered the first topological property: the 'Euler characteristic' establishes the genus of shapes (such as

Gedenkblatt zur sechshundert jährigen Jubelfeier der königlichen Haupt und Residenz Stadt Königsberg in Preußen.

Figure 5.1 Engraving of Königsburg (Bergin 1613, www.wikimedia.org public domain) 'circular' or 'linear' or 'cubic'). Regardless of how they are deformed (eg. by stretching or folding the space they are in), the sum of a shape's vertices, edges, and faces remains the same.

This idea was established through a discussion of the *Seven Bridges of Königsberg* (1736): in a famous example of public research driven by community curiousity Euler solved a problem which had been posed by the inhabitants and provided the basis for a general method of choosing routes efficiently (see Figure 5.2). Euler showed that it was impossible to find a route through the town that would cross each of its seven bridges across Pregel River (now named the Pregolya) exactly once. This is a topological problem in that connectivity is at issue, not the size of any one bridge or its distance from another bridge. Euler 'understood that the problem did not depend on the precise map of the city ... it was not a problem of geometry ... Euler establishes the new nature of the problem by using the term "geometry of position", an expression introduced for the first time by Leibnitz' (Kantor, 2005) as *geometriam situs*, or *analysis situs* 'another kind of analysis, geometric or linear, which deals directly with position, as algebra deals with magnitudes ... ' (Leibniz and Clarke, 2000, Letter to Huygens 1679). Euler presents his argument in 21 numbered paragraphs, beginning by saying:

1. ... Hence, when a problem was recently mentioned which seemed geometrical but was so constructed that it did not require the measurement of distances, nor did calculation help at all, I had no doubt that it was concerned with the geometry of position – especially as its solution involved only position, and no calculation was of any use. I have therefore decided to give here the method which I have found for solving this problem, as an example of the geometry of position.

2. The problem, which I am told is widely known, is as follows: in Königsberg ... (Euler, 1736/1741: 128)[4]

Euler concludes that 'If there are more than two areas to which an odd number of bridges lead, then such a journey is impossible' (1736/1741: para. 20, 139). To prove this, he develops a technique of assigning each area a capital letter *A–D* and each bridge a lowercase letter *a-f* and then asking about the path necessary to connect the areas, crossing each bridge only once (Figure 5.2). How many times does the letter for a given bridge appear when one connects the areas? 'A path signified by n letters corresponds to crossing $n-1$ bridges, so a solution to the Königsberg problem requires an eight-letter path' (Hopkins and Wilson, 2004: 204). More generally, if there is an odd number k of bridges then each individual bridge must appear $(k + 1)/2$ times. This frequency allows one to calculate a total for any given arrangement of areas or objects joined by bridges or links. This sums up the number of bridges required in any path that doesn't have to re-cross a bridge (Euler, 1736/1741: paras 8–12).

The strategically located town and most of its bridges were destroyed by aerial bombing and heavy fighting in 1945. After the Second World War, the town was used as a military base and was closed to foreigners for fifty years. It remains isolated; the area borders Poland along the Baltic Sea and is separated from the Russian Federation by the independent republics of Lithuania and Belarus. It is an exclave of Russia and an enclave within the European Union countries of Poland and Lithuania. Of the few buildings that have survived, the Cathedral with the grave of the philosopher Emmanuel Kant is still standing. To mark the tercentenary of Euler's solution, a number of mathematicians resurveyed the original location, now Kaliningrad, and concluded that 'Eulerian Walks' are still possible but not a perfect 'Eulerian circuit' as dreamt of. Despite the war-time destruction, a new Kaiserbrücke footbridge was rebuilt in 2005 and a motorway now spans right across Kneiphof Island but allows pedestrian access to the island.

> War, ironically, has led to the solution of the problem of the Seven Bridges. The case of Koenigsberg/Kaliningrad shows how politics affects spatialisation: what was once an abstract mathematical problem concerning space is completely altered due to politics. The city teaches an important lesson about how space is not simply a static, apolitical, mathematical entity, but rather a dynamic entity that is constantly changing due to natural, economic, social and political forces. ... To this day Kaliningrad remains a Russian 'island' and is now situated within the EU, sandwiched between Poland and Lithuania ...
>
> Kaliningrad Oblast is a living palimpsest, which complicates spatial questions concerning nationality, identity and homeland. Vesilind and Chamberlin describe Kaliningrad as haunted: 'The Russians and others who came here after World War II for a new life moved into the shell of a nation, into other peoples' homes and farms, to use other people's furniture and pots and pans' (1997: 110). The Russians living in Kaliningrad occupy a space with a German past, from which they are disconnected; a space, which is at the same time disconnected from their motherland. (Bailey, 2010: online)

Writing on the mathematical history, Mallion asks the speculative question whether, 'if the 1542 Honigbrücke [bridge *e* in Figure 5.2] had never been built, Euler would have been asked to look at this problem at all ... And if Euler had not intervened, topology and graph theory might have developed along different lines ... ' (Mallion, 2008: 34–5). Bailey's point is that Königsberg/Kaliningrad continues to provoke questions of relations between areas and cultural spaces as a type of what Blackwell (2004) calls *cultural topology* – a genuinely 'new type of analysis'.

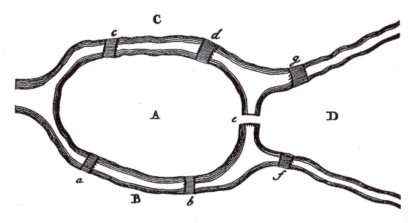

Figure 5.2 Euler's illustration of the bridges of Königsberg and Kneiphof Island, c.1736 (Euler 1736, after Mallion 2008: 26 and Faculty of Science University of Kragujevac 2007, public domain)

Non-Euclidean Space

What if M.C. Escher were to paint an imagined Königsberg in which one could find a Eulerian walk, crossing each bridge only once? This would require a weird painterly space in which the ground and bridges warped back on themselves to allow the flâneur to never cross his own path. Welcome to topological space. Escher's 1963 'Moebius Strip II' is often animated by amateurs online to show its ants infinitely following each other. Welcome to a *topological sensibility* that is not only already understood globally but in its diverse forms is a source of amusement – from computer animation students to the child in Kiev who plays a game of cat's cradle with a string.

Non-Euclidean 'topological spaces', a term introduced by Felix Hausdorff in 1922, are behind the visual tricks of Escher's paintings. However, they are studied as geometric wholes. Changing the parameters of spaces reshapes them by continuous stretching and bending, much as a potter could change their mind mid-creation to reshape an object. Topology focuses on spatial properties of these object-spaces that do not change under such 'homeomorphic' continuous deformations. For example, any object with one hole is 'homeomorphic' with any others with one hole. Similarly the angles of a triangle on a flat plane add up to 180 degrees. It is appropriate that in the front right of Figure 3.3 Raphael's 1505 *School of Athens* Euclid draws on a flat slate on the ground. Laid onto a sphere, one can still discern Euclid's triangles with three points. But because of the curvature introduced into its sides, the sum of the angles of a triangle will be greater, altering one of Euclid's *Laws*. So topology includes not only strict shape-invariance but also fuzzier, yet mathematically rigorous, 'shape-consistency' under deformation.

This can usefully be compared to other things that change yet are held to remain the same, such as a family or community or group – virtualities, that is intangible-but-real-entities that remain despite turnover in membership. Other examples include objects that age (a corroding automobile) but yet are still referred to as the same object. The virtual builds beyond a social constructionism to a post-structural empiricism that acknowledges the realism of entities such as a group or a mathematical set independent of the elements (e.g. the set of prime numbers versus the numbers that make it up – see Shields (2006b)).

Carl Friedrich Gauss (1777–1855) recognised the logical possibility of a non-Euclidean geometry that could displace Euclidean geometry and absolute three-dimensional space from its privileged position. Working on a geodetic survey, he became interested in geometrical figures on surfaces of different shapes. He wrote that an arithmetical 'number is a product of the mind but [geometric] space has a reality outside the mind whose laws we cannot prescribe a priori' (Gauss, 1863–1903: Vol. 8, 177, in Jammer, 1969: 147). Others, such as Nikolai Lobachevski (1792–1856) recognised that this relativised everyday physical space had opened the possibility of multiple topological spaces (Lobachevski, 2005). Rather than a single true geometry, the status of geometrical laws depended on the types of space in which they were applied (see Chapter 3). But proof might require observations on an astronomical scale and was frustrated by inaccuracies, even when Lobachevski tested his ideas by using an astronomical triangle whose base was the diameter of the earth's orbit and whose apex was at the star Sirius. Even on the scale of solar systems and galaxies, three-dimensional physical space might still be only one '*manifold*' embedded in the further dimensions of a more complex topology that we cannot know from within our own cosmological '*neighbourhood*'.

Topology has often borrowed cartographic metaphors: the structure of a manifold is encoded by a collection of '*charts*' that form an '*atlas*'. A chart is a local coordinate system. A topological atlas simply collects a set of charts of neighbourhoods to allow the broader differential structure of the manifold to be calculated. In the mid-1800s George Riemann (Göttingen, 1826–66) demonstrated that a subclass of *differentiable manifolds* existed, which allowed one to represent change between manifolds, such as when one translates a map of the Earth from a globe to a flat paper chart. Another example is when one maps one state in time to a new period (earlier or later) under the dimension 'time' (Riemann, 1854). These comparative manifold states model change of structure, form or properties through time. Time is imagined as a one-dimensional, differentiable manifold of instants, but not a true flow, *durée* or duration.

In the 1850's, Riemann discovered that while our reality seemed to be Euclidean, it was not ... Keeping the rest of Euclid's system intact, figures like Bolyai, Lobachevsky, and Riemann were able to create [self-]consistent geometries ... in which the parallel postulate [see above] did not hold. Early non-Euclidean geometries thus discovered that *the shape of space determines the kind of geometry that is possible within it*. (Blackwell, 2004: online, emphasis added)

Poincaré (1854–1912) noted that mathematics is not the study of objects, but instead, the relations between them. He not only opened up new areas of mathematics such as chaos (infinitely unpredictable behaviour) but brought non-Euclidean geometry into the mainstream by showing that different types of surfaces each had their own geometrical rules. One could not put a curved geometry onto a flat surface) and therefore each possible geometry that could be identified indicated every type of *manifold* – whether a surface or multi-dimensional space.

Working with curves is at the heart of computer rendering and the ability to engineer and build curved surfaces and architectural works. While working at the French Bureau des Longitudes on time zones and the synchronisation of local times in 1895, Poincaré wrote *Analysis Situs* (Greek-Latin for 'picking apart place') in which he pioneered the study of warped 'manifolds', such as the two-dimensional map surface of the world embedded in the three-dimensional space of the earth or of a globe (Poincaré, 2010). Manifolds may be Euclidean locally and familiar as everyday spaces. How one warps a square map onto a spherical globe is one example of how a manifold (the square map) can be warped by being embedded into other multi-dimensional spaces, referred to as the '*dimension*' of the manifold (in this case, moulding a flat map onto a sphere). The reverse process is to '*project*' a higher dimensional manifold onto a lower dimensional space, like flattening a globe onto a two-dimensional map. Another example is to think of three-dimensional physical space as the manifold of everyday life, set within a four-dimensional context which adds time to experience. We get the idea of a three-dimensional manifold with a fourth temporal dimension. Manifolds may be spaces of any n-dimensions. Thus in the context of physics, it is a four-dimensional time-space manifold that is being modified by extra dimensions – factors such as gravitational force that popular media often describe as 'curving' space.

Despite these deformations, any neighbourhood locally resembles another regardless of which dimensional system they are described in. Sticking with the example of the earth, any given location is surrounded by a circular region of the globe that can be flattened out into a plane (they have a 'neighbourhood homeomorphism'). We cannot tell in everyday life whether we live on a map-like plane or on a globe-like sphere. The problems that confronted Poincaré were both technical questions of how to mathematically and geometrically translate between the globe and flat charts, and philosophical questions such as how one might be able to prove the nature and number of dimensions of the space one was in, especially if one could not get 'outside' of it to assume a God's-eye view. This is analogous to the sort of issues sceptics raised during the time of Columbus – how could the roundness of the Earth be established within the apparent flatness of everyday locales? Was it a bounded shape, like a paper map, or were there no '*boundaries*' or edges, such as on the surface of a sphere? There are tests. For example, one test was whether or not a loop on the surface, beginning and returning to any given point could be shrunk to a point. Because, spheres are the only '*simply connected*' two-dimensional manifolds: a geographer on the surface of a spherical Earth could determine whether or not their world was a sphere. Some shapes, such as a torus or doughnut shape could have loops through the hole in the middle of the shape. These would not be shrinkable to points unless they were allowed to cut into the shape. Such a loop of string would tighten around the doughnut, pinching it.

It is generally thought that for everyday life and for quantum scales one dimension of time plus three or even two dimensions of space, respectively, are sufficient to model interactions. It was Poincaré, echoing Nietzsche's philosophical perspectivism, who first proposed an alternative to the absolute space of Descartes within the objective arena of scientific research. He argued that like geometric space, there were two dimensional perspectival visual spaces, but also tactile spaces, and motor spaces with as many dimensions as we have muscles. Each space is a manifold which has its own distinct characteristics (Poincaré, 1952: 50–8). In these manifolds, neighbourhoods are homeomorphic with small regions of Euclidean space, allowing one to represent two time zones, on the curved surface of the three-dimensional Earth, but separated by an hour of time distance – and yet still coexisting in one projection such as on a two-dimensional map. One could imagine the technical process as a light source inside of the spherical globe that shines through a window in the globe. Its rays project the features of the globe onto a flat wall.

The Topological Sensorium

In previous chapters, Lenin's attack on non-Euclidean geometry and spaces revealed the unease provoked by geometry and shapes that cannot be visualised in three dimensions (see Chapter 4). It is not just that the 'shape of space' is in doubt but that the answer cannot be resolved visually: there will be no 'now I see' moment of understanding. By defying the privilege of the visual, topology has pushed the cultural limits of our sensorium in a manner similar to a new technology or new media. First, the apparent movement of figures on a spinning zoetrope, then animation and cinema manipulated the passage of time in visualisation (Deleuze, 1986). The screen could be viewed as a clear window into a familiar three-dimensional space (despite the artifice and mechanisms required to produce the illusion of a space that continued off-screen). Shifting to a four dimensional time-space removed the three-dimensional ontology that underpins commonsense cause and effect, as well as the verities on which science and social science and thus politics are built. Such changes radically problematize understandings of the relationship between the body and work, the senses and labour, and the universality of pronounce-ments such as economic laws. That is, rather than a production process in which bodies move objects or where energy is consumed to smelt metal from ore, non-Euclidean geometries are at the heart of the sort of nano-scaled and probabilistic interactions one finds in the process of recording a DVD or other optical storage medium. The relationship between matter and energy (a laser beam in this case) is reconfigured in ways that chal-lenge the Euclidean world of everyday life and effort.

Does topology smooth out action into a field where we lose its texture and grain? No, topology shows us the importance of that field, temporal and spatial, and of its every lump and folding. While this will be explored further in the next chapter, it is worth noting that we must not be seduced by the ingrained Euclidean assumption that the milieu of social action is a 'smooth space' of power but remember that it involves striated and folded topologies. Nor is the 'point-free' field of topology a crowdless space. Rather it is an object of struggle by actors who seek to define the strategic relevance of specific scales of analysis in the framing and definition of social problems.

As noted in Chapter 2, notions such as warped space-time neighbour-hoods, or the notion that the universe could be difficult to envision, built on the work of early topologists. Just as it is necessary to leave the two-dimensional surface of the earth to see the curvature of the planet from space in its three dimensions directly, so it would be necessary to 'see' in four-dimensions in order to envision the three-dimensional 'shape' of the space of the universe and its curves. As it stands, radiation echoes of the early moments and outer edges of the universe allow us to 'see backward' in time because these low frequency radio waves have travelled millions if not billions of light years, aligning past time with distance. In the case of black holes where time becomes infinitely slow one could imagine that there is a local loss of time as a dimension (to the point that objects 'dis-appearing' into them are now hypothesised to never actually arrive at the 'event horizon', the point of being annihilated, although they effectively cease to exist because they are stalled in time). Does this suggest a point of critical departure for analysis of the late twentieth-century conservative rhetoric of the 'end of history'?

Figure 5.3   Reverse chronology and map of key figures in topology

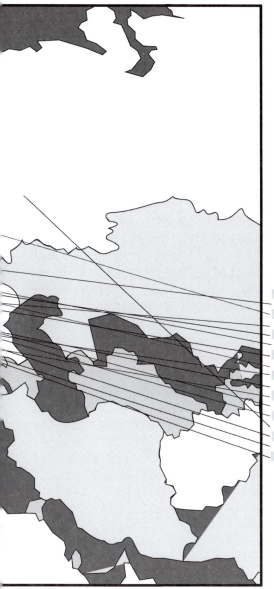

Lisa Randall (1962--) – Boston (not shown)
René Thom (1923-2002) – Strasbourg, Paris
Oscar Reutersvärd (1915 – 2002) – Stockholm
Karl Friedrich Gödel (1906-1978) - Vienna
Jan Brouwer (1881 – 1966) - Amsterdam
Albert Einstein (1879 – 1955) – Bern
Felix Hausdorff (1868 - 1942) – Bonn
Jakob von Uexküll (1864 – 1944) – Hamburg
Camille Jordan (1838 – 1922) – Paris
Ernst Mach (1838 – 1916) – Prague
Henri Poincaré (1854 – 1912) – Paris
Bernhard Riemann (1826-66) - Göttingen
Johann Benedict Listing (1808 – 1882) – Göttingen
Nikolai Lobachevsky (1792 – 1856) – Kazan
August Ferdinand Möbius (1790 – 1868) – Leipzig
Ferdinand Schweikart (1780 - 1857) – Marburg
Carl Friedrich Gauss (1777 – 1855) – Göttingen

Dimensionality and Orientability

Pure mathematics was not logically confined to three dimensions. As one of the first to formalise the field of topology, Brouwer (1881–1966) drew on Poincaré's work to show that the dimensionality of space is a topological invariant under any transformation of its coordinates. In the 1860s, Möbius discovered orientability as a topological principle of roundness. Orientation or the 'orientability' of figures varies from one topological space to another. Just as left and right are reversed when we look in a mirror, Möbius (1790–1868) discovered that triangles on the band that now bears his name changed their orientation by the time they make one circuit of the möbius strip (they are turned upside down). The shape of space determines what kind of orientation is possible. This property of the one-sidedness of the strip is 'non-orientability', and is different from the properties of apparently 'round' objects such as the Earth. Similarly, colouring a strip on 'the top' turns out to be colour on 'the bottom' after one circuit of the strip, and the inside is the same as the outside. Möbius had discovered a different kind of two-dimensional space which is a 'perpetual mirror world' in which it is impossible to tell which image is real and actual and which image is a reflection, that is, a virtuality. Up and down dominate as not only a gravitational but as a topological principle of material, despite the left-right reversals we observe in mirror-images, and despite the paradoxical idea that someone on the opposite side of the Earth must be standing 'upside down' in comparison to us.

With Gauss, Riemann was the first to present a mathematical analysis of the structure of space, whether curved or Euclidean. Rather than the axiomatic approach of his predecessors, Riemann generalised Gauss' work (Riemann, 1854). He introduced a classification of surfaces based on the number of folds along them. The equivalence of different knots provides a further example of manifolds and their transformations: 'knot theory' asks when should two knots be considered the same? Any knot is an embedding of a one-dimensional space, a loop of string, into the three-dimensional physical space of everyday life. We know that string can be unknotted and re-tied into a different type of knot. Geometrical topology would describe this as a one-dimensional manifold with three dimensions undergoing homeomorphic deformation of being tied in different ways. Dimensions can also be understood as degrees of freedom: the point has zero, the knot one; surfaces have two. If a manifold has a boundary, it is one dimension lower: a string (i.e. a one-dimensional line) tied in a knot has two boundaries at either end that are points (zero dimensional) unless its ends join (a circle), in which case it would have no boundaries; the boundary of a two-dimensional surface (a plane) is a line (one-dimensional), that is, an edge, and so on.

The itinerary that threads back and forth across Königsberg's bridges and island also have the quality of knots or of a cat's cradle game. Any knot is an embedding of a one-dimensional space or manifold, such as a loop of string, into the three-dimensional physical space of everyday life. We know that the string can be unknotted and re-tied into a different type of knot, making some knots equivalent to others. But a geometrical solution would be confined to one dimension – pulling the string out of the knot bit by bit. A topological solution would consider how to untie the knot using all the dimensions of everyday life. By extension it would consider the knots of everyday life in more dimensions: adding historical time is already a topological move, but consider the varying tempo of lived time and virtual temporalities such as Braudel's *longue durée* (1982), Benjamin's flash of *Jetz-zeit*, now-time, or Lefebvre's 'moment' that displaces the steady march of clock time. These are only a few established examples that may be seen as related in their resort to topological transformations and over-dimensioned shifts in the normative topologies of labour-time and the experience of the everyday.

Knots have been the basis for cross-cultural conceptions of complexity, from Piranesi's labyrinths, to fishing nets to children's games. Because topology offers the insight that it is possible to analyse systematically relationships and configurations themselves, it shows us that knots are more than metaphors: knots describe topologically not only complex networks but the twisted path a document might take through a bureaucracy, or that a decision-making process might follow. Topology maps across boundaries and interfaces where 'translations' that may recode, warp or recast objects, such as a document or terminology that is understood in different ways on either side of this border, a topological fold, held in place by power, that reorients the internal sense of a message. One might trace the experience of boundary-objects that have these qualities (Bowker and Star, 1999) as well as discursive sleights of hand in which meanings are realigned according the interpretation of different groups and their interests. For example, Stark, Vedres and Bruszt show how discursive meaning can be shifted to allow divergent local and transnational interests to engage in shared projects and narratives amongst groups in civil society (Stark et al., 2006).

However, Poincaré noted that three-dimensional manifolds could either be bounded (for example, a sphere or torus), or unbounded spaces. However, he became notorious for hypothesising that there could only be one four-dimensional manifold that is finite (like a sphere), but unbounded and simply connected. That is, every loop in it could be shrunk to a point: a topology known as the three-sphere.[5] If true, this would offer a means of testing, from the inside, whether the universe is a four-dimensional time-space manifold and thereby determining the shape of the cosmos, just as the Alexandrian geometers had sought to determine the shape of the Earth (see Chapter 2; see Perelman, 2002 for the famous proof). The object of Poincaré's 'Conjecture', the three-sphere is obtained from two everyday spheres. One representation of the three-sphere is said to appear in Gustave Doré's image of Dante's *Divine Comedy* (Peterson, 1979). However, this space can only be thought of as a virtuality, 'as if' the three-sphere. Other representations are provided by stereographic computer animations in which the three-sphere is projected into three dimensions much as we would project a one part or hemisphere of a globe onto a flat chart.

In the case of the four-dimensional three-sphere, the 3-D projection appears as a möbius strip twisted and looped into a 'trefoil knot' that then balloons out in a confounding Escher-like space in which surfaces merge into each other, like breaking open the seed pod of a plant and peering into the locules of the pod. But this three-dimensional projection condenses a four-dimensional entity – such projections make manifest the difference Lefebvre saw between representations of space, spatial practice and spaces of representation (see Chapter 2). Recall that by fixing spatialisations into historical modes of production, Lefebvre and all periodicising historians, produce a flattened projection of space into epochs ... a kind of Mercator projection of spatialisations. That is, they methodologically reduced the temporal dimension to a series of periods. As the word suggests, periods are precisely points: zero-dimensional. Earlier, Bergson had objected to the lack of duration in this approach to time. Unfortunately, in more ambitious attempts, the reintroduction of time has often tended to fix the spatial as a taken-for-granted stage for temporal action such as daily cycles in the medieval village analysed by E.P. Thompson (Thompson, 1980), or the itineraries and routines of Hägerstrand's time-geography (Hägerstrand, 1981; Pred, 1990). As rhythm in Lefebvre's late collaboration on 'rhythmanalysis', he attempted to correct for this at the scale of individual everyday life and urban society by envisioning rhythm as a time space figuration – a topology – with time grasped as tempo and metre within rhythm (Lefebvre and Regulier-Lefebvre, 1992).

Topological Archetypes: Folds, Bridges, Labyrinths

René Thom's (Strasbourg, Paris, 1923–2002) catastrophe theory models tendencies to stability in complex systems visualised as two- and three-dimensional graphs. These serve as archetypes that we have considered only as folds or knots up to this point. Thom's analysis was originally applied to linguistics. In his topological approach, objects subject to forces in a system are represented as points in these diagrams or spaces with the forces or other independent variables as the dimensions x, y, z, and so on. The 'catastrophe' is a position where the forces have *minimum potential* and the object tends to gravitate towards this point which has come to be referred to as an *attractor* and is often represented as a peak or depression in a field of points or as a fold in a field or surface across which sudden change is possible as the status of an entity moves from point to point across the topology. As a way of simplifying his approach, Thom identified seven basic spatial topologies in which catastrophes occur such as the fold, cusps, butterfly and swallowtail shapes, and 16 stable morphologies expressed diagrammatically showing the existence and interaction or differentiation of entities. In these archetypes (Wildgen, 1982), a line diagrams continuous existence (1); a line to or from a point diagrams (2) ending or (3) beginning respectively. Sudden change (4) appears as a fold or cusp which permits a leap across points on the surface, diagrammed as a line to a point, then a new line leaving from a point where the change is the leap across the points. The diagrams include merging and interacting lines as well (see Figure 5.4).

Thom focused on morphological structures in language (1975): sounds that analogically represent things in the world and are then built into more complex expressions such as verbs. Serres (1992) suggests that catastrophes

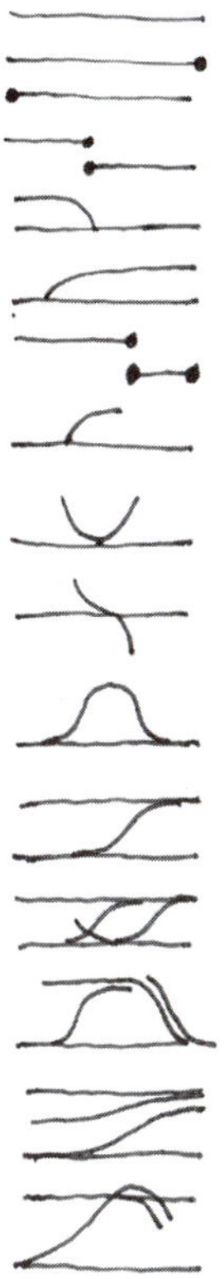

1 Exist, being (*être*, to be)

2 End, finishing (*finir*, to finish)

3 Begin (*commencer*, to begin)

4 Change (*changer*, to change)

5 Capture (*capturer*, to capture)

6 Emit, send, alienate (*emettre*, to emit)

7 Fall short, to almost do (*faillir*, to fail)

8 Spit, shoot (*cracher*, to spit)

9 Reject, rebuff (*rejeter*, to reject)

10 Cross (*traverser* to cross)

11 Jolt (*secouer*, to shake)

12 Give, produce (*donner*, to give)

13 Nudge, push, throw (*envoyer*, to send)

14 Take, expropriate (*prendre*, to take)

15 Link, connect (*lier*, to tie)

16 Cut off (*couper*, to cut)

Figure 5.4 René Thom's topological archetypes (after Thom, 1975 and Demers, 2010)

be applied to spatial constructions such as a bridge (discontinuity made continuous). Demers (2010) proposes that these diagrams can be applied to urban change as a complex historical system and summarises Serres' list as follows:

> *The Bridge*: a path that connects two banks, making a discontinuity continuous [e.g. archetype 4, sudden change].

> *The Well*: a hole in space, which can disconnect a trajectory that passes through and simultaneously connects piled spatial varieties and produces a new trajectory – the fall.

> *The Hotel:* organizes spatial extension into local domains of minimal differentiation.

> *The Labyrinth*: organizes global space into complex and intertwining relations.

> *The Prison*: defines a finite space within a global condition.

> *Death:* the cessation of existence. (Demers, 2010: 501)

Some of these are clearly attractors (such as the *Well*), others model the form of different catastrophe events. Wildgen (1982) contributes Frontiers, Heartbeat, Transience, Passage, Polarisation and so on. Serres' operators or archetypes are specific arrangements or topologies with the archetypes in Figure 5.4 'reproductions of constellated relations commonly found in myths, relations that comprise the series of important events described in the mythic narrative. These operators perform their work specifically on the spaces described in narratives' (Demers, 2010: 501, after Serres, 1992).

> Topologically, the *Well* works as a hole in space, cutting trajectories that cross it and simultaneously connecting diverse layers of space by forming new trajectories made locally possible by the working of the hole … any planning document that offers a general guide for the possible forms of the urban environment can be seen to operate on a discursive topology by forming a *Well*, augmenting existing local trajectories of development and supporting new trajectories through a process of gathering and funneling into determined local conditions.

> The richness of relations possible with the vocabulary of spatial operators allows us to see that a local operation that affects the space of the urban system in representation forms a *new space* or *topos*. The workings of the *Well* Operator can be seen to form a *Bridge*, connecting separate domains by a continuous path that was not previously possible. … stimulating rather than prohibiting a profusion of new idiosyncrasies and an infinite conception of scales within the confines of the domain

of operation. In short, such operations stimulate the perpetual variegation of a city and its narrative. In turn, each spatial operator contains multiple archetypal morphologies which, when postulated and examined individually, add a finer grain of specificity and rigor to the topological representations. (Demers, 2010: 504)

The 'Plushness' of the Real

'Plushness' captures extra micro-dimensions added on to everyday manifolds, like tiny loops on an apparently flat surface that one notices only at magnification. More recent uses of topology add extra dimensions that may be finite in size as ways of adding explanatory variables to explain the course of everyday phenomena. In the milieux of everyday experience, there is strong evidence for the utility of four dimensions, three spatial, one temporal. Although they are not usually felt, extra infinitesimally small, finite dimensions can usefully explain anomalies and deviations from the norm in particular circumstances. Topologically, it is as if they were like the loops that make the plushness of a terry cloth towel or a thick carpet. These are non-differentiable manifolds without metrics or scales. They could be understood as a lower-dimensional sub-space of a higher-dimensional space. At greater scales, the carpet covers the floor as a plane. At more detailed scale, the loops become significant. The higher dimensional manifold flattens out the sub-space, as if it were the surface of skin of a body without any attention paid to its depths or interior (cf. Randall, 2001; Randall and Sundrum, 1999).

By 2002, topological analysis could lucidly resolve complex representations such as those of quantum mechanics that challenge dominant spatialisations. Similar to the above example of the terry cloth towel, differential geometry models space not as one manifold but as a hierarchy of manifolds and metrics (Perelman, 2002) that are related at some scales but dissociated at others. That is, that while manifolds can appear to be smoothly and unremarkably curved for most purposes, they may at a greater degree of resolution involve singularities that disturb the regularity of the manifold. Imagine a surface that appears to be smooth but under magnification reveals many spikes, or many loops. Imagine at each spike that the timespace bifurcates or loops from one manifold into another (the sub-space) and back. Many are familiar with a particular case of geometrical singularity: catastrophe theory (Thom, 1975). This models sudden changes at 'bifurcation points' in the equilibrium of systems. They are projected into visualisations as spikes in a field of contours or in some cases folds and involutions. These are graphical visualisations of models that respond to practical questions, such as what will trigger the unpredictable timing and size of a landslide? While geographers of globalisation have questioned the necessity of thinking according to scale that disconnected the local and global scale (Jones et al., 2007; Woodward et al., 2010), mathematically, if space-time assumes different manifolds at different scales this allows an affinity between higher-dimensioned spaces and everyday three-dimensional milieux. Topologically, there is no interdiction. We can imagine the local as a subspace of the global. We can unpack a space at any scale to reveal internal sub-spaces that are subtended at any one point (on scale, see below).

This is an opportunity to extend and spatialise the hermeneutical tradition in critical theory, which has long worked with the contrast of surface appearance and deep structural forces. Rather than separating surface and depth where one discounts one level for a 'deeper', determining level, the texture of looped sub-spaces – the knots of the carpet – suggest multiple causal scales and always relativise the taken-for-granted power of forces at any given scale. For example, the common experience of duration stretching out like eddies in the flow of time can be mapped as extra temporal dimensions. Lower dimensional temporalities may be insignificant under most conditions but become the site of emergent psycho-political change. A prototype for this approach might also be found in the anthropology and psychology of time (respectively e.g. Lomnitz, 2001 and Csikszentmihalyi, 1990). It allows new practices of 'thick description' (Geertz, 1973; Ryle, 1968) that may also problematise the tendency for critique to focus on a retrospective present rather than the structuring of orientations to the future. It reminds us to relate, trace and contest the relationships between these multiple dimensions and to wonder at the priorities given to only certain of the time-space relations that make up the 'plushness' of the real.

Proceeding chronologically, this chapter has presented the historical development from Euclidean geometry to non-Euclidean topology; from spatial objects in up to three dimensions to time-space manifolds with minor dimensions; from static objects to dynamically changing relationships. Possessing the rigour of a clear terminology that conforms to both mathematical theory and GIS programming practices, we can turn to the topologies that are implied within contemporary social sciences and cases where this 'new kind of analysis' is applied.

Notes

1   I am grateful for the feedback of members of the Space and Culture Research Group, most currently, Ondine Park, Jim Morrow, Andriko Lozowy, Barret Weber, Petra Hroch, and particularly Dr Merle Patchett for her insightful reading of this chapter. Versions of this chapter were previously presented at the American Association of Geographers conference in Seattle, March 2010 and a discussion of the bridges of Königsberg published in the *Theory Culture & Society* special issue on Topology, 2012.

2   See http://en.wikipedia.org/wiki/File:Mug_and_Torus_morph.gif

3 See Halsted (1900) for a discussion of the developments of this theory by Gauss (1777–1855), Lobachevsky (1792–1856), and others.

4 Camille Jordan's (1838–1922) 'Jordan curve' theorem states that any closed path – i.e. a line that joins up with itself in a loop, however complex – divides a plane into an inside and outside area. Escher's use of complex Jordan curves allowed him to create impossible perspectives and objects derived from the möbius strip. An example is the familiar 'recycle' symbol created by Oscar Reutersvärd (1915–2002). The Jordan curve describes the creation of an inside and outside, as much a social as a mathematical phenomenon. It is thus fundamental to future methodologies for studying social divisions.

5 More technically, any compact three-manifold on which a closed loop can be shrunk to a point is homeomorphic to the three-sphere.

6

cultural topology

Despite the increasing number of texts that allude to a topographical character of their method, their theories or the entities they construct (power, the self and so on), they are not forthcoming on topology itself. Few introductions to topology exist outside of mathematical texts. Those in social sciences tend to take topology as a metaphor (see the critique of Inkpen et al., 2007) without mathematical roots – while describing it as a method. This has the effect of blurring not only the meaning of the term but also the work of disciplines and authors to whom it is applied. This trend can be observed in major interdisciplinary journals such as *Theory, Culture & Society*. For example, despite the topological aspects of his study of Foucault's late work, Collier applies topology as an epithet to describe systems or 'patterns of "correlation"' in a manner that is akin to a topological neighbourhood within a broader manifold he calls a 'problem space' (Collier, 2009: 180). He argues that the distinction between the micro and the macro (respectively, the body and population) has been glossed in the literature on governmentality (2009: 83; cf. Burchell et al., 1991). This emphasis on scales ignores the precise conformity to the terminology of mathematical topology that structures Deleuze's sensitive obituary to Foucault as a 'new cartographer' and Deleuze's discussion of Foucault's late work as a 'topology' and his methodology as a 'topography' (Deleuze, 1988b: 22–44). However, Collier makes a crucial observation: in Foucault's later work, 'what above all changes is ... the *system of correlation* between juridico-legal mechanisms, disciplinary mechanisms, and mechanisms of security' (Foucault, 2007: 8, emphasis added in Collier, 2009: 88).[1]

Diagrams

The relationality of multiple elements is properly topological. Both Foucault and Deleuze refer to a 'diagram': a matrix that is immanent to the entire social field, including the sense of time and space. For these and many other thinkers of French late modernity and postmodernity (one would include Maffesoli, Serres and Baudrillard) this is a logic, but not a transcendent abstraction such as a structure, or a determining ideology, or an economic 'base' which explains concrete reality or social interaction because it is 'above' or 'below' concrete reality. In place of reduction, they seek a logic that – like the mythical string payed-out by Theseus to find his way back in the Minotaur's labyrinth – traces the contours of a situation but remains within the tissue of the material world. C.S. Peirce is often cited as the seminal source in his observation that a diagram is a type of icon, for example a geometric drawing of a triangle is inseparable from an empirical triangle: 'we forget that abstractness in great measure, and *the diagram is for us the very thing*' (1885:181 italics added). Like a projection of a three-dimensional object onto a flat two-dimensional surface, there is an empirical transformation where it appears that the distinction between the original entity and its diagram is the abstraction, not the figure that has been produced on the page, 'there is a moment when we lose the consciousness that it is not the thing, the distinction of the real and copy disappears, and it is for the moment a pure dream, – not any particular existence, and yet not general' (Peirce 1885: 181). 120 years later, we are still explaining their power. Diagrams are immanent and are the consistent shape of forces rather than meta-level plans or blueprints (McCormack, 2005). Deleuze effectively 'diagrams' Foucault's work: he gives us a topological reading of Foucault's project.

> It would be feasible to say that capitalism and that form of sovereignty which is empire have a certain type of movement in common, that they develop and move across time and space in similar or even homologous ways, that they share in the same spatiotemporal categories, or – in short – that they conceptualize, structure, and measure time and space in the same ways. Aren't we dealing here with what Foucault would have called a diagram, that is, with an abstract mechanism and matrix that does not originate either in capitalism or in empire but that both nonetheless have in common? … an abstract principle whose myriad manifestations would include also the various and sundry apparatuses of real subsumption. (Casarino and Negri, 2008: 72)

According to Deleuze's topology, the diagram, like a plan, is a 'plane of consistency' or of immanence (rather than a 'plane of expression'), presenting the 'distribution of the power to affect and the power to be affected' (Deleuze, 1986: 73). A 'diagram is a map, or rather several superimposed maps' (Deleuze, 1988b: 44). In the language of mathematical topology it is a projection (see Chapter 6) of 'relations between forces, a map of destiny, or intensity' (Deleuze, 1988b: 36); 'the diagram, in so far as it exposes a set of relations between forces, is not a place but rather "a non-place": it is the place only of mutation' (Deleuze, 1988b: 85). The visual imagery that Deleuze uses to conjure the diagram as a plane of consistency in which the usual analytical and causal distinctions are collapsed is also a spatial language of maps and patterns which change over time, of forms and shapes, as if they were projected on screens, like shadow puppets (Rajchman, 1999). In Deleuze's language, it is abstract, but in the more Proustean terms of this book it also has *virtual* qualities – both real and ideal, rather than merely a question of the ideal and possible, as the abstract would designate (see the critique in Shields, 2003), the virtual is an image. The diagram's ideal quality indicates that it precedes the distinction between form and substance, discursive and non-discursive, expression and content (Deleuze, 1988b: 34). It is its virtuality that allows the diagram to act as a 'non-unifying immanent cause that is coextensive with the whole social field: like the cause of the concrete assemblages that execute its relations; and these relations between forces take place "not above" but within the very tissue of the assemblages they produce' (Deleuze, 1988b: 37). It becomes the map that precedes the territory (cf. Baudrillard, 1990: online); a schema like Beck's representation of the London Underground, that begins to determine life above ground based on the perceptions of distance, accessibility and centrality of various stations that it suggests to travellers.

Foucault refers to this diagrammatic evolution of forces as being interconnected with the 'articulable'. At the same time, the diagrammatic is paralleled by the archive, a 'history of forms' or what Deleuze refers to as institutions. These are 'allied with the "visible" (and material?) by Foucault in his texts ... Change is emergent from gaps, "non-places"', or blind-spots, to recall Lefebvre. These lie 'between the visible and the articulable ... where the informal diagram ... becomes embodied instead in two different directions that are necessarily divergent and irreducible' (Deleuze, 1988b: 38). Thus diagrams contrast with the archival as generative, abstract institutions that materialise and thereby reproduce culture.

> Thinking does not depend on a beautiful interiority that would reunite the visible and the articulable elements, but is carried under the intrusion of an outside that eats into the interval and forces or dismembers the internal (Deleuze, 1986: 87) ... it is impossible to tell parasite from host. This is apparent in his description of the madman on the sea, who is 'placed on the inside of the outside, or vice versa' (Deleuze, 1986: 11).
>
> His boat sails the twist on the Möbius sea ...
> ... a shift from a mutual exclusion, whose two sides are nontraversable, to a topological form where one side glides seamlessly into its other. (Hlibchuk, 2010, citing Blaser, 2006: 127, commenting on Spicer, 2008)

Foucault's most famous diagram was Bentham's Panopticon, a 'diagram of power' (Deleuze, 1988b). While Jeremy Bentham exhibited an architectural model for many years on his dining room table as a model of prison reform, this is argued by Foucault to be not just a model of prison surveillance but a mechanism of open sight lines that induced a state of self-conscious visibility. It assured order by making individuals police their own behaviour, regardless of who they are. If the Panopticon was originally an architectural model, and was subsequently built as prisons, it is diagrammatically a political technology that almost automatically induces a tendency to homogeneous orderly behaviour from a very heterogeneous group:

> It is a type of location of bodies in space, of distribution of individuals in relation to one another, of hierarchical organisation, of disposition of centres and channels of power, of definition of the instruments and modes of intervention of power, which can be implemented in Hospitals, workshops, schools, prisons. (Foucault, 1979: 205)

The Panopticon, as a diagram of disciplinary societies, is an analogue of the calculating, self-consciously value-maximising, subject and the qualitatively managed manifold of modern societies under capitalism and colonialism. These time-spaces of enclosure share spatio-temporal categories to conceptualise, structure, measure and project space and time. Recall that Lefebvre characterised this as an Abstract Space that both surveys and divides land into properties and estates and also analyses space as an abstract Cartesian grid divorced from its contexts. For example, Abstract Space puts objects in a conceptual space of latitude and longitude, survey grids and lot lines, private property and territorial nation states, while events are placed in an equally abstract, developmental temporality of continuous progress. Lefebvre describes Abstract Space as an inherent, accompanying refrain to capitalist modernity from its origins. It does not originate in either capitalism or colonialism but they nonetheless manifest it in common (Casarino, 2003: 72; see pp. 74–5, 176) and produced it as they expanded. When we speak of Abstract Space we are also referring to a diagram that emerges through an immanent critique of capitalist modernity and where the temporal dimension is strategically frozen into a singular period.

At the same time, it is worth recalling that the line connecting points or running from origin to terminus is a key element of the history of Abstract Space (Ingold, 2009). It appears not only as sight-lines but boundaries and edges. The line is a fundamental motif of the clarity of the diagram in that diagrams present a Euclidean order of lines arranged according to Euclidean logics of parallels, right angles and ordered intersections. For example, the Cartesian grid diagrams four-dimensional space-time as the frozen and infinite two dimensions of the x and y axis. *Extensio* is a net of parallel lines at right angles. Topologies transcend the restricted space of the diagram as well as the classical logic that traces relations and causalities as unilinear and unidirectional from one point to another. For example, knots trouble the assumptions of diagrammatic reason with lines in which the relation between their ends – origin and destination or any *a* and *b* – is overshadowed by the complexity and chaos of the relation in-between. Knots violate the very ethos of the diagram, suggesting that they can only be traced or disentangled by lifting them off the two-dimensional surface or the line be fished out of the diagram entirely. In so doing, knots demonstrate the importance of topological tools in the face of entanglements that are the stuff of social and economic life.

Deleuze Folding Foucault

Deleuze casts Foucault's genealogy as a 'theoretical topology', an *analysis situs* of the virtual, of the multiplicity of forces and potentialities immanent to an evolving situation rather than a mapping of external forces determining causal outcomes to the interaction of isolated, monadic objects. Here the entire context, the whole map, is significant. What are we to make of the diagram as a virtual mapping of 'immanent cause'? In his reading of Foucault, the virtual is expressed in material actualisation as an 'order of things' and as a realisation of an 'order of forms' (see Deleuze, 1988b: 37). Foucault's reading represents a shift away from the classical models of Marxist and Weberian sociological determination and causality. The diagram seems to limit the texture of historical and archival detail that one experiences in Foucault's work. Deleuze, however, is pointing to Foucault's distinctive praxis of focusing on moments of mismatch between the ideals and the actuality of the time. This often shows up as a characteristic relationship between the discursive and the material. This 'crack' in all things is not just 'how the light gets in' – as Leonard Cohen put it in his song 'Anthem' (Cohen, 1992) – but a constitutive feature of cultural formations where there is opportunity for creatively recasting the diagram and its expressions (Deleuze, 1988b: 46). Such gaps are not a failure of the diagram but a constitutive lacuna which unsettles social arrangements.

Perhaps the most enduring topological move that Deleuze makes with Foucault's oeuvre is his characterisation of Foucault's method as 'folding'. Indeed, Deleuze does not emphasise topology in his writing, but relies instead on the image of primary topological transformations of lines and surfaces as folding. 'Fold' allows what is distant across a surface to come into contact or distorts a straight line as it crosses a cusp (see Chapter 5). The fold is of course an illegitimate operation in a diagram as it turns a surface into the format of a 'pop-up book'. The intention is to disturb, to intervene, in the relationships depicted by the lines between any *a* and any *b* in the diagrams of surveillant modernity.

For example, a fold could be a temporal reflection back on an earlier time or works (Deleuze 1986: 31) such that a subject or entity comes into a new relation to themselves. That is, 'Subjectivation is created by folding' the material body, folding force back on itself as strategy creating an ethical relation with power, knowledge of identity creating truth, and ultimately

folding the outside itself by which the subject 'hopes for immortality, eter-
nity, salvation, freedom or death or detachment' (1986: 104). A fold could
be a doubling to form a pocket, as in the folds of drapery, that produces an
invaginated space that brings part of the outside within the fold of cloth
(1986: 96, 98, 110–11). The outside is gathered as an interior. 'Fold' dramatically changes a surface, introducing the quality of eventfulness into an
otherwise uniform field:

> ... any organisation (differentiation and integration) presupposed the pri-
> mary topological structure of an absolute outside and inside that encour-
> ages relative intermediary exteriorities and interiorities: every inside-space
> is topologically in contact with the outside-space, independent of distance
> and on the limits of a 'living'; and this carnal or vital topology, far from
> showing up in space, frees a sense of time that fits the past into the inside,
> brings about the future in the outside, and brings the two into confronta-
> tion at the limit of the living present ... between them there is a topologi-
> cal relation: the relation to oneself is homologous to the relation with the
> outside and the two are in contact ... (Deleuze, 1986: 118–19)

Using this topological operation, Deleuze imagines a matrix in which 'three
dimensions – knowledge, power and self – are irreducible, yet constantly
imply one another' (1986: 114). Each is a fold, with a doubled or inside-
outside quality: knowledge as articulable-visible. This allows Deleuze to
describe not just objects of research, or research problems, but Foucault's
topology as an overarching problem-space:

> *the way in which the problem appears* in a particular historical forma-
> tion: what can I know or see and articulate in such and such a condition
> for light and language? What can I do, what power can I claim and
> what resistances may I counter? What can I be, with what folds can I
> surround myself or how can I produce myself as a subject?

> To think is to fold, to double the outside with a coextensive inside. The
> general topology of thought, which had already begun 'in the neigh-
> bourhood' of the particular features, now ends up in the folding of the
> outside into the inside: 'in the interior of the exterior and inversely', as
> *Madness and Civilisation* put it. (Deleuze, 1986: 114, emphasis added)

Folding is also reversible. It produces an entanglement or what appears to be
a knot in Deleuze's re-telling of Foucault:

> intertwining of the visible and the articulable ... multiplied in both
> directions. ... It is still not the fold of Being, but rather the interlacing of
> its two forms. It is still not a topology of the fold, but rather a strategy
> of the interlacing ... double capture, the noise of words that conquered

the visible, the fury of things that conquered the articulable ... a hallu-
cinatory theme of Doubles and doubling that transforms any ontology.
(1986: 112)

'Unfolding' is the uncoiling of virtual capacities and latencies, actualised
in events. Unlike the production of an archive and forms of accumulated
knowledge,

> [p]ower ... is diagrammatic: it mobilizes non-stratified matter and func-
> tions, and unfolds with a very flexible segmentarity. In fact, it passes
> not so much through forms as through particular *points* which on each
> occasion mark the application of a force, the action or reaction of a
> force in relation to others, that is to say an affect like 'a state of power
> that is always local and unstable'. This leads to a fourth definition of
> the diagram: it is a transmission or distribution of particular features.
> (Deleuze, 1986: 73)

Like all topologies, the diagram concerns time as much as space. It is a set of
principles that are architectural and optical but that construct and charac-
terise an epoch and its sense of time and distinction in terms of ideal forms.
Foucault exposes the diagrams of the past while Deleuze looks towards
future 'societies of control'. The whole conception is embedded within a
comparative analysis of power in different historical periods and the transi-
tions between them.

However, there is also an option that brackets the tendency to dichot-
omise and periodise diagrams. While genealogy displaces the historical
search for transcendental foundations, it nonetheless still tends to ground
truth within an overarching temporal discourse of epochs and a sensibility
which is fundamentally historicising in its focus on transition and succession
of periods. A more topological approach takes up the radical contribution
of the diagram that lies in its spatiality to focus on continuous change over
successions of states. It emphasises contextual fields over monadic, detached
bodies and other entities. Instead these are actualisations in given events.
It problematises the entities that are the very focal points of genealogical
analysis while pursuing the ambition of tracing an immanent logic which
gives rise to situations and configurations of the social. We find intimations
of this conception in the work of Whitehead, who argues, 'Thus every occa-
sion is a momentary experience which "implicates" the whole structure as
a nexus or a "society" of actual occasions' (cf. Bohm, 1980; Stenner, 2008:
8–9; Toscano, 2008; Whitehead, 1922: 26):

> The fundamental concepts are activity and process. There are essentially
> no self-contained activities within limited regions. These passive geomet-
> rical relationships between substrata passively occupying regions have

passed out of the picture. Nature is a theatre for the interrelations of activities. All things change, the activities and their interrelations. To this new concept, the notion of space with its passive, systematic, geometric relationship is entirely inappropriate. It has thus swept away space and matter, and has substituted the study of the internal relations within a complex state of activity. (Whitehead, 1934: 36)

Heterotopias of Scale

'We simple blind people, simplistic, short-sighted, have not imagined implication, inclusion, fold; we have never known what a tissue is, never noticed or listened to women, never known what a melange might be, and never understood, or even imagined, time' (Serres, 1991: 82). The diagram of the present is elusive. The great strength of the diagram is its reduction to nodes and lines. What if one had to model the complexity of a foldable diagram where a fixed plot was less significant than the attenuation or contraction of points brought about by the fold or a mirror image that produces a virtual double such as one finds in web spaces? Building on Foucault, Landzelius suggests that we understand the difficulty of understanding the interwoven global, national and local scales of contemporary life and economic processes as a kind of 'global heterotopia':[2]

> The 'single real space' of Foucault's ... should be thought in relation to the scaling debate ... and generalized as a term referring to an overarching (global) scale. In that sense, we presently find ourselves living in a globally constituted (dystopic?) heterotopia of capitalism: a global space juxtaposing several spaces that are in themselves incompatible. (Landzelius, 2009: 63; see Foucault, 1986: 24)

In this topological confusion that is spatial and temporal, we are unable to depend on the 'memory-complex of traditional time and practice that constitutes the episteme' (Landzelius, 2009: 60) that we have inherited as Modernity, leading to what Lyotard referred to as a temporal condition affecting judgement (Lyotard, 1980), and Jameson later referred to as a postmodern spatial affect, disrupting our ability to cognitively 'map' the scales and relations of contemporary life (Jameson, 1984), in turn contributing to a malaise of affect and politics. In a similar vein, when Serres argues that the local is folded over into the global, much as dough is folded in kneading, the result is that:

> The route from local time to global time, from the instant to time, from the present to history, is unforeseeable; it is not integrable by reason, as analysis has shaped it. It seems to go crazily, no matter where, and

drunkenly, no matter how. If the baker knew how to write, she would lazily follow the fly's flight, the capricious foldings of proteins, the coast-line of Brittany or of Ile d'Ouessant, the fluctuating fringe of a mass of clouds. (Serres, 1991: 82)

Knowing position and path is not a question of analysis, 'separating of things one from another (for topological transformation disallows cutting)' (Connor, 2008: online). Instead it is a form of 'knowledge that multiplies gestures in a short time, in a limited space, so that it renders information more and more dense' (Serres, 1991: 78).

Massey has called these social spatialisations 'power geometries' (Massey, 1999). Power geometries are located, not stretched, and refer to capabilities as potentials. Massey is more obviously topological when she considers the remoulding of the Earth by tectonic forces and the rapid transformation of the relationships between distant places entailed by globalisation as a virtual 'shrinking' of the world achieved through closer ties and communications (cf. Shields, 2003, 2006b). Other examples could include Giddens' time-space dis-tanciation as the stretching out of social relations, or Harvey's time-space com-pression as a metaphor for theorising globalisation, or Virilio's emphasis on acceleration and the speed of travel and communications as having the effect of 'shrinking' our world (Virilio, 1986). How is it that these transformations in not only our understanding but our practices in space seem so commonplace? The implications of these theories have not been systematically understood thereby cutting short critique. Virilio goes on to assert 'The reduction of dis-tances has become a strategic reality bearing incalculable economic and politi-cal consequences, since it corresponds to the negation of space' (Virilio, 1986: 133). However, it is not a matter of negation of space but a change to conven-tional understandings and practices of space, a topological shift which involves time and space: a new cultural topology. These are questions of not just a single era's experience but of cultural topology in general which asks further – how is it that such global connectivity is mapped onto a local neighbourhood in which Euclidean and Cartesian rules of engagement and embodiment apply? More than a changing spatialisation, this appears as a multilayered 'hetero-topology' with different spatialisations applied at different scales. Malpas notes that phenomenologically,

We still await an adequate way of conceiving of time and space (whether or not such a conception can be achieved), being always pulled in the direction of a privileging of one over the other, of forgetting the way in which each always implies the other, even when we try to disentangle them. This is especially so in the context of contemporary thinking. The movement of modernity has thus been one that seeks to pull time and space apart, and to do so as it also tries to collapse both into a single homogenous measurability – a collapse that often appears as a collapse of time into space. As a result, the relation of time to space, and the relation of both to place, is made even more obscure, and yet the clarification of this relation becomes even more urgent. (Malpas, 2011: 308)

What in the topology of the late twentieth century makes the diagrammatic inaccessible and entangles the local and global scales in new knots?

Scale and Topology

In geography, scale has been debated as no longer useful. Brenner has argued that 'scales evolve relationally within tangled hierarchies and dispersed inter-scalar networks', contrasting the vertical of globalisation against the horizontal of everyday life and social process (Brenner, 2001). 'What is ignored in these associations is the everydayness of even the most [global and] privileged social actors who, though favourably anointed by class, race and gender, and while typically more efficacious in spatial *reach*, are no less situated than the workers they seek to command ... ' (Marston et al., 2005: 421). The problem is that scale is assumed in geography:

> In spite of Smith, Swyngedouw and Brenner, most empirical work is lashed to a relatively small number of levels – body, neighbourhood, urban, regional, national and global. Once these layers are presupposed, it is difficult not to think in terms of social relations and institutional arrangements that somehow fit their contours. (Marston et al., 2005: 422)

In a critical assessment of scale and the tendency to pit the local against the global in a reductive dualism, Marston, Jones and Woodward summarise approaches to scale under three general headings:

> [T]here are three choices we have for thinking about scale. We can, first, affirm hierarchical scale and, to the extent that it fails to capture the myriad socio-territorial configurations we encounter, augment it with some other concept(s); second, we can develop, as others have attempted to do, hybrid models that integrate vertical and horizontal understandings of socio-spatial processes; and third, we can abandon hierarchical scale in its entirety and put in its place some alternative. (Marston et al., 2005: 419–20)

The problem is that phenomena are preferentially selected for study based on a reification. A specific scale or range, such as the urban for example, is privileged despite the actual variability of the size of cities. However, notions such as place, region or city challenge standard forms of philosophical analysis, 'often seeming to dissipate like smoke at the first breath of inquiry, leaving us to turn to what may appear to be the more substantial and substantive notions of space and time' (Malpas, 2006: 295). Yet place is both experientially and logically grounded as a bounded area in which things, bodies and most importantly, qualities, may be *gathered* and are together. It is possible to experience oneself and a social group as en-placed, and as drawing on this assemblage in a place, and the processes of mutual co-evolution. This may be in close proximity, or place may be topologically stretched into region, expanding the assemblage. That is to say, that one can meaningfully and sensibly understand oneself to be 'in' a place as well as 'of' a place, and to understand events and change as 'taking place'. The construction of place is always a bounding and assembling that, like addition, is *an operation rather than a fact.*

Should bounding and relative location be privileged over scale? It is worth recalling that the notion of place or bounded region as a site of gathering opens on to the great philosophical themes of Being, emergence, history and things. Place is more than a simple concept with a clear denotation. Malpas explores this for Heidegger's work as a '*Topologie des Seyns*' (*Logos*, being (*Sein*). Malpas (2006) notes that place is figured as 'gathering' as far back as Heraclitus (λόγος – *logos*) and Aristotle (where it is read in terms of substance (Maley, 2008: 32)). Today λόγος continues to designate ratio, reason, a logic or cause, as well as speech or speaking. As Maley notes, in the Gospel of St. John gathering/saying, as it were, grounds metaphysical origins: 'In the Beginning was the Word (λόγος) and the Word (λόγος) was God'.

Topology formalises a methodological injunction not to become trapped by scale as boundedness. Against artificial Cartesian and Euclidean distinctions made between nested levels of the urban, nation state and global (Taylor, 1982), it offers the image of multiply-scaled spaces that are simultaneously pertinent to a situation, and which are tied together at significant bifurcation points. It casts the 'national', 'global' and 'local' as interacting and 'made through one another' (Gilmore, 2000, cited in Barad, 2001: 93). It avoids reifying scale as a fixed, reified thing against which to rank the size of other things (Landzelius, 2009), but it also avoids reducing scale to a fiction, to a folk-narrative or as simply a frame or platform (Smith, 2000) for framing other narratives and restricting what enters into relevance (see Herod, 2011 for a review). This allows multiplicity to enter into the heart of geography (cf. Lury, 2009).

If scale is not a material thing, neither is it merely an abstraction. For example, it is neither just 'a representational trope, a way of framing political spatiality that in turn has material effects' (Jones, 1998: 27), nor an abstract system of legal or organisational categories that may be taken as 'conceptual givens' (Howitt, 1993: 37). Groping towards a 'flat ontology', others believe that 'to deconstruct or otherwise analyse its deployments' (Marston et al., 2005: 421) will yield only concrete materialities, outcomes from which scale only serves to abstract and obfuscate.

However, the debate on scale is not over. Nanoscience reminds us that scale is a real property of actual processes. For example, the properties of any chemical element change as one breaks it down to the size of nano particles (10^{-9} and smaller). Melting points fall dramatically and materials become highly soluble. Because the same amount of a material ground into tiny, nano-particles has a greater surface area, it is more reactive, and everyone knows that ground coffee dissolves better than whole coffee beans, as an everyday example of solubility. While scale is the quality of larger compared with smaller, it is clearly a real relation. My argument is that topologically, all scales matter. We need a more fine-grained analysis, not a gross simplification.

It is a virtuality untheorised as such within geographical theory but well understood in the practical judgements of everyday life. That is, it is a relation of similarity or difference between entities or processes, some of which may be 'off-stage' in the analysis, such as in the concept of the global where there is clearly a reference to the planetary. Reduced to an abstract concept, scale becomes a category or identity rather than a quality or relation. It shifts from a virtuality, 'as if' or 'in contrast' to some other entity, into an idea, a pure possibility, an idea such as the planetary, or the global city, instantiated in a process or thing. As a set of differentials, the virtual is not about reproducing an essence or identity but is a medium of potentiality, of multiple forces and relations that are actualised or extended as the unfolding of time-space. What is significant about scale is that it both indexes and forms entities' capacity to enter into differential relationships relative to the scale of the other entities involved. Scale is about both thing and relation, *eidos* and *ethos* and thus about space, *topos* (to use the terms of Castoriadis' (1987) discussion of Plato in Chapter 4 above).

Topology, as the study of surfaces as well as spaces, speaks to attempts to flatten the ontologies and epistemologies of geography. In stressing the ongoing process of self-variation of curvature, it models complex relations and surfaces that generate singularities and regularity. It considers blockages and flows, patterns and homogenous planes. Against simply classifying objects and processes and filing them at different reified scales, topology offers a differential analysis of composition and the generation of typicality, but equally of decomposition, invention and change. These are localized, emergent processes and patternings that are contextualized in relation to a whole, not to a higher order, determining scale driving local events. Rooting analysis in a manifold that is simultaneously localised, or in multiple manifolds that bifurcate around a singular and located time-space event, allows agency and the subject to return to the scene of geography:

> Sites thus require a rigorous particularism with regard to how they assemble precisely because a given site is always an emergent property of its interacting human and non-human inhabitants. Seen as a manifold (DeLanda 2002) that does not precede the interactive processes that assemble it,

discussion of the site's composition requires a processual thought aimed at the related effects and affects of its n-connections ... we describe ... instances of articulation as material actualisations of potentialities that, given other combinations of potential and actual relations, would resolve themselves differently. (Marston et al., 2005: 425)

Topology's thick description of the local in the form of an over-dimensioned gaze embraces the active individual and their affects as part and parcel of the scene, contextualised and located in the emergent actualisation of a scene but not confined within it. Barad notes, 'Agency – rather than being thought in opposition to structures as forms of subjective intentionality and the potential for individual action – is about changing topologies, about reconfiguring the structural relations of power, about the possibilities and accountability entailed in reconfiguring material-discursive apparatuses' (2001: 80–1, and see 86–7), such as those partially diagrammed by Michel Foucault spatially as the Panopticon (although much less materially as an actual prison) or by Judith Butler discursively and temporally as the performative body (although much less spatially as an active agent).

This is distinct from celebrations of place, from global cosmopolitanism or from the fetishism of protected natural environments as the flip side to willful ignorance of global biosphere decline.

[T]he history of being is a history of place that is itself contained within, and unfolds from, the places in which we find ourselves. In this respect, the dominance of the technological – which consists not in the prevalence of technological devices, but rather in the holding sway of the system of ordering with which they are associated (more specifically, the globalized system of technological-bureaucratic economism) – occurs through certain specific transformations of place. Technological modernity gives priority to certain modes of place as it also covers over both the topological character of its own functioning, as well as the topological character of being as such. The tensions and obscurities that characterize modernity's appropriation of the concepts of time and space can be viewed as themselves reflections of the topological working out of modernity's own tensions and contradictions – tensions and contradictions that modernity cannot itself recognize or admit. Thus in the globalized world in which we live – a globalization that is itself invoked problematically by talk of 'our time' as a time that encompasses the entirety of the world – globalization appears only in and through the countless places by which the world is constituted, and yet it is those same places that it also seeks to efface. (Malpas, 2011: 309)

Scale suffers from what Serres calls sack or case logic (*valise*) – the rigid categorisation and ranking of nested boxes by volume. Against this he proposes an equally logical and rigorous but more flexible 'sack logic' in which under certain conditions larger sacks may be crumbled down within smaller sacks or smaller sacks inflated to include larger sacks. This cascading approach allows one to work with the global within the local or vice versa, responding to Malpas' call above and the geographical critiques of scale with a *new scalar logic of inclusions that is consistent, remains scalar but is more flexible* and which draws together different topologies and topological forms that may operate simultaneously within and around each other.

> The sack image allows for the existence of multiple scales and disparate and/or contradictory details [and] ... eliminates the mental picture of smaller 'fissures' undermining a larger narrative. ... The Grand Narrative [e.g. globalisation] becomes a *topos* that will hold a variety of contents ... the spatial metaphor of sack logic thus modifies the understanding and relevance and value of the narrative materials represented in the rhetoric of history. (Demers, 2010: 503–4)

Topology and the Social – Networks, Surfaces and Milieux

A topology of experience may be strategically sketched as a diagram of what happened or what happens, but the contingencies of the embodied flow of experience, and its knotting of the past as 'experiences' and the present as experiencing, suggest more multidimensional models of happening than a two-dimensional diagram would conventionally capture. As Vannini illustrates, travel and other mobilities are more complex than a mere line between departure and destination (Vannini, 2011). That is to say, that mobilities not only indicate the contours and dimensions of a topology, but are traced on or in topological surfaces that delimit the degrees of freedom of any movement: 'In truth, to change the world, one must change space' was Lefebvre's 'strategic hypothesis' (1974: 220, my translation).

Topology can shed new light onto familiar social science objects of research by mapping out how such objects change and how they relate, in this process, to other changing objects in multiple, relational spaces. Topology sets aside the privilege granted to Euclidean space in lay understandings of the social to problematise the spatio-temporal ironies and anomalies we do recognise in everyday life. That is, topology allows us to systematically adopt a critical stance to how notions such as a 'shrinking' or more closely tied world is represented and understood under conditions of neo-liberal globalisation. For example, how is it that the rapid changes introduced in only half a century by technologies of mobile computing, communications and travel are construed as unremarkable entwinings of distant places into a new spatialisation of the world as distinct but normatively de-differentiated? Topology provides methodological and conceptually precise frameworks for conceiving not only of relationships or the structure of activities or tasks such as crossing bridges. Topology also allows one to rigorously approach situations where the order of things is deformed by any given force. That is, it provides the mental hand-holds for working with situations where relationships are changed, distanciated, collapsed or distorted, reshaping the 'diagram' one might draw of the situation. This diagram would be paradigmatic, more a matrix than a single master principle or law.

The French philosopher Michel Serres offers philosophical studies of different forms of inter-relation and interdependence of human with non-human actors and the constraints imposed by material objects and the environment (Latour, 1987; Law, 1994; Serres, 1980; Serres and Latour, 1995). Particularly in the geography literature, citations are to Law and Latour rather than the foundations of topological methodologies or more recent deployments of topology such as in Serres' work (Herod and Wright, 2002: 130). Topology also appears in discussions of processes of continuous change and flux. In a key intervention marking the turn to topology in social theory, Lury comments on Deleuze and Guattari's observation that,

> '[i]t was a decisive event when the mathematician Riemann uprooted the multiple from its predicate state and made it a noun, 'multiplicity'. It marked the end of dialectics and the beginning of a typology and topology of multiplicities' ... I want to explore the implications of the decisive event described here. I aim to do this, not by trying to explain the mathematics of multiplicity in its own terms, but by finding ways to talk about the mathematics of this decisive event that reveal its sociological significance for cultures of change. A first point relates to space, a second to number, and a third to problems, or rather the relations between problems and solutions. (Lury, 2009: online talk)

Although they focus on a single spatial system that allows sets of objects to maintain their configuration despite being moved, John Law and Annemarie Mol offer one introduction to topology as a way of considering different forms of relationality that extend beyond stable network models. This is a key aspect of actor-network theories of the entwining of human and non-human actors or 'quasi-actants'. Law and Mol advance a topological approach as a corrective to the static, geometrical tendencies in lay conceptions of networks:

> Topology is a branch of mathematics which imagines different kinds of space. In particular, it invents spaces by thinking up different rules for defining the circumstances in which shapes will change their form or not. It is possible to devise indefinitely many rules for shape invariance,

but in the case of the immutable mobile we are dealing with just two forms of spatiality: space as Euclidean; and space as a network. In Cartesian, geographical or Euclidean space (we'll talk of Euclidean space) shape invariance is defined and achieved by holding constant a set of relative three-dimensional co-ordinates. If this is achieved then the shape holds. (Law and Mol, 2000: online)

Classically, the sciences assumed a three-dimensional space based upon Descartes' ontological thesis that all matter can be understood in terms of its 'extensiveness' (*res extensa*). Objects are static, measurable in terms of properties or dimensions that do not change. The notion that they might be elastic or mutable, or that objects do change (for example as they mature, age or flexibly respond to the pressures on them) is 'flattened' into a simplified topology, 'as if' or virtually a static three-dimensionality. That is, the space-time of everyday life, objects and contexts is idealised, mixing our own abstracted and simplifying stories and a virtual space where potentiality is artificially limited to what we can see and touch. It is this cultural constructionism that binds space-time with cultural texts and rhetoric (Noy, 2008).

Law and Mol consider four analytical approaches based on different relationalities, or topological systems: network, Euclidean, fluid and fire topologies, drawn from the phenomenology of Gaston Bachelard (1964). Each casts a given object in a different light, revealing them as sustained in different ways. These four rubrics allow them to argue that the technical configuration of objects be transferable and still function in geographical, three-dimensional space. But objects may also change incrementally to respond to shifts in relations in which they are embedded, being maintained and updated. They are additionally set within simultaneous absence and presence of a range of other materials and flickering discontinuities with surrounding conditions.

Law and Mol give the example of the Portuguese wooden ships on which fifteenth-century imperialism depended. Such technological objects must move in geographical space but maintain their geometric arrangement in their own technical 'network-space'. As 'immutable mobiles' they have to 'hold their shape' despite being moved from context to context, they are objects that have two faces. Analytically, they are embedded in two sets of relations. One set is technical and concerns a set of components that must work together in a fixed arrangement within a context of other elements: 'a network-object also implies a stable shape within a network space. The two go together' (Law and Mol, 2000: online). This first configuration is a mobile assemblage, moving through a second set of relations that are primarily spatial in the analysis, not temporal. This is the three-dimensional Euclidean space of ocean navigation. 'The mobility of the Portuguese ships only exists in Euclidean Space. There they move through an orthogonal box defined by X-Y-Z co-ordinates – a box in which there is a long distance between Lisbon and Calicut' (Law and Mol, 2000: online).

We might observe that space enters into this analysis twice: as an abstract, relational network-space and as an actual Euclidean space. They call this a 'double game' of participation in two spaces that are elided in any focus on objects such as the ship itself: 'it is that immutability in network space which affords the immutability and the mobility in Euclidean space. To put it more strongly, it is the interference between the spatial systems that affords the vessel its special properties. We are in the presence of two topological systems, two ways of performing shape invariance ... ' (Law and Mol, 2000: online).

'Networks have become the *de facto* spatiality of social movements, figuring as a precondition and an infrastructure ... and as an epistemic space through which to theorize the contested politics of social movements' (McFarlane, 2009: 362). However, recently there has been a broad effort to explore Law and Mols' Bachelardian topologies as a way of getting past the network as the sole spatialisation of social movements to better acknowledge their materialism and historicity as well as their dynamism and the importance of key divides across networks. McFarlane observes that a shift in terminology from network to assemblage might 'give intelligibility to new spaces by territorializing and deterritorializing milieu ... [as] a process of emergence, process and stablisation [sic]' (McFarlane, 2009: 561, commenting on Sassen, 2006: 5). We can place McFarlane's discussion of 'assemblage-as-a-topology' as akin to a discussion of a neighbourhood or a manifold torqued by an intervening dimension.

Most importantly, the 'assemblage-topology' has weak boundaries between inside and outside in contrast to most network approaches: 'assemblage-topology' again appears to be a topological neighbourhood that emerges through incorporation of elements that might be thought of as external or exterior.

> [It] emphasizes three inter-related sets of processes. First, assemblage emphasizes *gathering*, coherence and dispersion ... spatiality and temporality ... groups, collectives and, by extension distributed agencies ... Second ... an uneven topography of trajectories that cross or engage each other to different extents over time and which themselves exceed the assemblage ... Third, in contrast to Foucauldian notions like apparatus, regime or governmental technology, assemblage connotes *emergence* ... (McFarlane, 2009: 562 emphasis added)

This is a striking restatement of the phenomenological terms in which place, gathering, emergence and co-causality have been tied to philosophical concerns with being and signs. In Malpas' terminology, place and topology are 'irridescent' changing their qualities in response to the perspective and practical engagement of the observer (2006, 2011).

McFarlane uses this relational approach to consider the composites emerging when specific local movements connect and exchange ideas and resources to create a new trans-local, more-than-present, topology that re-spatialises activity and place in a way that exceeds a simple sum of the initial ingredients or movements. This involves multiple social spatialisations differentiated by scale but nested, interacting and including different ways of representing the process, contrasting imaginaries and material practices. A topological approach may change how agency is understood to be attributed (Bennet, 2005: 461; McFarlane, 2009: 366).

These assemblages represent a deformation from a simple network approach, a change in the 'angle of vision' (Li, 2007: 265, cited in McFarlane, 2009: 562) and a stress on the materiality of networks, but not a break. The understanding of topology is still limited to relatively consistent neighbourhoods and the possibility of radical catastrophe points or of ruptures is elided in the discussion. As a result, McFarlane unnecessarily worries that decisive explanatory causes will be obscured in the modelling of overall co-causalities and mediating relations. A false opposition is set up, harking back to Lenin's opposition to non-Euclidean spatial potential. This is a general problem in the literature. Some worry about 'topological relativism' versus realism or materialism (Blok, 2010: 898; Woodward, et al., 2010: 273). In McFarlane's work, topology is correctly understood to be materialist ('that emphasizes distribution of agency'), but against 'a tendency to centre the human, or groups of humans, as the basis or arbiter of causation and responsibility' (2009: 566) (for reassurance against this worry see the precision of Brown and Middleton (2005) on the agency of newborns and medical decision-making and procedure).

Diken also observes that different topologies sustain and are performed by quite different objects and milieux. The ship, above, is an immutable mobile that allows a colonial trading network with its social and political relations to be extended globally and sustained through time. Places may be related together in a social spatialisation as a diagrammatic chart. This mobility or relationality of every place or node referencing or relating to other nodes contrasts with the 'architectural' and Euclidean immobility of fixed geometric figures. Fluids, or flows are topologies of mutable mobiles, 'in movement and under transformation simultaneously' (Diken, 2011: 96; Shields, 1997). This is the topology of virtualities that are always in process: like a circulating cultural form, individual examples are each unique instances or singularities that only actualise a tendency or latent capacity (cf. Gaonkar and Povinelli, 2003; Lee and LiPuma, 2002).

The fourth topology identified by Law and Mol, that of 'mutable immobility' in the sense that it does not allow topological shifts in position, but rather flickers, is the essence of fire as a form (Bachelard, 1964). Winking in and out of existence as a specified entity draws on the non-metric idea of concrete actualities in non-Euclidean topologies that may not only exist in time and three-dimensional space but may have degrees of freedom that are, in effect, virtual dimensions. To oscillate between the virtual and actual suggests entities or cases that are and then are not, only to return in a subtly different actualisation. This is the topology of a syncresis on the cusp of the virtual and actual (see Chapter 2), and of ambivalent, liminal objects that cross boundaries to become not themselves, but something else, or to become a quality rather than a quantity.

In the process, this type of topology blurs the lines between not only the virtual and actual but other categories. '[i]n the lack of a calculus ... it is impossible to draw an absolute line between productive and unproductive, creative and destructive ... an irrational, "impossible" element' (Diken, 2011: 100; see also Žižek, 1992: 44) or, for that matter, between consumption and production, human and animal, place and space. The effect is to disconnect or render nodes un-connectable monads because they are ambivalently defined in the topological space. They cannot be positioned in a network space, the preferred, genetic topology for immutable mobiles and generic Actor Network Theory. Identifiable singularities are unplaceable according to normal metrics and relations. The problem, however, is not one of the object, that is, the individuals or nodes in a would-be network. Instead, it is a feature of the topology itself that lacks the coordinate structure to fix and define such nodes. It may be one where all their dimensions are degrees of freedom not amenable to measure. This is indicative of the importance of topologies that include non-metric, non-differentiable spaces or manifolds.

For example, the differential relationship between centres and peripheries is a second geographical commonplace, so much so that one could speak of a liminal spatialisation of the periphery (e.g. historical seaside Brighton compared to London (Shields, 1993)). Anthropologists have long posited a spatial aspect to rites of passage where a liminal zone of initiation is counter-posed to the space of everyday as a threshold zone in which the rules of the usual social environment do not apply but are suspended. A topological operation permits a sense of being 'betwixt and between' formal statuses and of 'time out of time'. Young initiates are removed from the tribe to be instructed, then 'reborn' back into the social world of the tribe as adults. Bodies move across a boundary beyond identity to become malleable subjects with flickering identities. While initiation may involve operations such as incisions, tattooing, circumcision and changes in self-conception, bodies remain materially more or less intact. The most significant change in their reality, in their being, is virtual not concrete (i.e. real-ideal not real-actual): the passage from childhood to adult. This is accomplished relative to a topology that bifurcates across a fold between the liminal and the everyday with dramatically different time-space norms across the manifold: the liminal is not a 'separate space' or time, but rather different topological neighbourhoods spanned by culture and flickering bodies.

The topology of flickering underscores the destructive and sustaining power of topologies. Actual, culturally stabilised and reified objects cannot sustain the relations of this 'fire topology', which breaks the dimension of time into that of binary singularity: on/off; visible/invisible; present/absent; a material *fort/da*. Reciprocally, without sustaining concrete objects, this impossible topology models atemporality: catastrophes, moments of rupture, that are instants that break the flow of chronological time and negate *durée*. They indicate not only stopping, but are in fact the antithesis of any passing or progressive time that may be likened, after classical thinkers, to a revolutionary break in historical flow or to the time of the messianic (see Diken, 2011: 98). Instead, they are the slipping glance that catches events in a flash, a single suspended moment.

Relations and Boundary Objects

There is no neutral topography which predates its recognition and take-up in social spatialisations or other more complex, *non-geographical* topologies. An immutable mobile is an object set within a theoretical approach that casts it analytically in two spaces: a technological network space of relations between components which is overlaid or folded over a geographical Euclidean space. Our interest is in how this sort of intersection happens at geographical sites such as we saw in the case of Québec City. This will invariably complicate the fixed three-dimensionality of Law and Mols' geography. Simmel, in his attention to shifting relationships and to the reversibility of boundary-drawing behaviour and symbols into ways of connecting, exhibits an early topology attention to temporality, spatiality and form. In much the same way that Simmel's early twentieth-century analysis of the ways that our trust in money binds us to distant strangers through markets, Serres' late century analysis of relations and relatedness reveals that mobile, travelling or traded objects bind societies. Their in-betweenness may be compared to the movement of a soccer ball that focuses and ties together competitors.

Network analyses of objects in flux, or 'boundary objects' which are 'different things' to different groups of people because they are caught between networks are challenging. They are 'plastic' enough to continue to function or maintain their sense despite different needs and constraints of different parties and contexts. They are able to remain recognisable when moved from one environment, cultural world or spatialisation to another (Bowker and Star, 1999; Star and Greisemer, 1989). not everything need change as spatialisations change, and boundary objects may maintain a sense of continuity and cohesion across ruptures and conflicts within and between spatialisations. This may allow actual collaboration, in fact, despite disagreements over the nature of the task or representations which portray the process in opposed terms (Stark et al., 2006). These liminal objects thus have a communicative and social role (Kimble et al., 2010).

'Fluid objects' such as those which vary depending on how they are assembled or maintained do not fit easily. Other anomalous objects tend not to feature in actor network analysis: for example, a toy that is immediately taken apart by a child and then played with, producing a 'toy fit to play with' through a process of dismemberment and experimentation. Scenarios of incorrect usage or hybridity concern not only trivial objects. Relativistic scenarios and quantum scales on which nanotechnologies and consumer items, such as CDs and DVDs, depend are also short-changed if network analysis becomes static, which might not be a problem in historical cases set in Newtonian physics and Euclidean space. Gamow notes: 'Einstein was probably the first to realize the important fact that the basic notions and laws of nature, however well established, were valid only within the limits of observation and did not necessarily hold beyond them' (Gamow, 1966: 106).

Some networks, processes and things escape the static bias of many network approaches governed by a synchronic focus on stasis and the immutability of 'scientific facts'. This can result in skewing key metaphors, and, by extension, the tools of these approaches towards situations where *fixity is maintained despite fluidity*, rather than where change occurs through deformation. It is a matter of strategic choice and power dynamics: studies of fixed logic may be useful in some cases, but in other cases, only a topological grasp of changing and intersecting logics and diagrams can grasp the significance of changes in networks or of consistencies in objects, such as the *Shan Hai Jing*, which move across historical moments of cultural stability and shift as they go from one such logical neighbourhood to another. Consider the fundamental case of light, which is indeterminately a wave and a particle, depending on the choice of experimental apparatus. This is a case where the social science interest in immutability would fail to come to grips with uncertainty in results (Heisenberg's Uncertainty Principle) and with an equivocal object of study that appeared differently depending on one's perspective and approach (Bohr, 1987: 72).

Serres proposes one such boundary-object, the *actant*, a quasi-object/quasi-subject that links people together in a chain of exchanges or relations. For example, a chain letter or the 'hot potato' in a game, or the available chairs that are sat on in turn by competing participants in a game of musical chairs. The importance of these quasi-objects is to mediate relations in a dynamic manner so that what lies between the nodes in a system is volatile and 'the whole is held together by what agitates it or keeps pulling it apart and back together' (Connor, 2002: online).

This quasi-object that is a marker of the subject is an astonishing constructor of intersubjectivity. We know, through it, how and when we are subjects and when and how we are no longer subjects. 'We': what does that mean? We are precisely the fluctuating moving back and forth of 'I.'

The 'I' in the game is a token exchanged. And this passing, this network of passes, these vicariances of subjects, weave the collection ... The 'we' is made by the bursts and occultations of the 'I.' The 'we' is made by the passing of the 'I.' By exchanging the 'I.' And by substitution and vicariance of the 'I'. (Serres, 1982: 227)

Rebelo takes up what Mejías refers to as the 'paranodal', a treatment of the interstitiality of relations that invests importance in the topological space betwixt and between crystalised moments or individuals, blurring them into their processes of transformation and emergence (Mejías, 2007). There is a drama to be found in these weavings that goes beyond the embeddedness and specificity of the stable moments formed when we reify, label and 'fix' cultural products and their author-creators. This dramaturgy considers the creative relations between traditional actors. But again it is necessary to move beyond simply applying the term 'topology' to a network. What cultural topology adds is the step beyond understanding 'linkages' between particular nodes in a given network as active transformers and connectors to consider this as a property of the space itself, affecting multiple individual bodies, actors or objects in a manner that can be defined and analysed.

In the 'emerging topological conditions and sensibilities of the modern world', Serres suggests a new universal in which 'the milieu arises in every place' (Serres, 1994: 128). In everyday life, these are often indicated by those prepositions that signal relations and relative positions 'on', 'with', 'under', 'in', 'through', 'beside', 'beyond':

Has not philosophy restricted itself to exploring – inadequately – the 'on' with respect to transcendence, the 'under', with respect to substance and the subject and the 'in' with respect to the immanence of the world and the self? Does this not leave room for expansion, in following the 'with' of communication and contract, the 'across' of translation, the 'among' and 'between' of interferences, the 'through' of the channels through which Hermes and the Angels pass, the 'alongside' of the parasite, the 'beyond' of detachment ... all the spatio-temporal variations preposed by all the prepositions, declensions and inflections? (Serres, 1994: 83)

This entails an attention to inclusions, foldings and attenuation. This is done by transcending classical binary logic to fuzzy sets that describe the continuum of 'conditions between inclusion and exclusion, thesis and antithesis' (Demers, 2010: 502). For Serres, a *milieu* is a context that is also literally a 'mid-place', an interface or membrane between inside and outside. The quasi-object, the chain-letter passed from hand to hand that is the material media of the social and communicative chain in the previous chapter, can be understood as a milieu, as a topological surface or front-line between the players. As a relation, it is syncretic, sliding between material 'thing' and virtual being (a quasi, 'as-if' object), and brings its own features and effects to the situation. In more complex terms, this virtual-material 'milieu-surface' can be understood as a liminal model of intersubjectivity and collectivity as a form of 'betweenness' and relationality.

> A milieu means literally a mid-place, a place that is in the middle. But its more common use, in both French and English, is as a context, a frame, a set of framing circumstances (what circles the stance, what stands around where one stands). It is in *The Parasite*, which is what is perhaps his wildest, wiliest, most difficult, and therefore in a sense his latest book, that Serres discovers himself as a philosopher of the circumstantial. The book has as its generative centre the proposition that there is no message or communication possible without a context ... Something always happens in the space of traversal to slow, deflect or deform the message; there is always noise on the line, a spanner in the works. (Connor, 2002: online)

Others go further to deploy topology as an analytical modelling that avoids reified objects while accommodating our desire to think in snapshot form. Topology allows an approach to phenomena that dissolves them and traditional sets of causes into a fluid becoming of forces and capacities which may then be understood at a micro level of interactions between specific elements rather than always a set of forces leading to a totalised, fixed state, object, or dependent and reified variable. This topological force field may be examined for its neighbourhoods of relative predictability, and this slightly displaced, diagonal glance, may then be strategically resolved back into the companion objects of our conventional experience and discourse.

Manning proposes that we rethink 'self' as an emergent form or moment rather than object and understand it as an aspect of a topology. I understand this as Deleuze's diagram of subjectivity folding an exteriority into an interiority materially defined by strata of knowledge and power – subjectivity is both continuous and discrete, outside and inside, objective and subjective. This means that via agency, understood as interactive and processual, space, objects and the subject are actively reconfigured, topologically, through a continuous enfolding and unfolding. Notions of subject and object lose their independence, space is no longer a container but a medium, and time is performatively measured by folding rather than by a linear metric.

The sense of self is a topographical entity that might be defined as an artificial snapshot of the entire network: a state rather than a thing that emerges across the structured fluidity of relations between factors rather than through a simple or even multi-causality. Manning works from touch and self-consciousness to a self that is topologically reduced to a diagrammatic topography of a surface, like a parchment or skin.[3] Seeking to evade the everyday language of things, Manning argues that the self is a singularity co-constituted with a 'worlding that becomes them' (Manning, 2009: 41), that suits them, and allows – like Bohm's eddies and nodes in an otherwise fluid stream – 'landing sites' as the space-time conditions for the actualisation of self and as a momentary folding or intensification within a field that evokes the Pre-Platonic *clinamen*.

> Individuation happens at the surface not of the skin ... of a flat multiplicity ... an accumulation of proximities ... [defining] a zone of indiscernability proper to 'becoming' (Deleuze & Guattari, 1987: 488). When the skin becomes not a container but a multidimensioned topological surface that folds in, through and across ... what emerges is ... the dynamic form of a worlding... Beyond the human, beyond the sense of touch or vision, beyond the object, what emerges is relation. (Manning, 2009: 42)

Spatialising the 'becoming' of individuation suggests a complex topology of experience that Manning projects onto a rippling surface ('skin') that separates subject and object but also enfolds and bulges out to the 'outside'. There is a latent reference to Deleuze and Foucault whose topology of folding is restated. This attempts to rhetorically complicate the Enlightenment dualism between subjectivity and an objective world outside and beyond the individual. For example, Kirsten Jacobson describes the spatialisation of hypochrondiacs and agoraphobia-sufferers as 'a sense of spatial contraction that mirrors the contraction in their abilities to engage with the people, the environment, and the situations that surround them' (2004: 31). The presumed Euclidean space of everyday life shrinks in a type of pathological and dysfunctional topology. 'The person's space contracts around them, corresponding to the reduced range of her responsibilities and possibilities; she has shrunk the space in which she can dwell' (Jacobson, 2004: 41). Lazzarato points out that subjectivity can find itself simultaneously on the side of the subject and the object' (Lazzarato 2006), which confounds the separation of subject and environment.

Cultural Topology

In practice, the significance of topological approaches is to focus attention on all aspects of relationality, whether in space or in time. In particular, it advances the actor network analysis that Law and Mol describe around technological objects by adding further dimensions and by focusing not on equilibrium, but on the life of the constellation of relations. They focus on the geographical context (for example, the geographical 'dimension' in which the actor-network 'manifold' of the ship, above, is embedded) and the way in which this impinges on the object itself. It is also possible to focus on the temporal dimension of change to these networks, bringing a diachronic aspect to an otherwise synchronic, static network. Topological approaches can describe stressors to networks as the stretching and warping of their relations and the ways these format the space within which a network and its features is then seen to be embedded.

> Topology describes social and cultural flows, fluidities and circulations as transformation processes without the usual reliance on ideas of text or discourse. Thinking topologically can also, more radically, encourage an embodied and relational understanding of the movement and flow of change. To do this, an auditory topology is proposed. This defines space as the depths and textures of the performance sound. (Henriques, 2009: online)

This is to suggest that topology might offer more than a metaphor for any study of continuous change – whether mathematical, spatial, material or social. Embedded within the idea of the homeomorphism of types of objects – such as our example of spherical objects earlier – is the idea of a form of kinship between similar entities even as they change dynamically and in non-linear, apparently random ways:

> On the other hand, there are topological spaces other than differentiable manifolds. In fact, there are spaces that do not possess a natural metric, a notion of distance between their points, let alone a metric that permits differentiation. Which means that topology in its generality offers models of continuous change that lie outside the horizons of calculus, and, indeed outside schemes of measurement and hence outside anything geometrical. Such spaces might be suitable candidates for capturing the a-metric dynamics of cultural change. Certainly, differential equations, however successful they are in modelling purely physical change, have little to say about the shape of cultural change, except perhaps as a constraint on their physicality, on their purely material actualisations as states of affairs. And much the same goes for numerical equations: one doesn't, except within quantitative forms of sociology (statistics, sociometrics), use numerical distance or employ metrical concepts as the primary means of characterizing the dynamics of *cultural* phenomena. (Rotman, 2009: 12)

This means that rather than assuming that topological neighbourhoods might resemble city neighbourhoods we should use topology as a tool for reimagining how entities might be related and how that 'nearness' or a figuration of elements can be modelled so that it can be understood. Drawing inspiration from Lefebvre (1991b: 117–18; 202), Ingold underlines that there is a crucial distinction between topological lines of flow that must be understood as possible vectors of action or interaction, compared to simple connections between entities found in most actor-network theories (Ingold, 2009: 151):

> The *acteur réseau* was intended by its originators (if not by those who have been beguiled by its translation as network) to be comprised of just such lines of becom-ing. ... the line of the web does not link the spider to the fly, neither does the latter's line of flight link it to the spi-der. Ensconced at the centre of its web, the spider knows that a fly has landed somewhere on the outer margins, as it sends vibrations down the threads that are picked up by the spider's super-sensitive, spindly legs. And it can then run along the lines of the web to retrieve its prey. Thus the thread-lines of the web lay down the *conditions of possibility* for the spider to interact with the fly, but they are not themselves lines of inter-action. If these lines are relations, then they are relations not *between* but *along*. (Ingold, 2009: 152; see Lefebvre, 1991b: 117–18)

The web is a 'meshwork' a topology of possible interactions that entangles the spider with its environment (Lefebvre 1991b: 118):

> The production of space, firstly, that of the body itself, continues until the secretions have produced a 'habitation' which serves, at the same time as an instrument ... The spider marks out directions, orients itself after angles, establishing symmetries and dis-symmetries and by this practice extends itself in space. For the living body, the fundamental sites ... [the 'signature'] of space, are immediately qualified by the body. (Lefebvre, 1991b: 202)

Rather than allowing ourselves to be seduced by a metaphor of topology or phase spaces and vectors or lines of flight, Rotman argues that we need to escape from the stereotyped smooth curves of change found in calculus and the simple notions of time as a linear fourth dimension. Returning us to the diagram – but now in a manner that is fundamentally new – Rotman asks if there might be an advantage to thinking relationally and 'diagrammatically about the dynamics of cultural transformation? ... then one has an opening perhaps to a different temporality; a mode of think-ing the dynamics of cultural change ... articulated as a flow of arrows at different morphic levels, a scaled and diagrammatic production of time' (Rotman, 2009: 13).

The continuous transformations of topologies can be seen to be a func-tion that preserves a certain nearness between specific entities that may be loosely coupled but hold their relative positions despite being deformed. This might capture 'continuity relative to a particular cultural form' in a way that escapes the over-determining expectations of a calculus of culture of what Urry has called a 'new social physics' (Urry, 2004). This might then escape the risk of cultural topologies being reduced to one temporality of a smooth differential calculus. Instead, one might consider a scaled (thus spatial) and diagrammatic (thus topological) *production* of time. Topology might respond to different forms of place attachment which bind people together in a community but which are changing incommensurably – meaning that at any point in time community is a fluid outcome and may look abruptly different: 'Like Wittgenstein's notion of family resemblance. There is a sameness, a shape constancy, which does not depend on any particular defining feature or relationship, but rather on the existence of many instances which overlap with one another partially' (Law and Mol, 2000: online).

Allen and Cochrane propose a topological account of state power with the idea that rather than the assumption of a 'centre' of authority extending out to regions and down to more specialised or local domains, it is helpful to think of a collapsed geography in which the state 'reaches' into different domains in different ways,

> [drawing] attention to the spatial reconfiguration of the state's institutional hierarchies and the ways in which a more *transverse* set of political interactions holds that hierarchy in place, but not in ways conventionally understood through a topographical lens. In contrast to a vertical or horizontal imagery of the geography of state power, what states possess, we suggest, *is reach, not height*. Topological thinking suggests that the powers of the state are not so much 'above us' as more or less present through mediated and real-time connections, some direct, others more distanciated. Indeed, what is arguably novel about the state's spatiality in the current moment is its ability to exercise its *hierarchical powers* of *reach* in ways that reflect a topological appreciation of space and place. (Allen and Cochrane, 2010: 1072–3; see John, 2009)

Hierarchies are not spatial (whether vertical or flattened horizontal arrangements) but institutional, allowing the state a presence across urban and regional structures:

> The ability to draw political actors within close reach through the simultaneity and succession of institutional arrangements provides a context within which negotiations may be brokered directly, rather than from afar or across a spatial divide that places the 'centre' of political power above everyone else. Little really happens at-a-distance, on this view, because the authority at the centre has already made its presence felt in its dealings with regional and local bodies, public, private and third sector ...

... Some of this interplay takes place indirectly by authorities *reaching into* the politics of regions and localities in an attempt to steer and constrain agendas; some of it operates in a more direct fashion by *drawing within close reach* those that are able to broker and influence decisions; whilst other forms of mediated interaction *reach out* beyond the region or locality to shape events within. (Allen and Cochrane, 2010: 1074–5)

There are more questions and possibilities to this topology. Reach is one practice of power. How does the spatial interleave with the time of the State – of election cycles, parliamentary sittings, budget years, bureaucratic work-plans, policy events and news media deadlines – and the time of crises, of peoples' needs and events?

Giaccaria and Minca build on Agamben's discussion of Schmidt's contrast between the topological and topographical (inside/outside, far/near, and so on) in describing Nazi concentration camps such as Auschwitz as not 'outside' of the Nazi social system but imbricated within it as an internal 'threshold, or a zone of indifference, where inside and outside ... blur with each other' (Agamben, 2005: 23–4, cited in Giaccaria and Minca, 2011: 4). It is not a simple space of confinement but of indeterminacy that breaks the linkage between location and identity (Agamben, 1998: 19–20). In Chapter 2 we saw how Solzhenitzyn described the Soviet Gulag system in similarly evocative terms as an 'archipelago' within the doorsteps of everyday life (1977), suggestive of a topological rationality deployed in the service of power that analysts continue to struggle with in the case of the CIA's extraterritorial network of holding cells, 'black sites' and flights, and programme of 'extraordinary rendition' after 9/11. This 'topological' rationality informs but escapes the topography that spatialises a set of policies as an actual environment. An overlapping, communication or tension is set up that potentially destabilises the self-consistency of ordered space.

Topological possibilities span social and cultural issues. Nortje Marres (2012) understands public debate as a topological 'issue space' that recasts objects of concern as each actor redefines them in a different way and relates them to other concerns – the objects are pulled around an elastic space changing as they come under the influence of other objects, bodies and epistemologies. As the deformation of one thing into another, topology offers a form of 'empirical critique' that operates in the actually-real, rather than at the level of abstractions. Delanda considers the latent qualities of objects and issues as topological virtuality. The dimensions of a manifold are 'degrees of freedom' for events and objects that are represented in and by it. This includes their participation in not only larger sets or groups but their membership in a genus that cannot be reduced to its individuals, as methodological individualism does (DeLanda, 2006; Harman, 2008: 370). Suggestively for sociology, Delanda likens genus to ideal type as a structure of a virtual space of possibilities outside of the individual members. This is intended as 'not conceptual but causal, concerned with the discovery of the actual mechanisms operating at a given spatial scale. [Yet] the topological structure defining the diagram of an assemblage is not actual but virtual and mechanism-independent, capable of being realized in a variety of actual mechanisms...' (DeLanda, 2006: 21, cited in Harman, 2008: 375). In this analysis, the individual case seems to merely crystalise or actualise the virtual and be a pretext for examining the non-linear, generative topology as a structuring environment, a kind of *Umwelt*.

A Topology of Experience

I am advocating a topological sensibility against merely using topology as a physical geography reference, using it aphoristically, or as a metaphor. Topological approaches work to contextualise objects and states, including cultural objects. They set cultural understandings and social status into institutional contexts that become the 'neighbourhoods' in which extremely complex totalities can be made sense of. A topological sensibility would provide the rules of connection from one local neighbourhood to an overall system. For example, as Gilmore notes, the limits of space as a container produces a politics of location rather than a politics of possibilities (1999).

> [The] view from somewhere, social location, positionality, standpoint, embodiment, contextuality, intersectionality, local knowledges and global capital are notions that line many a feminist toolbox for good reasons ... however thoughtfully modified, whatever caveats are offered to mitigate the limitations of these metaphors ... are constrained by a Euclidean geometric imaginary. (Barad, 2001: 75–6)

The topological also repositions the sensibility of space away from a naïve assumption of a three-dimensional literality. Generally, one finds spatialisation theorised as a contested but nonetheless hegemonic formation – a geography, not geographies. Case studies of given places and times tend not to focus on the plurality of social space-making. We want to ward off tendencies to focus on a single assumed spatialisation, even where it is presented as shot full of holes. Lefebvre's view, for instance, that each historical mode of production of space contains within it previous modes, so that the Abstract Space of capitalism includes both natural and feudal modes of spatiality, is locked within a teleological vision of history as progressive and developmental (see also Figure 3.2 in contrast to Raphael's trans-historical tableau of thinkers in Figure 3.3). A stress on his dialectical model for understanding phenomena suggested that previous modes of production of space are incorporated within each new historical synthesis.

This has left little room for developing an understanding of the co-presence of spatialisations despite his sketch of a utopian 'Differential Space'. The review of the small but growing number of examples reveals that many of the theorists of space are repeating themselves or remain within neoclassical models of spatiality and spatialisations. This is achingly evident in the critiques of scale and the persistent resort to strategic rhetorical constructions, such as the global and globalisation, despite their ontological and epistemological shortcomings. This leads to brittle theorisations that are easily outpaced by rival rhetorics in the media, such as the image of a borderless world or the shrinking globe. The point of this text is not to repeat the analysis of critical geographers. But professionally, the social sciences, and geography in particular, need to broaden their understanding of space to social spatialisation. That is, their understanding needs to be expanded to include multiple types of manifolds, such as diagrams, which are simultaneously germane to problems and used together to lend greater purchase on problems – not to mention a thicker description of what I have playfully called the 'plushness' of the real.

Topological approaches can take apart the static poles of ontology. Even the potential of conjoined problem spaces that are bifurcated around the singularity of a site opens up the closed world of empiricism and beckons a multiplicity of spaces of representation that truly expand the potentiality of each moment and place. Consider the following spatialisation of 'site' into a veritable event-space that embraces a set of possibilities rather than a single 'reality', drawing on Schatzki's spatial ontology (Schatzki, 2002) and Spinoza's discussion of the event:

> [E]ach site is a dynamically composed aggregate ... drawn according to its own internal 'logics' rather than any generalising laws. It makes no sense, therefore, to think of one's immediate surroundings as 'always already' or 'necessarily' a site, nor will one abstractly pre-exist the objects and bodies making up its composition. Likewise it makes no sense to privilege human agency in sites over the material force relations that draw them together ... We must approach sites as aggregating, negotiating and *working* materialities ...

> Sites are frequently held together, populated or even delimited by all sorts of obscure material 'bodies' – everything from percepts to sign systems (a body of sayings, a body of work, and so on) ... the material cooperation of the site is primarily affective and forceful (the 'constraint' and movement of cooperating bodies expressing reciprocality). That is, the comings-together of elements composing a site are always a matter of labour ... bodies do not merely *find* themselves in positions of relative or interlocking distribution, but *participate* in the production of the fields of force through which they aggregate. (Woodward, et al., 2010: 273)

Topology accounts for the proper and improper, the legitimate and the out-of-place. Building on the so-called 'spatial turn', a 'topological turn' in cultural studies is foreshadowed by proto-topologies such as Appadurai's description of globalisation as a series of 'scapes' of sectoral flows such as information, bodies or capital (Appadurai, 1996). Theorists have also mobilised topological insights: the role of 'attractors' as 'catastrophe' points to the 'bifurcation' or sudden phase change of complex systems (DeLanda, 2002; Deleuze, 1986; Mackenzie, 2005b; Massumi, 2002). On the social science side, the tendency has been to exploit only the metaphorical richness of topology, a cultural topology promises to allow generalisation across cases by drawing on the rigorous language and classification system already developed in mathematics. On the natural science side, no non-algebraic primers are available (but see Barr, 1989; Blackwell, 2004) and the tendency is to discuss the mathematical intrigue of the science (DeLanda, 2002; Mackenzie, 2005b).

In environmental politics, Blok (2010), following Ingold and Law, shows how the global in general, and global climate, in particular, are represented according to multiple topologies in which the global emerges as an object (sphere) and milieu (planetary, trans-national, etc.) with particular forms of relation, powers and vulnerabilities (Ingold, 1993; Law, 2004). In different social contexts, all these representations appear self-evident and as spaces of representation that frame further action and thought. Reflecting on Bachelard's topology of fire, Blok notes that, 'versions of climate change can seem to flicker chaotically ... an abruptly shape-shifting reality, embodied in a multiplicity ... of more-or-less place-specific and group-specific imaginaries of how social, technological and natural life interrelate' (Blok, 2010: 907; Tresch, 2007).

> If regions constitute the familiar surfaces of dominant geopolitical spaces, networks, by contrast, link regionally distant sites through powerful technoscientific and economic infrastructures of immutable mobiles ...
>
> ... Fluid spaces, defined in terms of graduate transformations, arguably come closest to capturing the peculiar contemporary status of global climate change as a grey box, hovering between stability and flexibility in weaving together social worlds of politics, economics, activist and publics across the world. Finally the fire spaces of continuous discontinuities help us make sense of critical NGO activities surrounding, for instance, the emissions trading of CDM markets, labouring to make otherwise absent overflows visible vis-à-vis dominant forms of regional and network climate-change topologies. (Blok, 2010: 908)

Topological analysis, when applied to cultural, rather than mathematical objects, provides a rigorous, yet unabashedly humble investigation of the nature of all forms of relation since the claims to consistency are no longer hidden in the assumptions of the system. They allow us to compare and contrast competing spatialisations and complex totalities that amount to alternate 'worldings' with alternate exclusions and inclusions. When viewed as a massively complex topological object, the system of cultural relations is far from simple. Yet, a topological approach views this complexity on the local level – the mathematical 'neighbourhood' – without reducing it to simple, quantitative functions of larger systems. The topological method systematically and formally interrogates how an object is defined, and in doing so,

> provides the *des res* and *ad hoc* grounds from which a concept of relation emerges ... [T]opology ... frames and contextualizes the conditions under which such claims are made. The extrinsic conditions that have traditionally bound certain cultural objects in terms of race or gender can be reconfigured topologically in non-totalizing, non-classical ways. (Blackwell, 2004: online)

Bachelard himself comments in other works on knots as a potential model of consciousness (Bachelard and Flocon, 1957). These and the previous cases of nested manifolds illustrate a knotting of spaces that itself requires a topological sensitivity. This would extend beyond the geometries of single objects and the performative dramas centred around them. Rather than actual objects, the less tangible but still real threads of relations and the ways in which these can be interwoven with other, more or less systematic sets of relations to produce complex patterns of behaviour and function as outcomes are the focus. This might be imagined as the weaving of warp and weft, two ordered sets of thread or yarn, to produce patterns on a loom.

The Cusp

These precedents suggest the potential of a topologically-informed cultural studies. While describing what topology is, the purpose here is not to systematically critique them but to establish an agenda for what a cultural topology can do. Topology offers cultural studies a new 'dimensionality' and level of precision regarding spatial and temporal relations, flows and transformations. As Massumi shows, the political is as much in the temporal dimension of anticipation – that is, in the structuring of futures in the form of anticipated outcomes, normalised desire and the governance of choice – not in a topologically Euclidean present. The strangeness of everyday life is precisely its disequilibrium as a knotting of topologies that entwine local with global, present with past and future, rather than being a result of its banality, presentism or constrained domestic space. Rather than solely relating to situations of ongoing or marked change or deformation, knotting multiply-imbricated spatial and temporal orders, a cultural topology exposes the complexity of the everyday, the settled. In setting the static or routine, if not in motion, then into an orbit that becomes a wobble of becoming, a cultural topology is as much about mobility as about the emergence of what is taken for granted as the actually real. Topology is the study of *poesis*, becoming.

Cultural topology offers five unique advances in contrast to network approaches. First, it encourages an approach that stresses not only relations in networks but that their nodes, rather than being 'sealed units', are alive and in process. Second, it develops the character of these nodes in relation to their engagement, their co-becoming, with a milieux of other nodes. Third, it allows for hitherto concealed dimensions of these nodes to open up in interaction. Fourth, it draws on a milieu that is both and at once spatial and temporal and has a range of dynamisms – a dynamic repertoire. Beyond this, fifth, it accommodates multiple milieux, spatialisations and temporalisations with different qualities so that they coexist and intersect in an object whether material or virtual, a site, or a geographic space. Not location, position and fixed shape: instead, *Relation, Connection, Boundary-drawing and crossing, Interaction* and *Dynamics*. While much of the literature focuses on contrasting representations and imaginaries, emerging work must pursue a frontier of material practices and capacities that produce social spatialisations and temporalisations, which unfold them as topologies that integrate time empirically with place, space and agency; knowledge, power and the subject.

Arjun Appadurai's cascading global-local 'scapes' of modernity (Appadurai, 1996), landscapes and flows of media, bodies or capital, suggest that a topologizing sensibility can provide a framework for exploring relations and processes at multiple scales. The focus on process means that this is not a proposal for a new structuralism, which depends on reference to bounded, hierarchical entities. As Lury, Parisi and Terranova (2012) have recently noted, culture itself is topological, endlessly establishing and transforming relations and equivalences, discontinuities and contrasts. They see topological approaches to social research in the ways in which we now trace out the continuities across what has been seen to be distinct and discontinuous: the body and society, technology and society, local and global, self and other. It allows us to understand mobilities as continuous flux rather than transmission of fixed entities across a static space.

Rather than the stress on the calculability of monadic entities and the division of spheres of life – work, family, public life – that characterized modernity, topological cultures operate as a changing field of entities in which feedback loops provide so much continuous 'live data' that they become a mediator that modifies the relations between objects and their development. They operate as a continuum that connects multiple entities, locations and scales and thereby becomes a new spatialisation and temporalisation – like one might have once said that television that is both 'in' your house and 'at' the scene, knotting together viewers and events, fans and shows, here and there, the local and the global (Butler, 2001 in Lury et al., 2012: 10–11).

Similarly, indicators or representations may no longer be fixed measures of stable entities out in a neutral environment but they participate together with their referents in a dynamically animated relationship to amplify the intensity of a phenomenon (positive feedback), to build new relationships between entities (by tagging or classifying them together with previously unlike entities) as if the field has been shrunk, bringing them together. A topological sensibility takes into account the intersection or 'transitive' relationships that arise between categories and their mutual constitution as aspects of the same temporal and spatial continuum. For example, Parisi (2012) notes that real time urban data and monitoring (such as traffic cameras, GPS, or measures of the flows of utilities such as electricity, gas or water) not only normalizes operations based on references to records of past conditions but can change the system on the fly (for example by continuously redirecting drivers). 'Connections here are not only relations between objects ... but also between possible (but not yet existing) objects.... The sequential running of algorithms ... the digital design of time and space is not only controlling or pre-empting the emergence of events, but it also unleashes random events' (Lury et al., 2012: 16) and novel reconfigurations into everyday life.

We are on the cusp. What are the methodological implications of a cultural topology? What is it to act topologically? How does a topological approach, such as diagramming the operations of power, reflexively alter the relationship between a world and agents, between objects and knowledge, to open up new possibilities, to actualize potentials and to realize ideals?

Notes

1   Rather than a given form of governance or power, Collier argues that Foucault is 'centrally concerned with how heterogeneous techniques, technologies, material elements, and institutional forms are taken up and assembled' (Collier, 2009: 89–90) in types of problem-making – or perhaps better, problem-recognition – that frame solutions, rather than with totalising epochs or functional needs that succeed one another in an historical sequence: 'In the frame of a topological analysis it is precisely the specific activity of thought that would have to be examined to understand the processes of recombination and reproblematisation through which contemporary government ... is being refigured' (Collier, 2009:100).

2   Landzelius argues that Foucault's description of the breakdown of normality in heterotopias builds on an image of the test given to aphasics to sort skeins of yarn by colour. In aphasia, other logics proliferate, leading to the continual rearrangement of the bundles that may easily be seen to be related to each other functionally and temporally in the manner of

a syntagm that ruptures official syntax and thus unveils the limits of order within the space of an episteme (Foucault, 1986: 27, in Landzelius, 2009: 60).

3 Drawing on Stern (1985), self is envisioned as a relational process together with the environment. The self does not develop so much in phases as in 'fractal phase-spaces composed of interweaving strata'. The self happens as 'foregrounding strata phasing toward organisation' intermeshed with 'the frustration of not being able to articulate the feeling of intensity that feeds this coherence – causing the foregrounding of strata phasing toward the virtual or immanence. Every becoming ... tinted with this double articulation' (Manning, 2009: 36; see Stern, 1985: 22) of the actual and virtual in a continual syncresis in which 'the subject' emerges only as a liminal phenomenon that cannot be pinned down like the corpse of a butterfly in a collection.

glossary of terms

abstract   Ideal and possible entities such as ideas and concepts.

Actual   Actively and tangibly existing as a phenomenon in the present moment, not just potentially, conceptually or latently. See Table 1.1.

Analysis Situs   Literally, analysis of situation. According to Poincaré, it describes topology as a branch of Geometry that describes the relative situation of points, lines and surfaces without consideration of their size.

Area   Quantity that expresses an extent of a surface, typically of two-dimensions.

Atlas   A collection of maps that covers the earth, the universe or a manifold.

Boundary   The edge of a manifold or the closure of a set minus its interior. If a manifold M has a boundary, then it is finite. The boundary is a manifold of one less dimension than the dimension of M.

Chart   A chart is a local coordinate system of a topological neighbourhood. A number of charts can be collected into an atlas.

Clinamen   Lucretius' name for the indeterminate and unpredictable swerve of atoms that founds the origin of freedom from predictability propounded by Epicurus.

Closed Path   A path (that is, a curve) on a manifold that begins and ends at the same point.

Compact   A manifold is compact if it has an atlas with a finite number of charts.

Concrete   (also Material): Real and actual entities with extension and effects, Descartes' *res extensa*. See Table 1.1.

Connected Sum   The manifold that results from cutting a solid ball out of each of two manifolds and identifying the points on the two spheres that bound the complements.

Continuous   A function from one space to another is continuous if the preimage or inverse of every open set is also open.

Complex Numbers   Set of numbers obtained by augmenting the real numbers with the square roots of negative numbers.

Corollary   A proposition that follows easily from a theorem or another proposition.

Curvature   A mathematical object that measures the deviation of the sum of angles of triangles from 180 degrees. In a two-dimensional manifold, the curvature at each point is a number.

Diagram   An icon, projection or visualisation of an entity, space or process using geometric and symbolic representation techniques to show relationships between elements within some sort of matrix or mechanism.

Differential Equation   An equation in which one specifies how rates of change (the 'differential') in one mathematical object (variable) is related to other objects. An example would be process affected by changing forces that determine the actual outcome in ways that are difficult to foresee by simply extrapolating from the current moment. The general solution is a 'function' whose various 'derivatives' satisfy the differential equation over a lengthy span of time..

Dimension   The number of independent degrees of freedom in a set. Or, the minimum number of real numbers (that is, the number of coordinates) that it takes to specify a proposition near a given point in a set.

Durée   The subjective experience of time as duration with a characteristic tempo proposed by Bergson as a critique of time measured as a series of instants, which loses the mobility of time.

Entourage   Set of elements or neighbourhoods.

Euclidean Space   For each positive integer n, Euclidean space of dimension n is n-space with distance defined by the Pythagorean theorem.

Field   An organised expanse or corpus of some integral quality that contains relations that either have a causative power (e.g. a magnetic field), or between causes and effects or other relations of dependency (social field, algebraic field).

Fifth Postulate   The fifth, and most complex, of the five postulates in Euclid's *Elements*: If a straight line falling on two straight lines makes the interior angles on the same side less than two right angles (that is, whose sum is less than 180 degrees), the two straight lines, if extended indefinitely, meet on that side.

Flat   A space is flat (a surface) if the sum of the angles of every triangle in the space is 180 degrees.

Geometrisation Conjecture   The conjecture that every three-dimensional manifold can be cut up along spheres and torn into pieces that have one of eight geometries.

Geodesic   A curve that traces the shortest distance between any two of its points.

Geometric Property   A property that depends for definition on a distance or symmetry (for example: straight, angle measure, circle).

Geometry   The structure that results from having a distance defined on a manifold.

Great Circle   A circle on the (two-dimensional, round) sphere cut out by intersecting the sphere with a plane through its centre.

Group (of Transformations)   A set of transformations with the properties that (1) the result of performing one transformation in the set, then another, is a transformation that again is in the set, and (2) the transformation that undoes a given transformation in the set is in the set. (That is, a group of a transformations is a set that is closed under the operations of taking products and forming inverses.)

Homeomorphism   A one-to-one correspondence between two manifolds in which nearby points correspond to nearby points. Homeomorphic objects can be remolded or deformed into each other without tearing being required. The most common example is of the transformation of a doughnut shape (a torus) into a mug where the hole in the doughnut becomes the hole in the handle while part of the body of the doughnut is hollowed out to form the cup.

Homogeneous   A manifold is homogeneous if the space looks the same at every point.

Ideal   Not actually present but considered as present when limits of infinity are included or when the intangible or pure form is included as part of existence. The Ideal includes both abstractions such as ideas and real but virtual entities. See Table 1.1.

Lemma   A mathematical result whose main purpose and interest is as a stepping-stone to proving another result.

Loop A path that begins and ends at the same point. More technically, a continuous mapping of an interval into a one-dimensional manifold in which both endpoints get mapped to the same point. That is, both ends 'loop back' to the same point.

Manifold A mathematical set that looks like Euclidean space at each point. (More formally, regions sufficiently near any point are homeomorphic to *n*-space.)

Map A representation of an area or field that normally has some one-to-one translation between the field and the representation itself, which may be a diagram. Maps may depict a real, imagined or virtual space.

Material See Concrete.

Metric A rule for specifying the distance between any two points of a set. In a manifold, a metric can be given by specifying a rule for measuring speed along curves.

Milieu Serre's notion of a medium that is between a communication channel and an environment. The milieu is an in-between transmission of space and time. It is thus a topology and is characterised by noise, mediation and intersections.

N-Space The set of all ordered *n*-tuples of real numbers.

Negative Curvature A region in a manifold has negative curvature if the sums of all angles of all triangles in that region are less than 180 degrees.

Neighbourhood The neighbourhood to point or set *x* is an open set that contains the *x*.

Non-Euclidean A space or mathematics in which Euclid's laws do not hold.

Open Set A set is open if any member or point in it can be varied or moved slightly and still remain within the set. Thus in topology an open set is the set of points *near* each other or a given point.

Partial Differential Equation A type of differential equation in which one specifies rates of change at different points in different directions. The solutions of partial differential equations are objects that have the desired rates change at all points in all directions. Many equations of mathematical physics are partial differential equations.

Path A continuous mapping within a manifold.

Phase Space Phase spaces are logically-defined spaces similar to those which allow us to visualise data in graphs; they have x-y-z or more dimensions. Each point corresponds to a unique state of a given system so that the phase space includes all possible states of the system.

Place a portion of space, a set or a field that has an assigned identity whether coordinates, location, or a name. Those defined in indefinite (unbounded) areas can be identified as places.

Place-image A specific image or representation associated with a place, either metaphorically, through action or history, or directly as in a photograph of a site.

Place-myth A set of place-images that constitute an overall representation of a place or location.

Poincaré Conjecture The conjecture, not proved, that every simply connected, compact three-dimensional manifold without boundary is homeomorphic to the three-dimensional sphere.

Positive Curvature A region in a manifold has positive curvature if the sums of angles of all triangles in that region are greater than 180 degrees.

Possible Entities that exist but without direct effect, such as abstractions (ideas, concepts that are ideal possibilities) and probabilities (mathematical objects such as percentages that indicate actual possibility). See Table 1.1.

Postulate An assertion accepted without proof. Synonymous with axiom.

Probable Actual and possible entities as in mathematical probabilities such as risks. See Table 1.1.

Proof A complete argument in which each assertion is an axiom or previously proved proposition, or else follows by formal rules of logic. It begins with axioms and known propositions and ends with the statement that was to be proved.

Proposition A statement that is derived from postulates and previously proved propositions using mathematical reasoning.

Pythagorean Theorem The statement that the square of the length of the hypotenuse of a right-angle triangle is equal to the sum of the squares of the two sides meeting at the right angle. (The hypotenuse is the side across from the right angle.)

Real   Entities that exist as realised, not as merely possible or thought. Real entities are defined by having tangible, material effects.

Res Extensa   Literally, extended thing (*res*). According to Descartes, 'corporeal substance' is one of three substances alongside ideas and God. Objects are combinations of these substance attributes, thus one can recognise a melted piece of dripping wax as another form of solid wax through knowledge of the idea, even as its corporeal substance changes in nature.

Riemann Curvature Tensor   A mathematical object that assigns a value to every planar direction through the point (which reflects how much angle sums of tiny geodesic triangles in that direction tend to deviate from 180 degrees).

Round Sphere   The word *round* refers to a sphere that has the same curvature at every point and is used when one wants to make a distinction between such spheres and topologically equivalent spheres that may have bumps. The surface of our earth is not a round sphere because it is flattened at the poles. A round sphere is isometric to the set of points at some fixed distance from a point in Euclidean space.

Simply Connected   A manifold is simply connected if any loop can be shrunk to a point. This is equivalent to the statement that the fundamental group consists of a single element (necessarily, the identity).

Social Spatialisation (Spatialisation)   The ongoing spatial organisation of all facets and scales of life, in the context of previously created spatial organisations to create a cultural formation that includes dispositions, representations and framings of the environment as a space of action. A 'spacing' of activities and ideas into 'places for this' and 'places for that'. Some archetypes of spatialisation include division into centre and periphery, binary divisions (here versus there, near versus far), division by scale (global versus local), and mosaic patterns.

Space   An extent or context defined by a social spatialisation. Spaces are manifolds characterised by a specific dimensionality.

Sphere   Without additional qualification, refers to a two-dimensional sphere which is any object homeomorphic to the set of points in three-dimensional space at a fixed distance from a given point. The surface of a ball is a sphere. There are, however, spheres of every dimension. The simplest definition of a sphere of a given dimension is as the set of points of fixed distance from a single point in the Euclidean space of one dimension higher. So, for example, the set of points at distance from a fixed point in six-dimensional Euclidean space is a five-dimensional sphere.

Surface A two-dimensional manifold.

Syncresis The interface of the ideal and the actual. Interaction across this interface or mobility between the ideal and actual as continuous actualisation and virtualisation. Syncresis is a porous, incomplete merging of different elements which preserves enough of the originals' identities to not fully subsume them into a new synthesis. This produces a flickering or equivocal states of real entities such as a 'flame'.

Tensor A mathematical object that assigns real numbers to a prescribed number of vectors (that is, velocities) at each point of a manifold.

Theorem An especially important proposition.

Three-dimensional Manifold (or Three-Manifold or Three-Space) An idealised mathematical volume that models the shapes that three-dimensional spaces, like our everyday universe, might have. The region around every point can be mapped onto the inside of a solid aquarium. Put differently, the region near every point looks like three-space.

Three-Sphere A manifold constructed by taking two solid balls and matching up the points on the (spherical) boundary of each. The set of points at a fixed distance from a point in four-dimensional space is a three-sphere.

Three-Torus The manifold constructed by connecting the opposite faces of a solid rectangular box.

Time A linear dimension ordering events sequentially within any given system or context. For modern cultures, time is normally progressive; that is, unidimensional and directional towards the future, but is also understood to be reversible, cyclical, divisible in epochs or phases, and to have varying velocity, or tempo, depending on the experience of durée. Its measurability is the subject of debate.

Topological Property (Topological Invariant) A property that is invariant under continuous homeomorphisms. Examples are connectivity, simple connectedness, dimension.

Topologically Equivalent Two manifolds are topologically equivalent if they are homeomorphic.

Topology The study of shapes and their transformation. The area of mathematics concerned with relationships between entities, points and lines, such that their properties are preserved under continuous deformations without tearing or suturing. It emerged from 'analysis situs' to become a study of manifolds and connectivity.

Torus The surface of a doughnut.

Two-Dimensional Manifold (or Two-Manifold) An idealised mathematical shape that models the surfaces of possible worlds. The region around every point can be mapped onto a sheet of paper (that is, the inside of a rectangle in the plane)

Two-Space The plane envisaged by Euclid that goes on forever in two independent directions. As a set, it is just the set of pairs of real numbers.

Umwelt The environment or world as detected, often partially, by the senses of a biological organism.

Virtual Real but ideal, or in Proust's definition, 'Real but not actual, ideal but not abstract'. Virtualities are the qualities or latent capacities of an entity, and of intangible but real entities such as 'community' or 'goodwill'. Virtualities are known through their actual effects, but do not have extension, therefore are not captured in the Cartesian understanding of reality. See Table 1.1.

references

Adams, P.C. (2011). 'A taxonomy for communication geography', *Progress in Human Geography*, 35(1): 37–57.

Agamben, G. (1998). *Homo Sacer: Sovereign Power and Bare Life* (D. Hellen-Roazen, trans.). Stanford, CA: Stanford University Press.

Agamben, G. (2004). *The Open: Man and Animal*. Palo Alto, CA: Stanford University Press.

Agamben, G. (2005). *State of Exception*. Chicago: University of Chicago Press.

Al Ghazali (Algazel) (1927). *Tahafot Al-Falasifat*. Beirut: Imprimerie Catholique.

Alexander, H.G. (1956). *The Leibniz-Clarke Correspondence*. New York: Philosophical Library.

Allen, J. and Cochrane, A. (2010). 'State power: Topological shifts in the organization of government and politics', *Antipode*, 42(5): 1071–89.

Anderson, B. (1991). *Imagined Communities: Reflections on the Origin and Spread of Nationalism* (2nd edn). London: Verso.

Anderson, B. (2002). 'A principle of hope: Recorded music, listening practices and the immanence of utopia', *Geografiska Annaler B*, 84(3–4): 211–27.

Appadurai, A. (1996). *Modernity at Large: Cultural Dimensions of Globalization*. Minneapolis: Minnesota University Press.

Ardener, S. (ed.) (1983). *Women and Space*. Cambridge: Cambridge University Press.

Aristotle (1964). *De Anima (Of the Soul)* (Vol. 3). Oxford: Clarendon Press.

Aristotle (1970). *Physics*. Oxford: Clarendon Press.

Aristotle (2007). *Categories* (E.M. Edghill, trans.). Available from http://ebooks.adelaide.edu.au/a/aristotle/categories/

Aristotle (350 BCE). *Metaphysics* (W.D. Ross, trans.). The Internet Classics Archive.

Azuma, T. (1981, Oct.). Three houses by Takamitsu Azuma, *Japan Architect*. 294: 17–42.

Bachelard, G. (1959). *La poétique de l'espace*. Paris: Quadrige/PUF.

Bachelard (1961). *The Poetics of Space*. New York: Basic.

Bachelard, G. (1964). *The Psychoanalysis of Fire*. Boston: Beacon Press.

Bachelard, G. and Flocon, A. (1957). *Châteaux en Espagne*. Paris: Cercle Grolier.

Bailey, S. (2010) 'The Spatial Questions Posed by Koenigsberg/Kaliningrad'. *SOC403*. Edmonton.

Bakhtin, M.M. (1970). *La Poëtique De Dostoïevski* (I. Kolitcheff, trans.). Paris: Editions du Seuil.

Bakhtin, M.M. (1981). *The Dialogical Imagination* (M. Holquist, trans.). Austin: University of Texas Press.

Barad, K. (2001). 'Re(con)figuring space, time and matter', in M. DeKoven (ed.), *Feminist Locations: Global and Local, Theory and Practice*. New Brunswick, NJ: Rutgers University Press. pp. 75–109.

Barr, S. (1989). *Experiments in Topology*. New York: Dover.

Baudrillard, J. (1990). *The Precession of Simulacra*. New York: Zone Books.

Beguin H. and Thisse, J.-F. (1979). 'An axiomatic approach to geographic space', *Geographical Analysis*, 11(4): 325–41.

Benjamin, W. (1989). *Paris Capital du XIXe Siecle: Le Livre des Passages*. (R. Lacoste, trans. Translation of W. Benjamin (1982) Frankfurt am Main: Suhrkamp Verlag, Vol. 5). Paris: Ed. Du CERF.

Bennet, J. (2005). 'The agency of assemblages and the North American blackout', *Public Culture*, 17(3): 445–65.

Bergson, H. (1948). *Essai sur les donnes immediate de la conscience*. Paris: PUF.

Bergson, H. (1970). *Ouevres*. Paris: Presses Universitaires de France.

Bergson, H. (1988). *Matter and Memory* (W.S. Palmer, trans.). New York: Zone Books.

Bhabha, H. (ed.) (1991). *Nation and Narration*. London: Routledge.

Bhabha, H. (1994). *The Location of Culture*. London: Routledge.

Bhaskar, R. (1991). *Philosophy and the Idea of Freedom*. Oxford, UK and Cambridge, MA: Blackwell.

Blackler, F. (1995). 'Knowledge, knowledge work and organizations: An overview and interpretation', *Organizational Studies*, 16(6): 1021–46.

Blackwell, B. (2004). 'Cultural topology: An introduction to postmodern mathematics', *Reconstruction*, 4(4). Available at: http://reconstruction.eserver.org/044/blackwell.htm

Blanchot, M. (1968). *Les Espaces litteraires*. Paris: Mouton.

Blaser, R. (2006). 'The practice of the outside', in M. Nichols (ed.), *The Fire: Collected Essays of Robin Blaser*. Berkeley: University of California Press. pp. 113–63.

Blok, A. (2010). 'Topologies of climate change: Actor-network theory, relational-scalar analytics, and carbon-market overflows', *Environment and Planning D: Society and Space*, 28(5): 896–912.

Blomley, N. (2010). 'Cuts, flows, and the geographies of property', *Law, Culture and the Humanities*, 7(2): 203–16.

Blum, V. and Secor, A. (2011). 'Psychotopologies: Closing the circuit between psychic and material space', *Environment and Planning D: Society and Space*, 29: 1030–47.

Bogdanov, A. (1904–1906). *Empiro-Monism*. Unpublished manuscript, London.

Bohm, D. (1980). *Wholeness and the Implicate Order*. London: Routledge.

Bohr, N. (1987). 'The unity of knowledge', *The Philosophical Writings Volume II: Essays 1933–1957 on Atomic Physics and Human Knowledge*. Woodbridge, CT: Ox Bow Press. pp. 67–82.

Bonazzi, A. (2002). 'Heterotopology and geography: A reflection', *Space and Culture*, (5)1: 42–8.

Bourdieu, P. (1972). *Esquisse d'un theorie de la pratique*. Paris: PUF.

Bourdieu, P. (1977). *Outline of a Theory of Practice* (R. Nice, trans.). Cambridge: Cambridge University Press.

Bowker, G. and Star, S.L. (1999). *Sorting Things Out: Classification and its Consequences*. Cambridge, MA: MIT Press.

Braudel, F. (1982). *Civilization and Capitalism, 15th–18th Century: The Structures of Everyday Life: The Limits of the Possible*. New York: Harper & Row. (originally entitled *La longue durée*).

Brenner, N. (2001). 'The limits to scale? Methodological reflections on scalar structuration', *Progress in Human Geography*, 25(4): 591–614.

Brown, S.D. and Middleton, D. (2005). 'The baby as virtual object: Agency and difference in a neonatal intensive care unit' [Proceedings Paper]. *Environment and Planning D: Society and Space*, 23(5): 695–715.

Butler, J. (2011) 'Bodies in alliance and the politics of the street', *Transversal: A Multilingual Web Journal*. Available at: http://eipcp.net/transversal/1011/ butler/ en (accessed 1 November 2011).

Bunge, W. (1966). *Theoretical Geography*. Lund: Gleerup.

Burchell, G., Godron, C. and Miller, P. (eds) (1991). *The Foucault Effect: Studies in Governmentality*. Chicago: University of Chicago Press.

Burke, K. (1969). *A Grammar of Motives*. Berkeley: University of California Press.

Burnet, J. (1920). *Early Greek Philosophy*. London: World.

Buroker, J. V. (1981). *Space and Incongruence: The Origin of Kant's Idealism*. Boston: D. Reidel.

Butler, J. (1993). *Bodies that Matter: On the Discursive Limits of 'Sex'*. New York: Routledge.

Cambre, M.C. (2011). *The Politics of the Face: Manifestations of Che Guevara's image and its collage of renderings and agency*. Ph.D. Thesis. Educational Policy Studies. University of Alberta. Edmonton. Available at: http://eipcp.net/transversal/1011/ butler/en (accessed 1 November 2011).

Camhis, M. (1979). *Planning Theory and Philosophy*. New York: Tavistock.

Campanella, T. (1620). *De sensu rerum et magia, libri quatuor*. Frankfurt.

Canadian Pacific Railway (1926). *The Ancient City of Quebec: Canadian Pacific Guide*. Montreal: Canadian Pacific Railway Company.

Câpek, M. (1961). *Philosophical Impact of Contemporary Physics*. Princeton, NJ: Van Nostrand.

Câpek, M. (1976). *The Impact of Physics on Philosophy*. New York: Van Nordstrand, Boston Studies in the Philosophy of Science.

Carrier, J. and Miller, D. (eds) (1998). *Virtualism*. New York: Berg.

Casarino, C. (2003). 'Time matters: Marx, Negri, Agamben and the corporeal', *Strategies*, 16(2): 185–206.

Casarino, C. and Negri, A. (2008). *In Praise of the Common: A Conversation on Philosophy and Politics*. Minneapolis: MN: University of Minnesota Press.

Castells, M. (1977). *The Urban Question*. London: Edward Arnold.

Castells, M. (1997). *Network Society* (Vol. 3). Oxford: Blackwell.

Castoriadis, C. (1978). 'La découverte de l'imagination', *Libre*, 3: 155–89 (Avertissement 151–155).

Castoriadis, C. (1987). *The Imaginary Institution of Society* (K. Blamey, trans.). Oxford: Polity.

Chalfin, B. (2007). 'Customs regimes and the materiality of global mobility: Governing the Port of Rotterdam', *American Behavioral Scientist*, 50(12): 1610–30. Available at: http://abs.sagepub.com/content/50/12/1610

Chang, C.-Y. (1984, Apr. May. Jun.). 'Japanese Spatial Concepts in 3 parts', *Japan Architect*, 324, 325, 326.

Cohen, A.P. (ed.) (1982). *Belonging: Identity and Social Organization in British Rural Cultures*. St John's, Newfoundland: Institute of Social and Economic Research.

Cohen, G. (1978). *Karl Marx's Theory of History*. Oxford: Oxford University Press.

Cohen, L. (1992). *Anthem. On The Future*: Columbia Records.

Collier, A. (1994). *Critical Realism: An Introduction to Roy Bhaskar's Philosophy*. London and New York: Verso.

Collier, S.J. (2009). 'Topologies of power: Foucault's analysis of political government beyond "Governmentality"', *Theory Culture & Society*, 26(6): 78–108. Available at: http://tcs.sagepub.com/content/26/6/78.abstract

Connor, S. (2002). 'Michel Serres's milieux'. Paper presented at the Brazilian Association for Comparative Literature.

Connor, S. (2008) 'Wherever: The ecstasies of Michel Serres'. Paper presented at the Digital Art and Culture in the Age of Pervasive Computing, Copenhagen. Available at: http://www.bbk.ac.uk/english/skc/wherever/

Cooke, P. (ed.) (1989). *Localities: The Changing Face of Urban Britain*. London: Unwin Hyman.

Copernicus, N. (1949). *Nicolai Copernici Thorunensis de revolutionibus orbitum caelestium libri sex*. Munich: Oldenbourg.

Csikszentmihalyi, M. (1990). *Flow: The Psychology of Optimal Experience*. New York: Harper and Row.

Cushing, F.H. (1896). 'Outlines of Zuñi creation myths', *Report of the Bureau of American Ethnology Extract*, 13: 325–446. Available at: http://www.archive.org/details/cu31924104094002

Davenport, T. and Prusak, L. (2000). *Working Knowledge: How Organizations Manage What They Know*. Cambridge, MA: Harvard Business School Press.

Davidson, T., Park, O. and Shields, R. (eds) (2011). *Ecologies of Affect*. Waterloo, ON: Wilfred Laurier University Press.

de Certeau, M. (1984). *The Practice of Everyday Life*. Berkeley: University of California Press.

de Cyon, E. (1901). 'Les Bases naturelles de la geometrie d'Euclide', *Revue philosophique*, 52: 1–30.

DeLanda, M. (2002). *Intensive Science and Virtual Philosophy*. New York: Continuum.

DeLanda, M. (2006). *A New Philosophy of Society*. London: Continuum.

Deleuze, G. (1981). *Difference and Repetition*. New York: Columbia University Press.

Deleuze, G. (1986). *Foucault*. Paris: Minuit.

Deleuze, G. (1988a). *Bergsonism* (B. Habberjam, trans.). New York: Zone Books.

Deleuze, G. (1988b). *Foucault* (S. Bove, trans.). Minneapolis: Univerisity of Minnesota Press.

Deleuze, G. (1989). *Cinema* (Vol. 2). London: Athlone.

Deleuze, G. (1992). 'Postscript on the societies of control', *October*, 59: 3–7. Available at: http://www.n5m.org/n5m2/media/texts/deleuze.htm

Deleuze, G. (2000). *Proust and Signs* (R. Howard, trans.). Minneapolis: Minnesota University Press.

Deleuze, G. and Guattari, F. (1987). *Mille Plateaux: A Thousand Plateaus* (B. Massumi, trans.). Minneapolis: University of Minnesota Press.

Deleuze, G. and Guattari, F. (1994). *What is Philosophy* (G. Burchell, trans.). New York: Columbia University Press.

Demers, M. (2010). 'Topology catastrophe: Catastrophe narrativization of urban morphologies', *Nexus Network Journal*, 12(3): 497–505.

Derrida, J. (1970). 'Ousia and Gramme: A note to a footnote in *Being and Time*' (E. S. Casey, trans.), in F.J. Smith (ed.), *Phenomenology in Perspective*. The Hague: Nijhoff. pp. 54–93.

Derrida, J. (1975). *Introduction to Husserl's 'The Origins of Geometry'*. London: Oxford University Press.

Derrida, J. (1994). *Specters of Marx* (P. Kamuf, trans.). New York: Routledge.

Derrida, J. (1998). Comme si c'etait possible (within such limits). *Revue Internationale De Philosophie*, 52(205): 495–530.

Descartes (1901). *Meditations*. Trilingual HTML Edition (John Veitch, trans.). Available at: http://www.cola.wright.edu/descartes/

Diken, B. (2011). 'Fire as a metaphor of (im)mobility', *Mobilities*, 6(1): 95–102.

Dorofeeva-Lichtmann, V.V. (1995). 'Conception of terrestrial organization in the Shan Hai Jing', *Bulletin de l'École française d'Extrême-Orient*, 82(82): 57–110.

Downs, R.M. and Shea, D. (1977). *Maps in Minds: Reflections on Cognitive Mapping*. New York: Harper and Row.

Dreyfus, H.L. and Rabinow, P. (1982). *Michel Foucault: Beyond Structuralism and Hermeneutics*. Chicago: University of Chicago Press.

Durkheim, E. (1912). *Les Formes élémentaires de la view religieuse* (2002 Online edn). Paris: PUF.

Durkheim, E. (1976). *The Elementary Forms of the Religious Life* (2nd edn). New York: George Allen & Unwin.

Durkheim, E. and Mauss, M. (1963). *Primitive Classification* (R. Needham, trans.). Chicago: University of Chicago Press.

Durkheim, E. and Mauss, M. (1973). *Primitive Classification*. Chicago: University of Chicago Press.

Einstein, A. (1961). *Relativity: The Special and the General Theory* (R.W. Lawson, trans.). New York: Crown Publishers.

Engels, F. (1970). *Socialism: Utopian and Scientific 1880*. Moscow: Progress.

Engels, F. (1973). *The Condition of the Working Class in England*. Moscow: Progress.

Engels, F. (1974). *Notes and Fragments for Dialectics of Nature, 1883*. Moscow: Progress Publishers.

Engels, F. and Kelley, F. (1892). *The Condition of the Working-class in England in 1844 with a Preface written in 1892*. London: George Allen & Unwin.

Euclid (1998). *The Elements* (T. Heath, trans.). Worcester, MA and New York: Clark University, Dover.

Euler, L. (1736/1741). 'Solutio problematis ad geometriam situs pertinentis (1736)', *Commentarii Academiae Scientiarum Imperialis Petropolitanae*, 8: 128–40.

Fearon, D. (2001). 'CSISS Classics – Georg Simmel: The sociology of space'. Available at: http://www.csiss.org/classics/content/75

Fisher, C.T. (2008). 'Repositioning the theorist in the Lower Ninth Ward', in P.E. Steinberg and R. Shields (eds), *What is a City? The Urban after Katrina*. Athens, GA: University of Georgia Press. pp. 159–71.

Foucault, M. (1979). *Discipline and Punish*. New York: Vintage.

Foucault, M. (1980). *Power/Knowledge*. New York: Pantheon.

Foucault, M. (1984). 'Space, knowledge and power', in P. Rabinow (ed.), *The Foucault Reader*. New York: Random House. pp. 239–56.

Foucault, M. (1986). 'Of other spaces' (J. Miskowiec, trans.), *Diacritics*, 16(1): 22–7.

Foucault, M. (2007). *Security, Territory, Population: Lectures at the Collège de France, 1977–1978*. New York: Palgrave Macmillan.

Futch, M.J. (2008). *Leibniz's Metaphysics of Time and Space*. New York: Springer.

Galison, P. (2003). *Einstein's Clocks, Poincaré's Maps*. London: Sceptre.

Gamow, G. (1966). *Thirty Years that Shook Physics: The Story of Quantum Theory*. New York: Dover.

Gaonkar, D. and Povinelli, E. (2003). 'Technologies of public forms: Circulation, transfiguration, recognition', *Public Culture*, 15(3): 385–97.

Gardiner, M. (1999). *Critiques of Everyday Life*. London: Sage Publications.

Gatrell, A.C. (1983). *Distance and Space: A Geographical Perspective*. Oxford: Clarendon Press.

Gauss, K.F. (1863–1903). *Werke.* Leipzig: Königliche Gessellschaft der Wissenshaften zu Göttingen.

Geertz, C. (1973). *The Interpretation of Cultures.* New York: Basic.

Geertz, C. (1996). 'Afterword', in S. Feld and K. Basso (eds), *Sense of Place.* Santa Fe, NM: School of American Research Press and University of Washington Press.

Genz, H. (1999). *Nothingness: The Science of Empty Space.* Reading, MA: Perseus.

Getis, A. (2008). A history of the concept of spatial autocorrelation: A geographer's perspective. *Geographical Analysis*, 40(3): 297–309.

Giaccaria, P. and Minca, C. (2011). Topographies/topologies of the camp: Auschwitz as a spatial threshold. *Political Geography*, 30(1): 3–12.

Gibson, J.J. (1982). *Reasons for Realism: Selected Essays of James J. Gibson.* Hillsdale, NJ: Lawrence Earlbaum and Assoc.

Giddens, A. (1979). *Central Problems in Social Theory: Action, Structure and Contradiction in Social Analysis.* London: Macmillan.

Gilmore, R.W. (1999). 'Queer publics: Transforming policy, scholarship, and politics'. Paper presented at the Opening Plenary, Local Parities and Global Change: Activists and Academies. Thinking about a Queer Future Conference.

Gilmore, R.W. (2000). 'Rosa and Ruth/Terror and Truth – Dialogue', Ruth Wilson Gilmore and Barbara Harlow. Rethinking Marxism Conference, Amherst, MA, September.

Gilroy, P. (2000). *Against Race.* Cambridge, MA: Harvard University Press.

Goffman,, E. (1973). *The Presentation of Self in Everyday Life.* Woodstock, NY: Overlook Press.

Goffman, E. (1974). *Frame Analysis.* Cambridge, MA: Harvard University Press.

Goldmann, L. (1971). *Immanuel Kant.* London: NLB.

Gottdiener, M. (1985). *The Social Production of Urban Space.* Austin, TX: University of Texas Press.

Gottdiener, M. and Lagopoulos, A.P. (1986). *The City and the Sign: An Introduction to Urban Semiotics.* New York: Columbia University Press.

Graham, S. and Marvin, S. (2001). *Splintering Ubanism.* London: Routledge.

Gregory, D. (1994). *Geographical Imaginations.* Oxford: Blackwell.

Greimas, A.J. and Courtés, J. (1982). *Semiotics and Language: An Analytical Dictionary.* Bloomington: Indiana University Press.

Greimas, A.J. and Fontanille, J. (1991). *Semiotique des passions. Des états de choses avec états d'âme.* Paris: Seuil.

Grönlund, B. (1993). 'Lefebvre's ontological transformations of space'. Paper presented at the Nordplan, 29 July.

Grosz, E. (1999). 'Thinking the new: Of futures yet unthought', in E. Grosz (ed.), *Becomings.* Ithaca, NY: Cornell University Press. pp. 15–28.

Hadden, R.W. (1997). *Sociological Theory: An Introduction to the Classical Tradition.* Peterborough, ON: Broadview Press.

Hägerstrand, T. (ed.) (1981). *Space and Time in Geography: Essays Dedicated to Torsten Hägerstrand.* Stockholm: CWK Gleerup.

Halbwachs, M. and Coser, L.A. (1992). *On Collective Memory.* Chicago: University of Chicago Press.

Hall, E.T. (1966). *The Hidden Dimension.* Chicago: University of Chicago Press.

Hall, E. (2003). 'Reading maps of the genes: interpreting the spatiality of genetic knowledge.' *Health & Place*, 9(2): 151–161.

Halsted, G.B. (1900). 'Gauss and the non-Euclidean geometry', *American Mathematical Monthly*, 7(11): 247–52.

Haraway, D. (1992). 'The promises of monsters: A regenerative politics for inappropriate/d others', in P. Treichler (ed.), *Cultural Studies*. New York: Routledge. pp. 295–337.

Harbison, R. (1977). *Eccentric Spaces*. New York: Avon.

Hardt, M. (1993). *Gilles Deleuze: An Apprenticeship in Philosophy*. Minneapolis: University of Minnesota Press.

Hardt, M. and Negri, A. (2000). *Empire*. Cambridge, MA: Harvard University Press.

Harman, G. (2008). 'DeLanda's ontology: assemblage and realism', *Continental Philosophy Review*, 41(3): 367–83.

Harré, R. (2002). 'Material objects in social worlds', *Theory, Culture & Society*, 19(5/6): 23–33.

Harvey, D. (1982). *The Limits to Capital*. Cambridge, MA: MIT Press.

Harvey, D. (1987). 'Postmodernism and the city'. Paper presented at the Urban and Regional Studies Seminar, University of Sussex.

Harvey, D. (1988). *The Condition of Postmodernity*. Oxford: Basil Blackwell.

Harvey, D. (1989). *The Urban Experience*. Oxford: Basil Blackwell.

Harvey, D. (1991). 'Afterword', in *Production of Space*. Oxford: Basil Blackwell. pp. 425–32.

Hausdorff, F. (1957). *Set Theory* (R. Aumann, trans.). New York: Chelsea.

Heidegger, M. (1962). *Being and Time* (J. Macquarrie and E. Robinson, trans.). New York: Harper and Row.

Heidegger, M. (1971). 'Building dwelling thinking' (A. Hofstadter, trans.), in *Poetry, Language, Thought*. New York: Harper Colophon Books.

Henriques, J. (2009). 'Auditory topologies, relationality and the diasporic propagation of culture'. Paper presented at Changing Cultures: Cultures of Change. ATACD – A topological approach to cultural dynamics.

Herod, A. (2011). *Scale*. London and New York: Routledge.

Herod, A. and Wright, M.W. (2002). *Geographies of Power: Placing Scale*. Malden, MA: Blackwell Publishing.

Herodotus (1962). *Herodoti Historiae*. Oxford: Oxford Classical Texts.

Hesiod (1914). *Theogeny* (H.G. Evelyn-White, trans.). Philadelphia: Pennsyvlania State University.

Hillier, B. and Hanson, J. (1984). *The Social Logic of Space*. London: Tavistock.

Hillis, K. (1999). *Digital Sensations: Space, Identity, and Embodiment in Virtual Reality* (Vol. 1). Minneapolis and London: University of Minnesota Press.

Hlibchuk, G. (2010). 'From typology to topology on Jack Spicer', *Contemporary Literature*, 51(2): 310–40.

Hodges, M. (2008). 'Rethinking time's arrow', *Anthropological Theory*, 8(4): 399–429. Available at: http://ant.sagepub.com/cgi/content/abstract/8/4/399

Hogan, T. (2002). 'Henri Lefebvre, everyday life in the modern world', *Thesis Eleven*, 71: 106–8.

Hopkins, B. and Wilson, R. (2004). 'The truth about Königsberg', *College Mathematics Journal*, 35(3): 198–207.

Howitt, R. (1993). 'A world in a grain of sand: towards a reconceptualization of geographical scale', *Australian Geographer*, 24: 33–44.

Hubbard, P., Kitchin, R. et al. (2004). *Key Thinkers On Space and Place*. London and Thousand Oaks, CA: Sage.

Hughes, E.C. (1928). *A Study of a Secular Institution: The Chicago Real Estate Board*. University of Chicago.

Husserl, E. (1962). *L'Origine de La Geometrie*. Paris: Presses Universitaires de France.

Idrisi Muhammad ibn Abd al-Aziz (Al Idrisi) (1990). *Kitab Nuzhat al-Mushtaq fi Ikhtiraq al-Afaq* (Vol. 2). Cairo: Maktabat al-Thaqafah al-Diniyah.

Idrisi Muhammad ibn Abd al-Aziz (Al Idrisi) and U. Sezgin (1988). *Kitab Anwar uluw al-ajram fi al-kashf an asrar al-ahram*. Frankfurt: Måhad Tåaråikh al-Ulåum al-Arabåiyah wa-al-Islåamåiyah.

Ingold, T. (1993). 'Globes and spheres: The topology of environmentalism', in K. Milton (ed.), *Environmentalism: The View from Anthropology*. London: Routledge. pp. 31–42.

Ingold, T. (2009). 'Point, line and counterpoint: From environment to fluid space', in A. Berthoz and Y. Christen (eds), *Neurobiology of Umwelt: How Living Beings Perceive the World*. Berlin: Springer-Verlag. pp. 141–55

Inkpen, R., Collier, P. and Riley, M. (2007). 'Topographic relations: Developing a heuristic device for conceptualising networked relations', *Area*, 39(4): 536–43.

Ivy, M. (1995). *Discourses of the Vanishing: Modernity, Phantasm, Japan*. Chicago: University of Chicago Press.

Jackson, J.B. (1984). *Landscapes* (E.H. Zube, ed.). Boston, MA: University of Massachusetts Press.

Jackson, P.J. (1999). *Virtual Working: Social and Organizational Dynamics*. London and New York: Routledge.

Jackson, P. and Smith, S.J. (1984). *Exploring Social Geography*. London: George Allen & Unwin.

Jacobson, K. (2004). 'Agoraphobia and hypochrondia as disorders of dwelling', *International Studies in Philosophy*, 36(2): 31–44.

Jakobson, R. (1980) *The Framework of Language*. Ann Arbor: University of Michigan Press.

Jameson, F. (1984). 'Postmodernism, or the cultural logic of late capitalism'. *New Left Review*, 146: 53–93.

Jammer, M. (1960). *Concepts of Space: The History of Theories of Space in Physics*. Cambridge: Harvard University Press.

Jammer, M. (1969). *Concepts of Space: The History of Theories of Space in Physics*. Cambridge: Harvard University Press.

Jardine, A. (1985). *Gynesis*. Cambridge: Harvard University Press.

John, A. (2009). 'Three spaces of power: Territory, networks, plus a topological twist in the tale of domination and authority', *Journal of Power*, 2(2): 197–212.

Jones, J.P., Woodward, K. and Marston, S. (2007). 'Situating flatness', *Transactions of the Institute of British Geographers*, 32: 264–76.

Jones, K. (1998). 'Scale as epistemology', *Political Geography*, 17(1): 25–8.

Jones, S.H. and Clarke, D.B. (2006). 'Waging terror: The geopolitics of the real', *Political Geography*, 25(3): 298–314.

Joyce, J. (1997). *Ulysses*. London: Picador.

Kant, I. (1910). *Gesammelte Schriften*. Berlin: G. Reimer.

Kant, I. (1953). *Prolegomena to any Future Metaphysics* (G.R. Lucas, trans.). Manchester: University of Manchester Press.

Kant, I. (1965). *Critique of Pure Reason* (N.K. Smith, trans.). New York: Macmillan and St Martin's Press.

Kant, I. (1968). 'Concerning the ultimate foundations of the differentiation of regions in space', in G.R. Lucas (ed.), *Selected Pre-Critical Writings*. Manchester: University of Manchester Press.

Kantor, J.-M. (2005). 'A tale of bridges: Topology and architecture', *Nexus Network Journal*, 7(2): 13–21.

Kern, S. (1983). *The Culture of Time and Space 1880–1919*. London: Weidenfeld and Nicolson.

Kimble, C., Grenier, C. and Goglio-Primard, K. (2010). 'Innovation and knowledge sharing across professional boundaries: Political interplay between boundary objects and brokers', *International Journal of Information Management*, 30(5): 437–44.

Knorr-Cetina, K. and Bruegger, U. (2002). 'Global microstructures: The virtual societies of financial markets', *American Journal of Sociology*, 107: 905–50.

Kojève, A. and Queneau, R. (1947). *Introduction à la lecture de Hegel; leçons sur la phenoménologie de l'esprit, professées de 1933 à 1939 à l'Ecole des hautes-études*. Paris: Gallimard.

Kolaja, J. (1969). *Social System and Time and Space*. Pittsburgh: Duquesne University.

Koyré, A. (1957). *From the Closed World to the Infinite Universe*. New York: Harper.

Kuratowsky, C.K. (1948). Topology 1. *Monografie Matematyczne*. Vol. 20. Warsaw-Lvov: Polish Mathematical Society.

Laclau, E. (1996). *Emancipation(s)*. London: Verso.

Lakoff, G. and Johnson, M. (1979). *Metaphors We Live By*. Chicago: University of Chicago Press.

Lañamme, J.-M. and Kaganski, S. (2010, Dec. 12). 'Entrevista con el director de cine Jean-Luc Godard', *El Cultural*, 12 December. Available at: http://www.elcultural. es/version_papel/CINE/28261/Jaen-Luc_Godard

Landzelius, M. (2009). 'Spatial reification, or, collectively embodied amnesia, aphasia, and apraxia', *Semiotica*, 175(1–4): 39–75.

Larsen, Ø. (1998). 'Imaginary democracy', in F. Collin (ed.), *Danish Yearbook of Philosophy* (Vol. 33). Copenhagen: Selskabet for filosofi og psykologi; Museum Tusculanum Press. pp. 31–54.

Latour, B. (1987). *Science in Action: How to Follow Scientists and Engineers through Society*. Milton Keynes: Open University Press.

Law, J. (1994). *Organizing Modernity*. Oxford: Blackwell.

Law, J. (2004). 'And if the global were small and noncoherent? Method, complexity and the baroque', *Environment and Planning D: Society and Space*, 22(1): 13–26.

Law, J. and Mol, A. (2000). 'Situating technoscience: An inquiry into spatiality', Available at http://www.lancs.ac.uk/fass/sociology/papers/law-mol-situating-technoscience.pdf (accessed December 2000).

Lazzarato, M., (2006). 'The Machine', *Transversal*. Available at http://eipcp.net/transversal/1106/lazzarato/en (accessed February 2013).

Le Doeuff, M. (1980). *L'Imaginaire philosophique*. Paris: Payot.

Lee, B. and LiPuma, E. (2002). 'Cultures of circulation: The imaginations of modernity', *Public Culture*, 14(1): 191–213.

Lefebvre, H. (1939). *Nietzsche*. Paris: Editions Sociales Internationales.

Lefebvre, H. (1947). *Critique de la vie quotidienne* (Vol. 1). Paris: Grasset.

Lefebvre, H. (1959). *La Somme et le reste*. Paris: PUF.

Lefebvre, H. (1961). *Critique de la vie quotidienne II. Fondements d'une sociologie de la quotidienneté*. Paris: L'Arche.

Lefebvre, H. (1962). *Introduction à la modernité*. Paris: Minuit.

Lefebvre, H. (1967). *Le Langage et la société*. Paris: Gallimard.

Lefebvre, H. (1968a). *La Vie quotidienne dans le monde moderne*. Paris: Gallimard.

Lefebvre, H. (1968b). *Le Droit à la ville* (2nd edn). Paris: Anthropos.

Lefebvre, H. (1970a). *Le Revolution urbaine*. Paris: Gallimard.

Lefebvre, H. (1970b). *Du Rurale a l'urbaine*. Paris: Anthropos.

Lefebvre, H. (1971). *Everyday Life in the Modern World*. London: Allen Lane.

Lefebvre, H. (1973). *La Suivre du capitalisme*. Paris: Editions Anthropos.

Lefebvre, H. (1974). 'La production de l'espace', *L'Homme et la société*, 31–32 (Jan–June): 15–31.

Lefebvre, H. (1976). 'Reflections on the politics of space' (M. Enders, trans.). *Antipode*, 8(2): 30–7.

Lefebvre, H. (1978). *De l'Etat: Vol. 4 Les contradictions de l'état moderne*. Paris: Union Generale d'Editions.

Lefebvre, H. (1979). 'Space: social product and use value', in J. Freiberg (ed.), *Critical Sociology, European Perspective*. New York: Irvington.

Lefebvre, H. (1981a). *Critique de la vie quotidienne. Vol. 3 De la modernité au modernisme*. Paris: L'Arche.

Lefebvre, H. (1981b). *La Production de l'espace* (2nd ed.). Paris: Anthropos.

Lefebvre, H. (1991a). *The Production of Space* (N. Donaldson-Smith, trans.). Oxford: Basil Blackwell.

Lefebvre, H. (1991b). *The Critique of Everyday Life, Volume 1* (J. Moore, trans.). London: Verso.

Lefebvre, H. (2003). *Urban Revolution* (R. Bonono, trans.). Minneapolis: Minnesota University Press.

Lefebvre, H. (2009). *State, Space, World: Selected Essays* (G. Moore, N. Brenner and S. Elden, trans.). Minneapolis: Minnesota University Press.

Lefebvre, H. and Regulier-Lefebvre, C. (1992). *Elements de Rhythmanalyse. Introduction à la connaissance des rythmes*. Paris: Ed. Syllepse et Archipel.

Leibniz, G.W. and Clarke, S. (2000). *Correspondence*. Indianapolis: Hackett.

Leibniz, G.W. and Holz, H.H. (1986). *Die Philosophische Schriften* (1. Aufl. ed.). Frankfurt am Main: Insel Verlag.

Lenin, V.I. (1908). *Materialism and Empirio-Criticism*. New York: International Publishers.

Lévêque, P. and Vidal-Naquet, P. (1996). *Cleisthenes the Athenian: An Essay on the Representation of Space and Time in Greek Political Thought from the End of the Sixth Century to the Death of Plato* (D.A. Curtis, trans.). Atlantic Highlands, NJ: Humanities Press.

Levi-Strauss, C. (1966). *The Savage Mind*. Chicago: University of Chicago Press.

Lévy, P. (1998). *Becoming Virtual: Reality in the Digital Age* (R. Bononno, trans.). New York: Plenum.

Lewin, K. (1964). *Field Theory in Social Science*. New York: Harper.

Lewis, M.E. (2006). *The Construction of Space in Early China*. Albany: State University of New York Press.

Li, T.M. (2007). 'Practices of assemblage and community forest management', *Economy and Society*, 36(2): 263–93.

Lipnack, J. and Stamps, R. (1997). *Virtual Teams: Reaching across Space, Time, and Organizations with Technology*. New York: John Wiley and Sons.

Listing, J.B. (1848). *Vorstudien zur Topologie*. Göttingen: Vandenhoeck und Ruprecht. http://babel.hathitrust.org/cgi/pt?id=hvd.32044018845610;seq=11;view=1up;num=1

Lobachevski, N.I. (2005). *Geometrical Researches on the Theory of Parallels* (G.B. Halsted, trans.). Ann Arbor, MI: University of Michigan Library.

Locke, J. (1690). *An Essay Concerning Human Understanding*. London: Thomas Basset. (Online based on the 2nd Edition, Books 1 and 2). http://www.gutenberg.org/cache/epub/10615/pg10615.html

Lomnitz, Claudio (2001) *Deep Mexico: An Anthropology of Nationalism.* Minneapolis: University of Minnesota Press.

Lucas, G.R. (1984). *Space, Time and Causality.* Oxford and New York: Oxford University Press.

Lucretius. (1997). *De rerum natura* (W.E. Leonard, trans.): Project Gutenberg.

Lugones, M. (2003). *Pilgrimages – Peregrinajes.* New York: Rowman and Littlefield.

Lundvall, B.A. (ed.) (1992). *National Systems of Innovation: Towards a Theory of Innovation and Interactive Learning.* London: Pinter Publishers.

Lury, C. (1997). 'Marking time with Nike, or, "He was thrilling to watch, and was the only one with his own shoe"', unpublished manuscript.

Lury, C. (2009). 'Topology: The engaging of multiplicity'. Paper presented at Changing Cultures: Cultures of Change.

Lury, C., Parisi, L.and Terranova, T. (2012). 'Introduction: The becoming topological of Culture', *Theory, Culture & Society* 29(4–5): 3–35.

Lynch, K. (1956). *The Image of the City.* New York: Harper.

Lyotard, J.-F. (1980). *The Post-Modern Condition* (B. Massumi, trans.). Minneapolis: University of Minnesota Press.

Lyotard, J.-F. (1984). *Les Immateriaux.* Paris: Centre Georges Pompidou.

Lyotard, J.-F. (1988). *The Differend.* Minneapolis: University of Minnesota Press.

Mach, E. (1901). *Space and Geometry in the Light of Physiological and Psychological and Physical Inquiry.* Chicago: University of Chicago Press.

Mackenzie, A. (2005a). 'The performativity of code: Software and cultures of circulation', *Theory Culture & Society*, 22(1): 71–92.

Mackenzie, A. (2005b). 'The problem of the attractor: A singular generality between sciences and social theory', *Theory, Culture & Society*, 22(5): 45–66.

Maffesoli, M. (1981). *Le Temps des Tribus.* Paris: Meridiens-Klinckseick.

Maley, K. (2008). *Heidegger's Possibility: Language, emergence – Saying be-ing.* Toronto: University of Toronto Press.

Mallion, R. (2008). 'A contemporary Eulerian walk over the bridges of Kaliningrad', *BSHM Bulletin: Journal of the British Society for the History of Mathematics*, 23(1): 24–36.

Malpas, J. (2011). 'The place of topology: Responding to Crowell, Beistegui, and Young', *International Journal of Philosophical Studies*, 19(2): 295–315.

Malpas, J.E. (2006). *Heidegger's Topology: Being, Place, World.* Cambridge, MA: MIT Press.

Mandelbrot, B. (1967). 'How long is the coast of Britain? Statistical self-similarity and fractional dimension', *Science Technology & Human Values*, 156: 636–8.

Manning, E. (2009). 'What if it didn't all begin and end with containment? Toward a leaky sense of self', *Body & Society*, 15(3): 33–45.

Marres, N. (2012). 'On some uses and abuses of topology in the social analysis of technology (or the problem with smart meters)', *Theory, Culture & Society,* 29(4–5): 288–310.

Marston, S.A., Jones, J.P. and Woodward, K. (2005). 'Human geography without scale', *Transactions of the Institute of British Geographers*, 30(4): 416–32.

Martins, M.R. (1982). 'The theory of social space in the work of Henri Lefebvre', in R. Forrest, J.W. Henderson and P. Williams (eds), *Urban Political Economy and Social Theory.* Epping: Gower. pp. 160–85.

Marx, K. (1859). *Critique of Political Economy.* Available at: http://www.marxists.org/archive/marx/works/1859/critique-pol-economy/ch01.htm

Marx, K. (1973a). *Economic Manuscripts: Grundrisse – Introduction 1857* (online edition). Available at: http://www.marxists.org/archive/marx/works/1857/grundrisse/ (accessed 2 May 2011).

Marx, K. (1973b). *Grundrisse*. London: Penguin.

Marx, K. (1973c). *Karl Marx: Surveys from Exile. Political Writings* (Vol. 2). Harmondsworth: Penguin.

Marx, K. (1976). *Capital* (Vol. 1). Harmondsworth: Penguin.

Marx, K. (1981). *Capital* (Vol. 3). Harmondsworth: Penguin.

Marx, K. and Engels, F. (1964). *The German Ideology*. Moscow: Progress Publishers.

Marx, K., Engels, F. and Jones, G.S. (2006). *The Communist Manifesto*. New York: Penguin Books.

Maskell, P. and Malmberg, A. (1999). 'Localised learning and industrial competitiveness', *Cambridge Journal of Economics*, 23: 167–86.

Massey, D. (1999). *Power-Geometries and the Politics of Space-Time,* Heidelberg: Department of Geography, University of Heidelberg.

Massumi, B. (1998). 'Sensing the Virtual, Building the Insensible.' *Hypersurface Architecture, special issue of AD Architectural Design* (Profile no. 133) 68 (5/6): 16–24.

Massumi, B. (2002). *Parables for the Virtual*. Durham, NC: Duke University Press.

Massumi, B. (2005). 'The future birth of the affective fact'. Paper presented at Genealogies of Biopolitics, University of Montréal.

Matoré, G. (1962). *L'espace humain*. Paris: La Colombe.

Matusik, S. and Hill, C. (1998). 'The utilization of contingent work, knowledge creation, and competitive advantage', *Academy of Management Review*, 23(4): 680–97.

McCarthy, C. (2002). 'Camoflage: Military uphoulstery and interior disguise', *Space and Culture*, 5(4): 320–32.

McCormack, D.P. (2005). 'Diagramming practice and performance', *Environment and Planning D: Society and Space*, 23(2): 119–47.

McFarlane, C. (2009). 'Translocal assemblages: Space, power and social movements', *Geoforum*, 40(4): 561–7.

Mejías, U.A. (2007). *Networked Proximity: ICTs and the Mediation of Nearness*. New York.: Columbia University.

Merleau-Ponty, M. (1962). *Phenomenology of Perception*. London: Blackwell.

Merleau-Ponty, M. (1968). The intertwining – the chiasm (A. Lingus, trans.), in *The Visible and the Invisible*. Evanston, IL: Northwestern University Press. pp. 130–55.

Merrifield, A. (1993). 'Place and space: A Lefebvrean reconciliation', *Transactions of the British Institute of Geographers*, 18(4): 516–31.

Miller, R., Lessard, D., Michaud, P. and Floricel, S. (2000). *The Strategic Management of Large Engineering Projects: Shaping Institutions, Risks and Governance*. Cambridge, MA: MIT Press.

Monferran, J.-P. (2003). 'La révolte et le crime', *La Somme et le reste. Etudes lefebvriennes – Réseau mondial*, 2: 2–3.

Morrissette, B. (1972). 'Topology and the French nouveau roman', *Boundary* 2(1): 45–57.

Newton, I. (2009). *Philosophiae Naturalis Principia Mathematica* (J. Ingram and K. Edkins, eds), Project Gutenberg Ebook. Available at: http://www.gutenberg.org/ebooks/28233

Nicholas of Cusa [Cusanus] (2001). *De Docta Ignorantia* (J. Hopkins, eds). Available at: http://jasper-hopkins.info/DI-II-12-2000.pdf

Norberg-Schulz, C. (1980). *Genius Loci: Towards a Phenomenology of Architecture*. London: Academy Editions.

Noy, C. (2008). 'Pages as stages: A performance approach to visitors' books', *Annals of Tourism Research*, 35(2): 509–28.

O'Connor, D. (2003). *Mediated Associations: Cinematic Dimensions of Social Theory*. Montreal: McGill-Queen's University Press.

O'Kelly, M.E. and Grubesic, T.H. (2002). 'Backbone topology, access, and the commercial internet, 1997–2000', *Environment and Planning B: Planning and Design*, 29: 533–52.

O'Shea, D. (2007). *The Poincaré Conjecture*. New York: Walker and Co.

Ockam, W. of (1494). *Summulae in libros physicorum*. Bologna.

Olma, S. (2004). 'Physics unbound', *Mute*, 27: 11–14.

Parisi, L. (2012). 'Digital design and topological control', *Theory Culture & Society*, 29(4–5): 165–92.

Park, R. (1925). 'The city: Suggestions for the investigation of human behaviour in the urban environment', in R.D. McKenzie (ed.), *The City*. Chicago: Chicago University Press. pp. 1–46.

Patriotta, G. (2003). *Organizational Knowledge in the Making: How Firms Create, Use, and Institutionalize Knowledge*. Oxford: Oxford University Press.

Peirce, C.S. (1885). 'On the algebra of logic: A contribution to the philosophy of notation', *American Journal of Mathematics*, 7(2): 180–96.

Perella, S. (1998). 'Hypersurface theory: Architecture >< Culture', in M. Toy (ed.), *Hypersurface Architecture*. London: Academy Editions.

Perelman, G. (2002). 'The entropy formula for the Ricci flow and its geometric application'. Available at: http://arxiv.org/abs/math/0211159

Perrin, C. (1977). *The Politics of Zoning*. Baltimore: Johns Hopkins.

Petchevsky, R. (1981). 'NeoConservativism and the new right', *MF*.

Petersen, V.C. (2002). *Beyond Rules in Society and Business*. Cheltenham: Edward Elgar Publishing.

Peterson, M.A. (1979). 'Dante and the 3-sphere', *American Journal of Physics*, 47(12): 1031–5.

Piaget, J., Inhelder, B. and Szeminska, A. (1964). *The Child's Conception of Geometry*. New York: Harper.

Plato (1925). *Timaeus* (W.R.M. Lamb, trans.) *Plato in Twelve Volumes* (Vol. 9). Cambridge, MA: Harvard University Press.

P'o Kuo (Guo Pu) (1985). *Shan Hai Jing; Legendary Geography and Wonders of Ancient China*. Taipei: National Institute for Compilation and Translation.

Poincaré, H. (1914). *Science and Method* (F. Maitland, trans.). London: T. Nelson.

Poincaré, H. (1952). *Science and Hypothesis*. New York: Dover.

Poincaré, H. (2010). *Papers on Topology: Analysis Situs and its Five Supplements* (J. Stillwell, trans., Vol. 37). Providence, RI: American Mathematical Society.

Portoghesi, P. (1982). *Post Modernism*. New York: Rizzoli.

Pred, A. (1990). *Lost Words and Lost Worlds: Modernity and the Language of Everyday life in Late Nineteenth-century Stockholm*. Cambridge: Cambridge University Press.

Preziosi, D. (1979). *Architecture, Language and Meaning*. New York: Hawthorne.

Preziosi, D. (2003). *Brain of the Earth's Body: Art, Museums and the Phantasms of Modernity*. Minneapolis: University of Minnesota Press.

Priestley, J.B. (1964). *Man and Time*. London: Aldus.

Ptolemy (1969). *Geographia*. Amsterdam: Theatrum Orbis Terrarum.

Rajchman, J. (1998). *Constructions*. Cambridge, MA: MIT Press.

Rajchman, J. (1999). 'Diagram and diagnosis', in E. Grosz (ed.), *Becomings: Explorations in Time, Memory and Futures*. Ithaca, NY: Cornell University Press.

Randall, L. (2001, July/Aug). 'MIT's Lisa Randall: Two branes are better than one', *Science Watch*, 12(4). Available at http://www.sciencewatch.com/july-aug2001/sw_july-aug2001_page3.htm (accessed 27 June 2011).

Randall, L. and Sundrum, R. (1999). 'Large mass hierarchy from a small extra dimension', *Physical Review Letters*, 83(17): 3370–3.

Ratzel, F. (1903). *Politische geographie: oder, Die geographie der staaten, des verkehres und des krieges* (online edn). München: R. Oldenbourg.

Reclus, E. (1892). *The Earth and its Inhabitants*. New York: D. Appleton and Co.

Riemann, G.F.B. (1854). 'On the hypotheses which lie at the bases of geometry', *Nature*, 8(183–4): 14–17, 36, 37. Available at http://www.maths.tcd.ie/pub/HistMath/People/Riemann/Geom/WKCGeom.html

Rogers, T. (2000). 'Applying the spatial critique to theory in psychology: Toward a useful third space', *Trumpeter*, 16(1). Available at: http://trumpeter.athabascau.ca/index.php/trumpet/issue/view/28 (accessed 29 February 2013).

Ross, K. (1988). *The Emergence of Social Space: Rimbaud and the Paris Commune*. Minneapolis: University of Minnesota Press.

Rotman, B. (2009). 'Topology, algebra, diagrams'. Paper presented at the ATACD.

Ryle, G. (1968). 'The thinking of thoughts. What is "Le Penseur" doing?', *University Lectures* (Vol. 18). Saskatoon, Sask: University of Saskatchewan. Available at: http://lucy.ukc.ac.uk/CSACSIA/Vol14/Papers/ryle_1.html

Sack, R. D. (1980). *Conceptions of Space in Social Thought: A Geographic Perspective*. Minneapolis: University of Minnesota Press.

Sartre, J.P. (1960). *Critique of Dialectical Reason*. Paris: PUF.

Sassen, S. (2006). *Territory, Authority, Rights: From Medieval to Global Assemblages*. Princeton, NJ: Princeton University Press.

Saunders, P. (1981). *Social Theory and the Urban Question*. London: Hutchinson.

Sayer, A. (1985). 'The difference that space makes', in J. Urry and D. Gregory (eds), *Social Relations and Spatial Structures*. London: Macmillan. pp. 49–66.

Schatzki, T.R. (2002). *The Site of the Social*. University Park, PA: Pennsylvania University Press.

Schweikart , K.(1818). *Astralgeometry*. Marburg.

Serres, M. (1980). *Le Passage du Nord-Ouest* (Vol. 5 of Hermes). Paris: Editions de Minuit.

Serres, M. (1982). *The Parasite* (L.R. Schehr, trans.). Baltimore: Johns Hopkins University Press.

Serres, M. (1991). *Rome: The Book of Foundations*. Stanford: Stanford University Press.

Serres, M. (1992). 'Language and Space: From Oedipus to Zola'. *Hermes: Literature, Science, Philosophy*, in J. V. Harari and D. F. Bell, (eds) and trans. Baltimore: The Johns Hopkins University Press. pp. 39–53.

Serres, M. (1992). 'The Origin of Geometry.' *Aut Aut* (250): 66–75.

Serres, M. (1994). *Atlas*. Paris: Julliard.

Serres, M. and Latour, B. (1995). *Conversations on Science, Culture and Time*. Ann Arbor: University of Michigan Press.

Shapiro, M. and Lang, A. (1991). 'Making television reality: Unconscious proccesses in the construction of social reality', *Communication Research*, 18(5): 685–705.

Sharkey, A. and Shields, R. (2005). 'Technology, communication and citizen participation in a rural town youth centre'. Paper presented at the Canadian Sociology and Anthropology Association Annual Conference, University of Western Ontario, London, Ontario.

Sheringham, M. (2000). 'Attending to the everyday: Blanchot, Lefebvre, Certeau, Perec', *French Studies*, 54(2): 187–99.

Shields, R. (1986). *Notes Toward a Theory of Social Spatializations: Henri Lefebvre, the Problem of Space and the Postmodern Hypothesis*. Ottawa: Carleton University.

Shields, R. (1989). 'Social spatialization and the built environment: The West Edmonton Mall', *Environment and Planning D: Society and Space*, 7(2): 147–64.

Shields, R. (1991). *Places on the Margin: Alternative Geographies of Modernity*. London: Routledge Chapman and Hall.

Shields, R. (1992). 'A truant proximity: Presence and absence in the space of modernity', *Environment and Planning D: Society and Space*, 10(2): 181–98.

Shields, R. (ed.) (1993). *Lifestyle Shopping: The Subject of Consumption*. London: Routledge.

Shields, R. (1997). Flow. *Space and Culture – Theme Issue on Flow*, 1: 1–5.

Shields, R. (1998). 'Raumkonstruktion und Tourismus', *Voyage: Jahrbuch für Reise und Tourismusforschung*, 2: 53–72.

Shields, R. (1999). *Lefebvre: Love and Struggle – Spatial Dialectics*. London: Routledge.

Shields, R. (2003). *The Virtual*. London: Routledge.

Shields, R. (2006a). 'Knowing space/spatialization', *Theory Culture & Society*, 23(2–3): 146–9.

Shields, R. (2006b). 'Virtualities', *Theory Culture & Society*, 23(2–3): 284–86.

Shields, R. (2011). 'The tourist affect: Escape and syncresis on the Las Vegas strip', in *Ecologies of Affect: Placing Nostalgia, Desire and Hope*. Waterloo, ON: Wilfred Laurier University Press. pp. 103–24.

Shields, R. and Sharkey, A. (2008). 'Abject citizenship – rethinking exclusion and inclusion: Participation, criminality and community at a small town youth centre', *Childrens' Geographies*, 6(3): 239–56.

Shields, R. and Taborsky, E. (2001). 'The new knowledge speak: Implications of contested definitions of knowledge and information', *Australian Journal of Information Systems*, 8(2): 142–9.

Simmel, G. (1908). *Soziologie Untersuchungen: Über die formen der vergesellschaftungpp*. Leipzig: Verlag von Duncker & Humblot. Available at: http://ebooks.library.ualberta. ca/local/soziologieunters00simmuoft

Simmel, G. (2007 [1908]). 'The social boundary'. *Theory, Culture & Society*, 24(7–8): 53–6.

Simmel, G. (2009). *Sociology: Inquiries into the Construction of Social Forms* (A.J. Blasi, A.K. Jacobs and M.J. Kanjirathinkal, trans.). Leiden and Boston: Brill.

Simmel, G., Frisby, D. and Featherstone, M. (1997). *Simmel on Culture: Selected Writings*. London: Sage.

Simplicius (1992). *Simplicius: Corollaries on Place and Time* (J.O. Urmson, trans.). Ithaca, NY: Cornell University Press.

Sklar, L. (1974). 'Incongruous counterparts, intrinsic features and the substantivality of space', *Journal of Philosophy*, 71(9): 277–90.

Smirnov, O. (2010). 'An analytical approach to geographic space', unpublished manuscript, Toledo, Ohio.

Smith, D. (1987). *The Everyday World As Problematic: A Feminist Sociology*. Boston, MA: Northeastern University Press.

Smith, M. (2001). 'Repetition and difference: Lefebvre, Le Corbusier and modernity's (im)moral landscape', *Ethics Place and Environment* 4(1): 31–44.

Smith, N. (2000). 'Scale', in R.J. Johnston, D. Gregory, G. Pratt and M. Watts (eds), *The Dictionary of Human Geography*. Oxford: Blackwell. pp. 724–7.

Soja, E. (1980). 'The socio-spatial dialectic', *Annals of the American Association of Geographers*, 70(2): 207–25.

Solzhenitzyn, A. (1977). *The Gulag Archipelago*. New York: Harper and Row.

Sorokin, P.A. (1937–41). *Social and Cultural Dynamics* (Vol. 1). New York: American Book Company.

Sorokin, P.A. (1943). *Sociocultural Causality, Space, Time*. Durham, NC: Duke University Press.

Spengler, O. (1926–28). *The Decline of the West*. New York: Alfred Knopf.

Spicer, J. (2008). *My Vocabulary Did This to Me: The Collected Poetry of Jack Spicer*. Middletown, CT: Wesleyan University Press.

Stanek, L. (2011). *Henri Lefebvre on Space. Architecture, Urban Research, and the Production of Theory*. Minneapolis: University of Minnesota Press.

Star, S.L. and Greisemer, J.R. (1989). 'Institutional ecology, "translations" and boundary objects: Amateurs and professionals in Berkeley's Museum of Vertebrate Zoology 1907–1939', *Social Studies of Science*, 19(4): 387–420.

Stark, D., Vedres, B. and Bruszt, L. (2006). 'Rooted transnational publics: Integrating foreign ties and civic activism', *Theory and Society*, 35: 323–49.

Stenner, P. (2008). 'A.N. Whitehead and subjectivity', *Subjectivity: International Journal of Critical Psychology*, 22(1): 90–109.

Stern, D. (1985). *The Interpersonal World of the Infant: A View from Psychoanalysis and Developmental Psychology*. New York: HarperCollins.

Strambach, S. (2002). 'Change in the innovation process: New knowledge production and competitive cities – the case of Stuttgart', *European Planning Studies*, 10(2): 215–31.

Strathern, M. (1996). 'Cutting the Network', *Journal of the Royal Anthropological Association,* 2(3): 28–68.

Strauss, C. (2006). 'The imaginary', *Anthropological Theory*, 6(3): 322–44.

Tafuri, M. (1976). *Architecture and Utopia* (B.L. La Penta, trans.). Cambridge, MA: MIT Press.

Tafuri, M. (1980). *Theories and History of Architecture* (G. Verrecchi, trans.). New York: Granada Publishing through Harper and Row.

Taussig, M.T. (1998). 'Viscerality, faith and skepticism: Another theory of magic', in N. Dirks (ed.), *In Near Ruins; Cultural Theory at the End of the Century* Minneapolis: University of Minnesota Press. pp. 221–56.

Taylor, P. (1982). 'A materialist framework for political geography'. *Transactions of the British Insitute of Geographers*, 7(1): 15–34.

Teymur, N. (1980). *Environmentalism*. Edinburgh: University of Edinburgh Press.

Thom, R. (1975). *Structural Stability and Morphogenesis*. Boulder, CO: W.A. Benjamin, Westview Press.

Thompson, E.P. (1980). *The Making of the English Working Class*. London: Gollancz.

Tobler, W.R. (2004). 'On the first law of geography: A reply', *Annals of the Association of American Geographers*, 94(2): 3004–10.

Toscano, A. (2008). 'The culture of abstraction', *Theory, Culture & Society*, 25(4): 57–75.

Tresch, J. (2007). 'Technological world-pictures: Cosmic things, cosmograms', *ISIS*, 98(1): 84–99.

Turetzky, P. (1998). *Time*. London: Routledge.

Urry, J. (2000). *Sociology Beyond Societies; Mobilities for the Twenty First Century*. New York: Routledge.

Urry, J. (2004). 'Small worlds and the new "social physics"', *Global Networks – a Journal of Transnational Affairs*, 4(2): 109–30.

Vannini, P. (2011). *Ferry Tales: Mobility, Place, and Time on Canada's West Coast*. New York: Routledge.

Vesilind, P. J.and Chamberlin, D. (1997). 'Kaliningrad: Coping with a German past and a Russian future'. *National Geographic* (March): 110–23.

Virilio, P. (1986). *Speed and Politics: An Essay on Dromology*. New York: Semiotext(e).

Virno, P. and Hardt, M. (1996). *Radical Thought in Italy: A Potential Politics*. Minneapolis: MN: University of Minnesota Press.

von Uexküll, J. (1909). *Umwelt und Innenwelt der Tiere*. Berlin: J. Springer.

von Uexküll, J. (2011). *A Foray into the Worlds of Animals and Humans: With A Theory of Meaning* (J. O'Neil, trans.). Minneapolis: University of Minnesota Press.

Waters, M. (2001). *Globalization*. London: Routledge.

Weber, M. (1966). *The City*. Glencoe, IL: The Free Press.

Weiner, A.D. (1980). 'Expelling the beast: Bruno's adventures in England', *Modern Philology*, 78(1): 1–13.

Whitehead, A.N. (1922). *The Principle of Relativity*. New York: Cosimo Classics.

Whitehead, A.N. (1934). *Nature and Life*. Cambridge: Cambridge University Press.

Widder, N. (2000). 'What's lacking in the lack: A comment on the virtual', *Angelaki*, 5(3): 117–38.

Wildgen, W. (1982). *Catastrophe Theoretic Semantics: An Elaboration and Application of Rene Thom's Theory*. Philadelphia: John Benjamins Publishing.

Woodward, K., Jones, J.P. and Marston, S.A. (2010). 'Of eagles and flies: Orientations toward the site', *Area*, 42(3): 271–80.

Zevi, B. (1969). *Architecture as Space*. Princeton NJ: Princeton University Press.

Zieleniec, A. (2007). *Space and Social Theory*. London: Sage.

Žižek, S. (1989). *The Sublime Object of Ideology*. London: Verso.

Žižek, S. (1992). *Enjoy Your Symptom!* London: Routledge.

Znaniekci, C. (1950). *Social Space*. New York: Methuen.

index